Fiscal Reform and Structural Change in Developing Countries

Volume 1

Also edited by Guillermo Perry, John Whalley and Gary McMahon

FISCAL REFORM AND STRUCTURAL CHANGE IN DEVELOPING COUNTRIES
Volume 2

Fiscal Reform and Structural Change in Developing Countries

Volume 1

Edited by

Guillermo Perry
Chief Economist, Latin America
World Bank, Washington

John Whalley
Professor, University of Western Ontario, Canada, and
University of Warwick

and

Gary McMahon
Consultant, World Bank, Washington

in association with
INTERNATIONAL DEVELOPMENT RESEARCH CENTRE
CANADA

First published in Great Britain 2000 by
MACMILLAN PRESS LTD
Houndmills, Basingstoke, Hampshire RG21 6XS and London
Companies and representatives throughout the world

A catalogue record for this book is available from the British Library.

ISBN 0–333–58883–5

First published in the United States of America 2000 by
ST. MARTIN'S PRESS, LLC,
Scholarly and Reference Division,
175 Fifth Avenue, New York, N.Y. 10010

ISBN 0–312–23580–1

Library of Congress Cataloging-in-Publication Data
Fiscal reform and structural change in developing countries / edited by Guillermo
Perry, John Whalley and Gary McMahon.
    p. cm.
Includes bibliographical references and index.
ISBN 0–312–23580–1 (v.1)   ISBN 0–312–23581–X (v.2)
    1. Taxation—Developing countries. 2. Fiscal policy—Developing countries. I.
Perry, Guillermo. II. Whalley, John. III. McMahon, Gary.

HJ2351.7 .F567 2000
336.3'09172'4—dc21

                                                                00–033331

This book is printed on paper suitable for recycling and made from fully managed and sustained
forest sources.

10   9   8   7   6   5   4   3   2   1
09   08   07   06   05   04   03   02   01   00

Printed and bound in Great Britain by
Antony Rowe Ltd, Chippenham, Wiltshire

Contents

Notes on the Contributors

Richard M. Bird is Professor of Economics at the University of Toronto, Canada. He previously taught at Harvard and has been a visiting professor in the UK, Australia, the Netherlands and Japan, and has acted as adviser to the government of Columbia and as consultant to the IMF, the World Bank, USAID and other national and international organizations. Bird's major research interest has long been the fiscal problems of developing and transitional countries and comparative public finance in general. His current research interests include work on various aspects of taxation and fiscal decentralization, tax administration and international taxation. He is the author of *Tax Incentives for Investment in Developing Countries*.

Robin Boadway is Sir Edward Peacock Professor of Economics, Queen's University, Ontario, Canada. He is the author of *Public Sector Economics* and *Welfare Economics* and various articles on public economics, fiscal federalism and welfare economics. He has served as President of the Canadian Economics Association and as editor of the *Canadian Journal of Economics*.

Chia Ngee Choon is Senior Lecturer at the Department of Economics, National University of Singapore and Visiting Professor at the University of Western Ontario. Her current research interests include the environmental impact of motor vehicle taxes. She has published several articles using computational general equilibrium modelling techniques.

Omar O. Chisari is Director of the Instituto de Economia Universidad de la Empresa, Buenos Aires, Argentina. His research areas include microeconomics, regulatory economics and CGE modelling.

Catherine Enoh is Technical Advisor to the Ministry of Planning and Industrial Development, Côte d'Ivoire. She is also Professor of Macroeconomics, ENSEA in Abidjan, Côte d'Ivoire.

Ephrem Enoh is Economic and Financial Adviser to the Prime Minister of Cote d'Ivoire. He is also Professor of Modelization, ENSEA, in Abidjan, Côte d'Ivoire.

Edmé Koffi is Technical Adviser to the Ministry of Planning and Industrial Development, Côte d'Ivoire.

Gary McMahon is a consultant at the World Bank, Washington. He works primarily in the area of macroeconomics and environmental economics for developing countries.

Guillermo Perry is presently Chief Economist for the Latin America and Caribbean region of the World Bank. He has been Minister of Finance and Public Credit, Minister of Mining and Energy and Director of two of the leading economic think-tanks in his country (Colombia): FEDESAR-ROLLO and CEDE. He has published a number of books on structural reform and economic policy.

Sandra Roberts was a consultant at the World Bank while a doctoral candidate in economics at Queen's University, Kingston, Ontario.

Guillermo Rozenwurcel is Professor, School of Economics, University of Buenos Aires, Senior Researcher, Center for the Study of the State and Society (CEDES) and Researcher at the National Council for Scientific and Technological Research (CONICET), Buenos Aires, Argentina. He specializes in macroeconomics and monetary and financial issues in developing countries.

Anwar Shah is Principal Evaluation Officer with the Operations Evaluation Department at the World Bank, Washington. He has previously served the Ministry of Finance, Government of Canada and Government of Alberta, Canada. He has advised the governments of Brazil, Indonesia, China, South Africa, Pakistan, Argentina and Mexico on fiscal federalism issues. His current research interests are in the areas of governance, fiscal federalism, fiscal reform and global environment. His books include *Fiscal Incentives for Investment and Innovation*.

Horacio Sobarzo is Director of the Center for Economic Studies, Mexico City, Mexico. His areas of research include public finance, international trade and applied general equilibrium.

Carlos M. Urzúa is Professor at El Colegio de México, Mexico and Director of Doctoral Programs at Technologico de Moneterrey, Campus Ciudad de Mexico.

John Whalley has worked extensively in the tax and other policy areas and is known for his work on developing countries. A Research Associate of the National Bureau of Economic Research, he holds positions at the University of Western Ontario, Canada and the University of Warwick, UK. He is also a Fellow of the Economic Society.

Preface

The two volumes of *Fiscal Reform and Structural Change in Developing Countries* analyze the experience of countries involved in major tax reforms in the 1980s and first half of the 1990s by a combination of qualitative and quantitative country studies and over-arching thematic studies. The emphasis is on the role of fiscal reform in stabilization and structural change, as well as the effects that policy for stabilization and, especially, structural change can have on the fiscal deficit under different types of tax systems. The authors argue that the strong movement towards more simple tax systems is primarily due to administrative reasons and adaptation of the tax systems to the economic structures of the countries. Complex tax systems constructed in the import-substitution era, with some support from institution-free optimal tax theory, have been found to be very costly to administer. Moreover, with the move to more open economies, it is recognized that improperly designed fiscal systems can magnify the effects of domestic or external shocks. Nevertheless, it is important to note that, even when institutional factors are taken into account, *optimal tax systems* will vary across countries due to a variety of reasons, including historical factors or initial conditions, political economy considerations, institutional matters, economic structure, the macroeconomic background, and different social welfare functions.

All of the researchers and editors would like to thank the International Development Research Centre of Canada for its generous financing of the project behind these books.

1
Introduction

Guillermo Perry and John Whalley

Introduction

What constitutes tax reform in developing countries, and how does it differ from comparable reform in developed countries? How important is tax reform for economic performance in these countries? How does it contribute to growth, macroeconomic stability, poverty alleviation, resource mobilization, trade and other economic performance characteristics? What kind of reforms are sustainable and which are not, given the often turbulent macroeconomic environment in these countries? How important is enforcement of existing tax laws through improved compliance, as against changes in tax structure? How are the evolution of the impacts of tax reforms in developing countries affected (relative to developed country experience) by such common characteristics as price and quantity controls, labour market distortions, black markets, credit rationing and other factors? Is the widespread adoption of VAT in these countries a good or bad idea; and how much do such changes merely reflect the adaptation of the tax structure to a maturing economy as against reform *per se*? Similarly, is tax structure determined primarily by economic structure, theoretical developments or global pressures, including imitation effects?

This and the companion volume discuss these and other related issues in the context of a series of country case studies and broader thematic chapters. The project combines model-based numerical evaluation of tax reforms in a number of developing countries with a group of more qualitative country pieces which emphasize macroeconomic, structural adjustment and political economy considerations. It also draws together relevant factual information in comparative form on recent and current tax reforms in project countries.[1] In five of the seven countries – Argentina, Colombia, Côte d'Ivoire, Mexico and the Philippines – both quantitative and qualitative studies were undertaken, while only a quantitative analysis was carried out for Singapore and a qualitative study for India.[2] In addition, the thematic chapters capture broader issues not easily covered in the country studies.

General equilibrium modelling has the great virtue of capturing economy-wide interacting effects associated with tax reform. Modellers are able to trace through the implications for production, demand, trade and other economic performance characteristics of changes in tax structures. These can include reforms in indirect taxes such as VAT, extension of direct taxes including income and corporate taxes, or changes in the tax mix away from, for example, trade taxes to more broadly based consumption taxes. Modelling work of this type has been extensively used in developed countries and has yielded important insights on the interacting effects in terms of efficiency and distributional implications of tax reform. This volume thus presents analyses which examine developing country tax reform issues using general equilibrium techniques in ways which take account of developing country characteristics, both in terms of model structure and in terms of tax patterns.

At the same time, fiscal reforms are often guided or inhibited by macro-economic and political economy considerations, aspects of a country's economy which are not easily captured by general equilibrium models. Accordingly, our book balances the more technical modelling approach with comparative analyses focusing on the often complex macroeconomic and political situations in which many reforms have taken place in the last two decades.[3] By providing analyses which consider both the longer-run structural features of an economy and the (often) short-run considerations which can dominate reform, it is hoped that a clearer picture of the processes will be generated. In fact, as will be seen, one of the conclusions of the volume is that macroeconomic and political economy factors generally dominate reforms in the short run; however, over time the structural factors play an increasingly powerful role.

Fiscal reform issues in developing countries

Tax reform is a widely used but surprisingly imprecise term in both developed and developing countries. The word 'reform' conveys major change, but tax change occurs on an ongoing basis in most countries around the world, developing countries being no exception. It is, therefore, highly judgemental as to when one crosses the borderline between tax change and tax reform. While generalization is difficult, tax reform in developing countries is none-theless clearly different from what is often understood in developed coun-tries. In particular, given the importance of the state in the productive sectors of the economy, it is often the case that significant and sustainable headway can only be made on the budget deficit by looking at the entire fiscal situa-tion. Hence, although the analysis in this volume will focus on the tax component, it will often be necessary to discuss the entire fiscal system.

Within developed countries tax structures are fairly uniform, with a heavy reliance on personal income taxes, consumption taxes, social security taxes and property taxes. In developing countries tax structures are more diverse.

They typically evolve from a heavy initial dependence on trade taxes (still common in some of the lower income countries in Africa) to more reliance on specific excises, and from there to a heavier dependence on more broadly based indirect taxes – initially manufacturing-level VATs and subsequently more broadly based VATs. Next comes growth in the use of income and corporate taxes, frequently with a slow phase-out of special tax arrangements such as tax holidays and other tax-based incentive schemes. In the more rapidly growing developing countries, such as Korea and Taiwan, growth itself has led to a clear maturation in tax structure over time. Because of the growing number of such countries, especially in Asia, it is often hard to disentangle tax reform from tax maturation in the developing world. It may be the case that tax reform in developing countries more often follows changes in the economic structure rather than leads them.

Gillis (1989) surveys tax reform efforts in a number of developing countries and both classifies and draws lessons from these efforts. He emphasizes the important distinction between comprehensive and partial reforms, suggesting that most tax reforms in developing countries are partial, concentrating on just one major tax source. He also draws a distinction between changes in tax structure (changes in the relative importance of component taxes) and changes in tax systems (introduction of new taxes or a fundamental redesign of existing taxes), suggesting most developing country reforms are the former with the exception of VAT introduction. In addition, he emphasizes the difference between revenue-enhancing and revenue-neutral reforms, suggesting that in the majority of developing country tax reforms, revenue enhancement is one of the major objectives. He also discusses distributional aspects of reforms, as well as whether objectives are interventionist or more towards economic neutrality; that is, whether the intention is to actively drive resource allocation in particular ways through tax reform. He concludes with a discussion of contemporaneous (or package) versus sequential tax reforms, suggesting most developing country reforms are the latter.

In surveying tax structures in eight East Asian economies, Tanzi and Shome (1990) argue that distortions in tax structure only become major impediments to growth once macroeconomic stability prevails, and their removal only motivates tax reform if macroeconomic imbalances are small. They also argue that, typically, distortionary taxes that deal with fiscal instabilities are preferable to persistent public sector deficits. They examine macroeconomic instability in East Asian countries with both high and low levels of taxation. They find that once stability had been won, tax reforms that substituted broadly based taxes (such as VAT) for more distortionary taxes (such as trade taxes) seemed to attract support.

More recently, in examining tax reforms in a number of developing countries, Burgess and Stern (1993) suggest that developing-country tax reform usually occurs in response to a number of related pressures: overreliance on particular tax sources such as natural resources or trade taxes; narrow tax bases such as income tax which create loopholes and evasion; complications in indirect tax arrangements involving a series of *ad hoc* measures; and weak administration.

In their analysis of reform in four Latin American countries, Perry and Herrera (1994) emphasize the entire fiscal dimension of the problem. Budget deficits in Latin America were often as much due to deficits of state-owned enterprises, quasi-fiscal deficits of the central bank and Olivera–Tanzi inflationary effects as due to deficiencies in the tax systems *per se*. Fiscal reform in Latin America has relied heavily on privatization, both to close the fiscal gap in the short run and to reduce state obligations in the long run. The large reductions in macroeconomic instability have also played an important role in both the short run (via a reverse Olivera–Tanzi effect) and the long run (by eliminating this problem entirely). Central banks have generally (but not always) got out of the subsidy game, with respect to commercial banks, industrial firms and foreign currency markets. Finally, and similar to Burgess and Stern (1993), Perry and Herrera stress that reform of the tax system itself is still to a considerable extent constrained by the economic structure of the country.

The chapters in this volume discuss the hypotheses of the various authors above as well as others with respect to both what causes and defines fiscal reform as well as the effects that accompany reform. We suggest that, despite this earlier literature, what is meant by fiscal reform in developing countries remains surprisingly ill-specified, and the reasons for the occurrence of reform are more varied than widely believed. We also emphasize how, despite attempts in the current literature to summarize and categorize reforms, there has been little quantitative assessment of the impact of reforms. Insights emerging from the work in this volume suggest, for example, that:

1 reforms that appear on paper to restructure substantially the tax system may have little effect on revenues and even effective rates (Mexico);
2 redistributive impacts on socioeconomic groups can be pronounced even if by income range little redistribution seems to occur (Côte d'Ivoire);
3 estimated redistribution from tax reform depends crucially on key assumptions regarding such features as urban/rural migration, and whether taxes on price-controlled items are shifted forward (Colombia); and
4 macroeconomic stability generated by major privatization initiatives can be a key precondition to significant tax reform (Argentina).

As countries have grown and tax systems matured in a number of countries, there has often been as much emphasis placed on improvements in compliance and tax administration as there has been on choosing the most appropriate tax structure. Improved compliance has been crucial in recent tax reforms in such countries as Argentina, the Philippines and Mexico, and probably more important than structural changes in the system. Unlike in the developed world, the words 'tax reform' in developing countries can often be disguised language for announcements of increased administrative efforts.

As Gillis (1989) emphasizes, developing country tax reform also does not generally follow the same pattern as in developed countries. It is common to think of major tax reforms in the developed world as comprehensive system-wide reforms, restructuring income, corporate, sales and other taxes – such as the reforms proposed by the Carter Commission in Canada in 1966 or the reforms implemented in 1986 in the United States. In these and many other cases extensive background work and consultations took place before a government proposal emanated, usually involving simultaneous tax change in multiple tax sources.

In the case of the developing world there have been relatively few system-wide tax reforms, with most so-called reforms focusing only on individual taxes.[4] Indeed, in recent years tax reform in developing countries has been almost synonymous with the introduction of VAT. In many countries income tax is only a small and somewhat inconsequential source of revenue due to exemptions or outright evasion. Tax reforms in Uruguay in 1974–5 actually abolished the income tax because of its limited role in the tax system compared to presumptive and other taxes. Similarly the corporate tax, while typically raising more revenue than the income tax, has remained relatively small, with changes largely occurring in investment, sectoral and regional incentives. Thus, on the surface partial tax reforms seem the rule of the day as far as the developing world is concerned, with reforms specifically focused on VAT, often in conjunction with a realignment in trade taxes.

Nevertheless, one of the key results emerging from the thematic and more qualitative studies in this volume is that a broadly defined fiscal reform is occurring with increasing frequency in recent years. When privatization, reductions of quasi-fiscal deficits, movements away from inflation and financial repression taxation, large cuts in subsidies to industry, large reductions in the civil service, the revamping of fiscal federalism, increased attention to administrative concerns, and other issues are taken into account, it can be strongly argued that system-wide fiscal reform has taken place in many developing countries.

Accordingly, the effects of tax reforms in developing countries, as compared to developed countries, are more difficult to distinguish from changes in wider government intervention in the economy. Income or losses and liabilities from government-owned assets are frequently significant elements in public finances. In India, for example, prior to recent reforms over 80 per cent of the manufacturing sector was government-owned. We have already noted that privatization initiatives, such as those recently undertaken in Argentina and Mexico, can be a temporary source of new revenues which sharply reduce deficits without corresponding short-run tax increases. In addition, other instruments such as price controls, regulatory and quantity interventions can have effects similar to taxes in developed countries, but the transfers are directly from one agent to another, rather than via governments. Other effects not associated with more conventional tax policies (such as rent-seeking) can also be prevalent. As a result, tax reform in its narrower sense and as understood in the developed world to involve base-broadening in the income tax, changes in indirect taxes and the like, can lead in the case of developing countries to an excessive focus on what is only one component of a wider set of public interventions.

Moreover, the macroeconomic context within which the tax policies operate can be crucial in the analysis of developing-country tax reforms in some cases. In some of the Latin American countries, such as Brazil and Argentina, monthly inflation rates have been as high as 30 to 40 per cent. In such circumstances, the timing of tax collections becomes a major determinant of the size of the public sector deficit (the Olivera–Tanzi effect) and the real tax rates can be highly variable. Policy changes which accelerate tax payments may have more impact on economic performance than those that, in developed countries, might be conventionally construed as tax reform. Changes in macroeconomic policy which dramatically lower the inflation rate, such as tax and privatization measures in Argentina in 1991, can have a large effect on public finances, with potentially more significant impacts on performance than changes in statutory tax rates. The sustainability of fiscal reforms can depend crucially on the macroeconomic environment, since lower tax revenues and increased macroeconomic imbalances often go hand in hand. In fact, another key result of the qualitative and thematic studies is that fiscal reform must adapt itself to the changing macroeconomic environment, especially in the short run.

Finally, the studies here indicate that there is a number of emerging issues with regard to fiscal reform in developing countries. While the recent past has seen a general convergence of fiscal systems in developing countries, it has also witnessed the more or less successful resolution of macroeconomic instability and structural adjustment in a large number of countries, primarily in East Asia, although Chile and Colombia are also of note. This success has brought a new confidence to these countries and also given them a greater freedom of policy choice and action. In the fiscal area these efforts are beginning to turn towards fiscal federalism and the related strengthening of local taxation, environmental taxation and stabilization funds in order to stabilize public expenditures, questions of income distribution and tax harmonization in integration treaties. This volume contains full chapters on the first two issues and discusses the other three in various chapters. Another conclusion of the qualitative and thematic studies is that the convergence of fiscal systems across developing countries is likely to be temporary. As individual countries grow in wealth and confidence, issues like the ones noted above will increasingly be put (back) on the plate.

We conclude this introduction with a brief discussion of the organization of the book. As each of the first two parts contains a synthesis chapter, we will not at this time highlight particular chapters and authors. Volume 1 of this book contains the country studies on Argentina, Mexico, Côte d'Ivoire and Singapore. In addition it contains thematic papers on fiscal federalism and tax incentives for investment. Volume 2 begins with an overview of the results of the more qualitative country chapters and the thematic chapters. It continues with the country studies on Colombia, the Philippines and India. These are followed by thematic chapters on environmental taxation, the interaction of macroeconomic and tax policy, economic structure and fiscal policy, trade and fiscal policy, tax incentives and tax structure in rapidly growing countries.

Notes

1 See also the recent survey on taxation and development by Burgess and Stern (1993), as well as the edited volumes by Gillis (1989) and Khalilzadeh-Shirazi and Shah (1991).

2 These two volumes also contain two chapters which analyse in a comparative fashion specific features of the South Korean and Taiwanese fiscal systems. However, as these studies concentrate on particular aspects of the systems and not on reform as a whole, these have been included in the thematic papers.

3 For three countries – Argentina, Colombia and Mexico – the modelling and more qualitative analyses are presented separately. In two others – Côte d'Ivoire and the Philippines – they are integrated in the same chapter. Finally, as noted above, the Singapore and Indian studies only contain a general equilibrium and qualitative analysis, respectively.

4 Gillis (1989) notes actual or proposed reforms in Venezuela (1958–9), Colombia (1968, 1974, 1986), Liberia (1969), Indonesia (1983–4), Jamaica (1985–7), Bolivia (1986) and Pakistan (1986–7) as the only examples of full-scale reform of which he was aware at the time of writing.

References

Ahmad, E. S. and N. H. Stern (1991) *The Theory and Practice of Tax Reform in Developing Countries*, Cambridge University Press.

Burgess R. and N. Stern (1993) 'Taxation and Development', *Journal of Economic Literature*, vol. xxxi, no. 2, pp. 762–831.

Chang, C. and P. W. H. Cheng (1992) 'Tax Policy and Foreign Direct Investment in Taiwan', in T. Ito and A.O. Krueger (eds), *The Political Economy of Tax Reform*, NBER, University of Chicago Press.

Choi, Kwang (1992) 'Comment on "An Appraisal of Business Tax Reform in Taiwan: The Case of Value-Added Taxation" by Chuan Lin', in T. Ito and A. O. Krueger (eds), *The Political Economy of Tax Reform*, NBER, University of Chicago Press.

Chia, N. C., S Wahba and J. Whalley (1992) 'Assessing the Incidence of Taxes in Côte d'Ivoire', Mimeo University of Western Ontario, London, Canada.

Clarete, R. (1991) 'A General Equilibrium Analysis of the Tax Burden and Institutional Distortions in the Philippines', in J. Khalilzadeh-Shirazi and A. Shah (eds), *Tax Policy in Developing Countries*, Washington, DC: World Bank.

Gillis, Malcolm (ed.) (1989) *Tax Reform in Developing Countries*, Durham, North Carolina: Duke University Press.

Khalilzadeh-Shirazi, J. and A. Shah (1991) *Tax Policy in Developing Countries*, Washington, DC: World Bank.

Kwack, T. and K. S. Lee (1992) 'Tax Reform in Korea', in T. Ito and A. O. Krueger (eds), *The Political Economy of Tax Reform*, NBER, University of Chicago Press.

Perry, G. and A. M. Herrera (1994) *Finanzas Publicas, Estabilización y Reforma Estructural en América Latina*, Washington, DC: Inter-American Development Bank.

Tanzi, V. and P. Shome (1990) 'The Role of Taxation in the Development of East Asian Economies', in T. Ito and A. O. Krueger (eds), *The Political Economy of Tax Reform*, NBER, University of Chicago Press.

2
Tax Reform, Tax Compliance and Factor Mobility: A CGE Model for Argentina

Omar O. Chisari[1]

O23 H26 H25
O21 E62
O16 D58

Introduction

During the 1980s many Latin-American countries experienced both high financial instability and fiscal restrictions. Though external indebtedness was probably a main cause of the fragility of public accounts, reduced tax compliance was also of importance. This led to inflationary financing and the use of a complex set of distortive taxes.

The stabilization programmes that have been launched during the 1990s, have placed a lot of emphasis on improving government revenues by increasing compliance, reducing evasion, limiting the variability of effective tax rates, and substituting export duties and turnover taxes. In fact, what has been observed is a remarkable increase in revenues from existing taxes, a tendency to reduce the variance of effective tax rates and only partial movements towards tax reform. These efforts have been particularly successful for the value-added tax (VAT) and for taxes on personal income.

Accordingly, the purpose of this chapter is to examine the welfare and allocative effects of:

1 The replacement of effective VAT rates with a lower uniform statutory rate to simulate increased tax compliance.
2 A partial tax reform encompassing replacement of existing distortive taxes with a uniform VAT.
3 A complete replacement of the current tax system with a uniform VAT. Most of the experiments performed are 'equal-yield' tax replacements; that is, they eliminate or reduce a tax rate while exactly compensating the government for lost real revenues by adjusting the rate of the VAT.

In some cases, however, an 'option value' of the reform for the government is also computed. Holding the utility index of private agents at least to their initial level, a decrease in the government's utility can be interpreted as a reduction in the quantity of public goods produced in the economy; a reform will be accepted only if it saves administrative costs of a similar magnitude. The exercises are done under assumptions of perfect and imperfect capital mobility. This is justified by the special features of the Argentine economy, which, due to financial instability experienced a huge capital flight during the 1980s. Because of this, examining the effects on the results of the various tax reforms mentioned arising from different assumptions on capital mobility is of particular interest. Would a tax reform improve welfare in the presence of capital rationing? How would the specificity of domestic capital influence the welfare gains of domestic agents? Are assumptions on capital mobility important for tax incidence issues?

The computable general equilibrium (CGE) model used to conduct the study consisted of ten domestic production sectors, five domestic consumers, a domestic investor, the domestic government and an external sector represented by a consumer and a producer. Domestic industries are broken down to take into account tax rate differences according to the destination of the products. The analytical model is calibrated to a 1986 data-set, and it is consistent with recent national accounts.

The chapter is organized as follows. The next section presents the data sources and the calibration procedure. The consequences of partial tax reforms are then discussed, followed by a summary of the main results of an overall tax reform where the current tax system is replaced by a uniform VAT. The final section presents the main conclusions of the experiments.

Data sources and calibration procedure

The main source of information is the 1984 input–output matrix for Argentina, updated for 1986 and consistent with the latest national accounts. The matrix includes 223 sectors and is, itself, an update of the corresponding 1973 matrix. Due to the surveying procedure, the transactions in this matrix are presented in gross current prices, meaning that taxes are already included in the price. This is particularly troublesome for the fiscal credit that originated in the VAT method in Argentina.[2] Thus, it was necessary to separate true production coefficients from the taxes originating in these transactions, and this was accomplished by using the estimates of the effective taxes paid by each sector as it is presented in Santiere's study (1989a).

Table 2.1 reports the tax revenue as a proportion of GDP and total public sector income. All taxes are presented in ad valorem terms for modelling and computational needs. This is a common procedure in the literature and helps to avoid problems like nonexistence or multiplicity of equilibria. One of the most salient characteristics of the tax system in Argentina during the 1980s, not captured in this table, is the complexity associated with the high variability and ineffectiveness of the tax rates; a variance that depended not only on the existence of special regimes but also on the ability of each sector to

Table 2.1 Tax yield as a proportion of total revenue and GDP, 1986 (%)

Taxes	Tax/total rev.	Tax rev./GDP
VAT	13.9	2.4
Indirect and specific taxes	11.0	1.9
Turnover tax	8.8	1.5
Tax on fuels	11.9	2.1
Export duties	4.7	0.8
Tariffs	9.8	1.7
Taxes on labour (firms)	9.9	1.7
Taxes on capital (firms)	17.9	3.2
Personal income tax (labour)	11.3	2.0
Personal income tax (capital)	0.9	0.2
Total	100.00	17.6

Source: Instituto de Economía, UADE, according to Santiere (1989a).

evade or elude a specific tax. Therefore that complexity was not necessarily a product of the statutory rates.

The inflationary tax (not included in Table 2.1) amounted to 1.4 per cent of GDP, one of the lowest levels of the decade. The reason was that, though inflationary finance was a recurrent fiscal instrument during that period, after the Austral Plan was launched in 1985 there was a reduction in the national deficit. This resulted in a reduction in the rate of inflation during 1986, which was chosen as the benchmark year for this study.

Revenue from export duties and tariffs represented about 2.5 per cent of GDP; however, from the point of view of their nominal and effective impact on exports and imports their impact was much more significant. On average, export duties amounted to more than 20 per cent of agricultural export prices.

Domestic production

Ten sectors of production are considered in this chapter, listed in Table 2.2 along with their share in GDP for 1986. Each sector is divided into five sub-sectors, which include two producers of intermediate goods (necessary to determine a tax base for turnover and other indirect taxes); an investment producer; an exporting sub-sector; and a domestic consumption goods producer. The proportion of these sub-sectors in total industry production is summarized in Table 2.3.

Several assumptions are made with respect to domestic production. First, industries of the same type (producing the same good but to different destinations) use the same technology (same ratio between intermediate consumption and value added and the same elasticity of substitution between labour and capital – the value added production function). Although the sub-sectors do not exhibit technological differences, they do differ with respect to tax

Table 2.2 Industry share in GDP (%)

Sector no.	Production sectors	Share (%)
1	Agriculture, forestry and fisheries	8.1
2	Mining	2.5
3	Food beverage and tobacco	6.3
4	Textiles, apparel and leather	3.8
5	Paper and printing; petroleum refining; chemical, rubber and plastics; lumber, furniture and glass	10.5
6	Metals, machinery and instruments	4.6
7	Electricity, water and butane	1.7
8	Construction	6.4
9	Trade and transportation	22.6
10	Finance and insurance; services	33.6

Table 2.3 Sub-sector composition of domestic industries (%)

Production sectors	Intermediate goods	Investment goods	Export goods	Consumption goods
Agriculture	58.20	2.93	23.90	14.97
Mining	99.69		0.31	
Food, beverage and tobacco	37.74		16.65	45.62
Textiles and leather	48.25	0.60	7.59	43.57
Paper, rubber, petroleum refining	78.22	0.04	5.01	16.73
Metals, machinery and instruments	57.33	23.10	5.44	14.13
Electricity, water and butane	76.47		0.01	23.53
Construction		100.00		
Trade and transport.				100.00
Finance and insurance; services	25.12			74.88

Source: Instituto de Economía, UADE, according to Secretariá de Industria (1989).

treatment. For example, investment and export sub-sectors do not charge a VAT and thus the impact is fully on domestic consumption goods. Second, labour and capital are used to 'produce' sector-specific value added by means of CES (constant elasticity of substitution) production functions. The elasticities of substitution were gathered from literature or based on econometric estimates. The exceptions were sectors 9 and 10 which were assumed to be unitary as there was no available information; it seemed reasonable to assume that the substitution between labour and capital is easier in these sectors than in the rest of the economy. Third, intermediate inputs and value added are combined in fixed proportions according to the available information on the input–output matrix (Secretaría de Industria, 1989).[3]

Domestic consumption

Domestic consumers are split into five brackets according to their share of total income (bracket 1 corresponds to the poorest). Each bracket is assumed to behave according to Cobb–Douglas utility functions; treating domestic and imported consumption goods as Armington goods. The exception is 'Trade and Transportation', which is assumed to be consumed in fixed coefficients with the rest of the 'goods'.

Personal income distribution and the share of each good in total expenditures are presented in Table 2.4. 'Construction' is assumed to be an investment good not included in expenditure plans of domestic consumers.

Savings and investments

It is supposed that each agent makes independent investment decisions. They receive a constant proportion of total income available to the private-sector and devote it to the purchase of a 'composite' investment good. The public sector also purchases this investment good. Producers maximize profits by selecting quantities of domestic and imported investment goods to produce the investment good using a Cobb–Douglas production function.

External sector

On the consumption side the external sector is represented by a single consumer with a Cobb–Douglas utility function. Production is determined using a constant elasticity of transformation (CET) function.

Table 2.4 Household expenditure composition and personal income distribution (%)

	Income bracket				
	1st	2nd	3rd	4th	5th
Agriculture, forestry and fisheries	2.46	2.64	2.18	2.09	1.25
Mining					
Food, beverage and tobacco	13.85	13.96	11.81	11.56	8.5
Textiles, apparel and leather	3.56	4.64	4.57	4.92	5.30
Paper and printing; petroleum refining; chemical, rubber and plastics; lumber, furniture and glass	3.82	4.86	4.39	4.98	4.06
Metals, machinery and instruments	0.47	1.03	1.39	2.01	2.33
Electricity, water and butane	1.79	1.70	1.45	1.30	0.88
Construction					
Trade and transportation	60.80	49.16	46.98	37.62	28.13
Finance and insurance; services	13.25	22.01	27.23	35.51	49.48
Income share	6.51	10.0	15.02	19.79	48.61

Source: UADE, according to information of CEPAL and INDEC (1988).

Calibration procedure

MPSGE (see Rutherford, 1989) was used to calibrate the model and to perform the exercises, accommodating units so that initial prices are all unitary. The 'calibration' procedure endogenously determines the missing parameters of the analytical model to replicate the base-year accounts.[4] For example, the parameters of the Cobb–Douglas utility functions (share of every good in total expenditure) are computed in the first solution of this model. In a similar way, the scaling and share parameters used in the CES production functions and CET frontier of the foreign sector are determined.

Partial reform: replacement of domestic VAT with uniform VAT

The model is used to appraise the impact of an equal-yield replacement of the domestic VAT with a uniform VAT. Thus, the VAT rate is included as an endogenous variable to be determined by solving the corresponding counterfactual exercise. The exercise is computed complying with a constraint imposed on fiscal revenues: they must equal the initial utility of revenue for the government (see Shoven and Whalley (1977) for a discussion of the theoretical foundation for this simulation).

First, the effective VAT rate is replaced with the statutory rate in order to simulate increased tax compliance. The substitution of a 'heterogeneous' VAT with a uniform VAT has, however, been defended on administrative grounds; there are enforcement and monitoring costs involved with a uniform VAT.[5] Since it is easier to monitor and apply a homogeneous tax not plagued with special treatments, a second exercise is performed to evaluate the 'option value' for the government of the tax replacement.

Movement to uniform VAT: welfare changes of private agents

The results of the substitution are presented in Table 2.5. Changes in utility levels of private agents are indicated by rows C1 to C5, and the modifications in activity levels are given by rows A1 to A10. G stands for the utility level of public sector and CI for investors' utility index. The relative prices of labour to capital (L/K) and to capital specific to agriculture (L/KA) should be compared to a value of one, their value at the benchmark equilibrium. Column (N) corresponds to the case of domestic capital mobility only, column (K) shows the results when capital is freely mobile internationally, and, finally, column (A) depicts the changes in welfare and allocation of resources when this mobility is matched with capital specificity in agriculture.

It can be seen that there are no simultaneous welfare gains for all consumers. Moreover consumers in the first bracket experience reductions in their utility level in all scenarios, a behaviour almost certainly associated with a reduction of the price of labour relative to the capital rate of return; this effect is partially compensated in case (K) since capital mobility favours an

Table 2.5 Partial reform: equal-yield replacement of domestic VAT with uniform VAT

| | Capital mobility category | | |
	N	K	A
Change in welfare (%)			
C1	−0.33	−0.11	−0.33
C2	0.04	0.18	0.0
C3	−0.3	0.0	−0.23
C4	−0.3	−0.17	−0.30
C5	0.19	0.0	0.19
CI	0.70	0.68	0.68
G	0.0	0.0	0.0
Changes in activity levels (%)			
A1	0.74	1.76	0.0
A2	1.87	2.11	2.0
A3	3.2	3.81	3.26
A4	4.96	5.28	5.2
A5	1.95	2.2	2.0
A6	1.30	1.44	1.43
A7	1.38	1.51	1.43
A8	1.23	1.26	1.25
A9	−0.2	0.0	−0.12
A10	−3.4	−2.3	−2.3
Relative Factor Prices L/K	0.986	0.988	0.987
Relative Factor Prices L/KA			0.980

appreciation of domestic 'non-tradeable' factors. Investors' welfare is enhanced because the uniform VAT rate is not placed on investment goods.

Notice also that primary and industrial sector activity levels (sectors 1–8) are increased while activity levels of sectors 9 and 10 are reduced. This outcome is due to the fact that the initial effective VAT rate for services was very low: 3.4 per cent for trade and transportation and 0.5 per cent for finance, insurance and other private services.

The assumptions on factor mobility are not critical for the changes observed in activity levels, except for agriculture. However, it must be taken into account that cases (K) and (KA) correspond to a 'bigger' economy, whereas case (N) is computed without allowing production sectors to expand their size by 'importing' capital from abroad.

Summarizing, this exercise showed that there were no significant improvements in private welfare levels as a result of the substitution of the heterogenous VAT for a uniform VAT without exemptions. Moreover, some of the brackets experienced reductions in their utility levels, which can be interpreted as the costs to be paid by private agents in order to obtain a reduction in administrative and monitoring costs. Those costs are not explicitly modelled here; this is a shortcoming in the general equilibrium presentation of the economy, since the administrative activities absorb resources that are taken out of the process of production of consumption and investment goods – see Mayshar (1991) for a discussion in an optimal taxation model.

Movement to uniform VAT: 'option value' for the government

One way to surmount the above difficulty is to assume that the administrative activities are conducted by the government removing resources for the provision of 'true' public and collective goods. Adopting this methodology implies that it is necessary to determine the value for the VAT that yields the smallest reduction in government utility necessary to leave every agent at least indifferent to the initial position, after the tax replacement.[6] Assume, for example, that this reduction amounts to 10 per cent of initial utility; for the reform to be undertaken, the corresponding administrative cost savings should be at least 10 per cent.

Table 2.6 shows the welfare levels when the government progressively reduces the tax rate and its utility level in order to reach a non-blocked reform, assuming domestic capital mobility. The reform becomes acceptable, *ceteris paribus*, for every domestic consumer when the utility of the public sectors is reduced by approximately 4 per cent; in other words, the administrative gains should amount to more than 4 per cent – in utility terms – for the reform to be accepted. Notice that although the government is persistently reducing its welfare through reductions in the VAT rate, it is difficult for agents in the first bracket to obtain welfare gains. This is due to the impact that government expenditure has on labour market conditions and the important proportion that labour income represents for the agents belonging to the first bracket. They behave like partners of the public sector since the wage rate is strongly responsive to changes in public sector revenue.

Table 2.7 reports the welfare levels, under perfect international capital mobility, when the government progressively reduces the VAT rate. In this case, the required decrease in government utility is less significant; it is necessary to sacrifice about 1 per cent of public sector welfare to offset private losses. This leads to the conclusion that a VAT reform motivated by a desire for increased efficiency would be less costly in a scenario of capital mobility than in a situation of capital rationing or immobility. This result seems to be the case for Argentina in the 1980s.

Another exercise was considered assuming all consumers in the economy to have identical sources of income. In this case every consumer's endowment of labour and capital is proportional to their share in total income distribution and only preferences differ between brackets. In fact, putting aside income distribution considerations, it is easier to accept a tax reform under any assumption on capital mobility. Table 2.8 reports the results.

Table 2.6 Option value of the partial VAT reform (domestic capital mobility)

	Tax rate (%)					
	4.3	3.5	3.0	2.5	2.0	1.0
C1	0.996	0.997	0.997	0.998	0.998	0.999
C2	1.000	1.002	1.003	1.004	1.005	1.007
C3	0.997	0.9995	1.0006	1.0018	1.002	1.005
C4	0.997	0.9988	1.0	1.001	1.0022	1.004
C5	1.0018	1.007	1.01	1.014	1.017	1.024
CI	1.007	1.007	1.007	1.0071	1.0071	1.0072
G	1.0	0.99	0.984	0.987	0.971	0.959

Table 2.7 Option value of the partial VAT reform (international capital mobility)

	Tax rate (%)		
	4.3%	4.0%	3.5%
C1	0.999	0.9996	1.0008
C2	1.0017	1.0027	1.004
C3	0.999	1.00	1.0016
C4	0.998	0.999	1.0009
C5	1.0008	1.002	1.0055
CI	1.006	1.0067	1.0067
G	1.0	0.997	0.991

Table 2.8 The single consumer case

	Tax rate (%)			
	7.0%	5.0%	4.5%	4.0%
Domestic capital mobility				
C	0.989	0.997	0.999	1.0012
G	1.031	1.008	1.002	0.996
International capital mobility				
C	0.988	0.997	0.999	1.0014
G	1.030	1.008	1.003	0.996

Partial reform: replacement of distortive taxes for an equal-yield VAT

This section examines the effects on welfare arising from the elimination of distortive taxes for an equal-yield VAT.

Elimination of tariffs and export duties

Tariffs and export duties are eliminated by a VAT in order to consider the following questions:

- What is the impact on private agents?
- Is there a Pareto-improving movement under any assumption on factor mobility?

The results of the counterfactual simulation are shown in Table 2.9. The results indicate that there is no Pareto-improving movement under any assumption on factor mobility. It is interesting to note, however, that the identity of winners and losers changes according to the assumptions on factor mobility. This is clearly the case when capital is freely mobile internationally (K); after the reform, the flow of capital to the economy is accompanied by an appreciation of labour which causes a reduction in welfare for those consumer brackets whose income depends heavily on the performance of capital. Case (A) further illustrates this effect; the relative price of labour to

Table 2.9   Partial reform, replacement of tariffs and export duties for an equal-yield VAT

	N	K	A
Changes in welfare (%)			
C1	−5.8	10.56	−1.9
C2	−3.3	6.86	−1.3
C3	−3.6	6.34	−1.4
C4	−3.5	6.16	−1.4
C5	3.0	−5.9	0.12
CI	3.56	4.6	3.6
G	0.0	0.0	0.0
Changes in activity levels (%)			
A1	65.15	224.81	0.48
A2	1.08	17.01	15.03
A3	−6.0	22.2	−1.1
A4	−1.5	12.25	16.82
A5	1.2	18.15	15.69
A6	4.3	11.73	19.22
A7	−3.3	5.78	3.46
A8	1.5	4.13	4.18
A9	−9.4	−3.4	−4.7
A10	−9.5	−7.0	−4.4
Relative factor prices L/K	0.905	1.173	1.01
Relative factor prices L/KA			0.75

Note: Column headings have the same meaning as in previous sections.

capital specific to agriculture (L/KA) substantially decreases and thus increases the reward of 'Land'. This fosters an increase in the welfare of agents belonging to the fifth category.

The modification of the activity levels is certainly related to the tax reform. Since export duties have been completely abolished there is a big incentive for industries to reallocate their resources towards exporting sectors, and this implies an increase in their activity levels. The behaviour of agriculture (sector S1) is apparent in this sense; in fact export duties represented 0.8 per cent of GDP in 1986 (see Table 2.1), but they amounted to 22 per cent of total agricultural exports. However, the results of case (K) are not realistic since they correspond to the possibility of increasing capital in agriculture, including land, whose productivity is specific to its geographical conditions – the same comment holds true for Table 2.11.

Elimination of turnover and other indirect taxes

What are the consequences of replacing the turnover tax and other indirect taxes with an equal-yield VAT? This issue is particularly interesting for Argentina since the elimination of provincial turnover taxes has been one of the objectives of the federal administration; the tax is considered a distortive tax which hurts exports and favours imports.[7]

The results of the CGE simulations are presented in Table 2.10. While there are no generalized welfare gains from the substitution, a comparison can be made with the results from Table 2.5 where the domestic VAT is replaced by a uniform VAT. In the case of domestic capital mobility (N), the welfare of all agents worsens under the current simulation. For example, agents in the fifth bracket experience an increase in welfare when turnover and other indirect taxes are replaced by an equal-yield VAT; this is not true in the case of Table 2.5. There are two possible explanations for this effect: (1) indirect taxes are working like tariffs and export duties and there is an 'optimal tariff' for the economy; (2) in the presence of other distortions, the elimination of indirect taxes worsens the utility levels of agents (a second-best effect). The first alternative cannot be accepted since the elimination of trade taxes is shown to be welfare-enhancing for the agents in the fifth bracket (Table 2.9). This suggests that the second argument is correct.

The first three quintiles experience increases in their utility levels due to reductions in relative prices of those goods that enter in an important proportion in their budget. The fourth and fifth quintiles, instead, suffer a reduction in their utility levels since they consume 'services' (see Table 2.4 above), taxed with a VAT after the reform. Under any assumption of capital mobility, it is clear that the activity levels of the industrial sectors (sectors 2 to 8) increase relative to the rest of the sectors. This is due to the neutralization of the 'cascade-effect', which artificially affected intermediate costs.

Table 2.10   Partial reform: replacement of turnover and other indirect taxes for an equal-yield VAT

	N	K	A
Changes in welfare (%)			
C1	−0.47	0.98	0.16
C2	−0.18	0.74	0.17
C3	−0.82	0.66	0.12
C4	−1.4	−0.52	−1.1
C5	−0.59	−1.4	−1.0
CI	2.9	3.35	3.43
G	0.0	0.0	0.0
Changes in activity levels (%)			
A1	0.46	7.7	0.0
A2	3.49	5.4	5.0
A3	7.59	12.37	10.0
A4	8.97	11.53	11.4
A5	3.55	5.54	5.2
A6	4.63	5.86	5.8
A7	1.65	2.65	2.3
A8	3.37	3.95	3.6
A9	−0.9	−0.37	−0.61
A10	−4.6	−4.4	−4.27
Relative factor prices L/K	0.976	0.999	0.990
Relative factor prices L/KA			0.958

Regarding agriculture, its activity level cannot be augmented as it was increased when there was perfect flexibility of capital. Only labour can be reallocated under the assumptions of column (A), but there is a very limited substitutability between capital and labour in that sector. In accordance with that assumption the production levels of sectors 9 and 10 (non-tradeables) are reduced more smoothly than in the case of full flexibility of capital.

An overall reform: complete replacement of the current tax system with a uniform VAT

This section analyses the effects on welfare arising from the complete replacement of the current tax system with a uniform VAT charged on domestic and imported consumption goods. The results of the first simulation are presented in Table 2.11. When capital is immobile internationally (N), the substitution of the entire tax system for a uniform VAT is Pareto-inferior for consumers; their utility levels are reduced by 2 to 3 per cent. Since it is assumed that VAT is not charged on investment goods, investors experience a welfare gain since there is a reduction in the price of investment goods

Table 2.11 An overall reform

	N	K	A
Changes in welfare (%)			
C1	−2.8	22.2	−22.2
C2	−2.4	11.72	−11.6
C3	−3.1	10.32	−10.0
C4	−3.3	9.49	−11.2
C5	−3.5	−20.5	−25.4
CI	15.19	18.11	35.0
G	0.0	0.0	0.0
Changes in activity levels (%)			
A1	48.7	363.0	−66.0
A2	3.4	30.19	26.85
A3	−2.1	50.55	−40.2
A4	1.5	21.89	−7.8
A5	3.0	31.43	24.98
A6	10.6	21.71	60.45
A7	−0.2	12.77	1.73
A8	11.4	16.90	39.26
A9	−7.5	−1.6	−19.0
A10	−12.0	−11.4	−11.8
Relative factor prices L/K	0.916	1.4138	0.899
Relative factor prices L/KA			0.1441

relative to the rest of the goods in the economy.[8] Notice also the dramatic changes of the results when it is accepted that agricultural capital is specific.

One of the big issues of discussion during the late 1980s was the impact of the burden of external debt honouring on public finances. Some authors argued that devaluations could influence in a very important way public accounts, since most of the external debt had been passed on – through a variety of mechanisms – to the public sector.[9]

Table 2.11 was computed by assuming that the government was honouring a debt in a specific factor different from capital used in produc tion. Assume instead that this hypothesis was removed so that the debt would have to be repaid according to the rate of return of productive capital; this assumption implies not only full international mobility of capital, but also that public sector accounts would be improved if the 'relative price' of tax revenue (defined in terms of domestic goods) were to appreciate after a tax reform. This is the result that could be expected after observing the appreciation of domestic goods – and labour – observed in column K. In fact, this is what happens under scenario K when the new assumption is introduced. Instead of an equal-yield outcome, the public sector experiences an improvement of about 2.5 per cent in its utility level, while the rest of the numbers show only slight modifications.[10]

A second simulation is performed to evaluate the 'option value' for the government of the overall tax reform. Assuming domestic capital mobility only, Table 2.12 illustrates that it is quite difficult to obtain a Pareto-improving movement by progressively reducing the VAT rate (and therefore the provision of public goods). Another shortcoming of substituting the current tax system for a uniform VAT is that the necessary VAT rate is very high (40.5%); this creates an incentive for tax evasion or lobbying.[11]

It is interesting to see that while the government is reducing its own welfare by decreasing the tax rate, it is difficult for consumers in the first bracket to experience a utility gain. This can be explained by the idea that labour income of agents in the first bracket depends on the public sector demand for labour; sacrificing government revenue and hence welfare causes a decrease in the wage rate.

The results in Table 2.13 assume that capital is freely mobile. In this case, it is almost impossible to increase the welfare of those brackets which depend heavily on the rate of capital return (the fifth quintile).

Table 2.12   Option value of the overall VAT reform (domestic capital mobility)

	Tax rate (%)				
	40.5%	35.0%	20.0%	10.0%	5.0%
C1	0.972	0.974	0.979	0.98	0.985
C2	0.976	0.985	1.012	1.031	1.042
C3	0.969	0.929	1.008	1.029	1.040
C4	0.966	0.976	1.006	1.027	1.038
C5	0.965	0.996	1.009	1.17	1.213
CI	1.1519	1.15	1.1489	1.149	1.15
G	1.0	0.947	0.766	0.59	0.478

Table 2.13   Option Value of the overall VAT reform (international capital mobility)

	Tax rate					
	49.7%	40.0%	35.0%	20.0%	10.0%	5.0%
C1	1.22	1.25	1.27	1.32	1.36	1.38
C2	1.117	1.148	1.165	1.22	1.26	1.28
C3	1.103	1.135	1.152	1.20	1.25	1.27
C4	1.09	1.126	1.143	1.20	1.24	1.26
C5	0.795	0.829	0.848	0.911	0.96	0.986
CI	1.18	1.1797	1.179	1.178	1.179	1.18
G	1.0	0.919	0.872	0.70	0.538	0.43

Concluding remarks

Under the assumptions of this chapter, a partial reform of the VAT – involving the elimination of special treatments, reduction of the nominal tax rate and widening of the tax base – does not increase private welfare. Moreover, it is found to be regressive when capital is not perfectly mobile. With perfect capital mobility, instead, the VAT behaved progressively.

In fact, two types of partial tax reforms have been considered. The first reform replaced domestic VAT with an equal-yield uniform VAT in order to simulate increased tax compliance; and increased compliance led to ambiguous welfare implications for private agents. When capital was immobile, the reform became acceptable for every agent when the utility of the public sector was reduced by 4 per cent. In the case of perfect international capital mobility, the government had to sacrifice 1 per cent of its welfare to offset private losses.

The second partial reform eliminated distortive taxes for an equal-yield VAT; two cases were discussed:

- When tariffs and export duties were eliminated, assuming capital was immobile, the fifth bracket experienced a welfare gain while all others exhibited a welfare reduction. The opposite result occurred when capital was assumed mobile; the fifth quintile in whose income depends more heavily on capital rate of return was the only bracket to suffer a welfare loss.
- When turnover and other indirect taxes were eliminated, all agents suffered a welfare loss if capital was assumed immobile. However, when capital was perfectly mobile the lower quintiles experienced welfare gains but the upper quintiles suffered a reduction in welfare.

An overall tax reform consisting of a complete replacement of the current tax system with an equal-yield uniform VAT was also studied. When capital was immobile, all agents experienced a welfare loss. However, under international capital mobility only agents in the fifth bracket (the wealthiest sector) suffered a reduction in welfare. It is also observed that in both cases the VAT rate necessary to compensate government income was extremely high, resulting in important incentives for tax evasion.

Notes

1 Instituto de Economía Universidad Argentina de la Empresa, Lima 717 Piso 5to. (1073) Buenos Aires, Argentina. Tel: (541) 372–5454; Fax: (541) 383–4309.
2 The tax credit method is illustrated by Shoup (1990). The VAT in Argentina is an income-type VAT based on the destination principle (see Schenone, 1990). The VAT liability is computed by subtracting the fiscal credit (tax already included in the price of inputs) from the fiscal debit (tax multiplied by the value of the good or service sold).

3   A full description of the analytical model may be requested from the author.
4   Mansur and Whalley (1984) present a description of the method.
5   This is not only the case of VAT in Argentina; the recent Canadian experience with the Goods and Services Tax (GST) shows that administrative issues play a significant role on the full evaluation of the workings of a tax.
6   That means that the replacement should determine a Pareto-improving movement – in a weak sense – not to be blocked by the agents in any bracket. Alternatively, it could be argued that under a kind of Rawlsian justice criterion, the least favoured agent should be assisted not to suffer a welfare loss.
7   Several alternatives have been mentioned to compensate for the lost revenue. On the one hand, the federal government favours the implementation of a sales tax at the retail level, which is considered very difficult to monitor and particularly discriminatory for those provinces oriented to production activities rather than to the location of consumers. On the other hand, some provinces have proposed the use of a provincial VAT to be charged on top of the federal VAT; in this case the federal government objects that the increase in the nominal value of the rate would determine incentives for evasion and elusion.
8   When this assumption is removed, we get different results. Consumers in brackets 1 to 3 experience welfare improvements (0.5 per cent, 0.8 per cent, 0.1 per cent respectively), while consumers in brackets 4 and 5 suffer welfare losses (0.2 per cent and 0.7 per cent respectively). Investors still have a utility gain but of a smaller magnitude (1.6 per cent).
9   A summary of the impacts that this could have on public sector functioning and on the economy's performance can be found in Damill *et al.* (1989).
10 However, this exercise does not capture the consequences of the so-called *third gap*, the constraint on the rate of growth determined by the public sector financial difficulties. The three-gap literature adds, in general, two assumptions to the hypothesis that there is a significant public sector external debt: the government is rationed in credit markets and there is some complementarity between private and public investment.
11 In the context of a model of optimal taxation, Chisari and Navajas (1992) show that an increase of nominal tax rates could determine an increase of the incentives to allocate resources to evasion or elusion activities.

References

CEPAL, 'Indicadores macroeconómicos de la Argentina', various issues.

Chisari, O. O. and F. Navajas (1992) 'Public Inputs, Tax Collection Costs and Fiscal Constraints', Fifth Annual Inter-American Seminar on Economics, National Bureau of Economic Research and Instituto Di Tella, Buenos Aires.

Damill, M., J. M. Fanelli, R. Frenkel and G. Rozenwurcel (1989) *Deficit Fiscal, Deuda Externa y Desequilibrio Financiero*, Buenos Aires: Ed. Tesis.

FIEL (1991) *El Sistema Impositivo Argentino*, Fundación de Investigaciones Económicas Latinoamericanas, Buenos Aires: Ed. Manantial.

FIEL/CEA (1990) *El Gasto Público en la Argentina*, Buenos Aires.

INDEC (1988) 'Encuesta de gastos e ingresos de los hogares', Buenos Aires.

Mansur, A. and J. Whalley (1984) 'Numerical Specification of Applied General Equilibrium Models: Estimation, Calibration and Data', in H. E. Scarf and J. B. Shoven (eds), *Applied General Equilibrium Analysis*, Cambridge: Cambridge University Press.

Mayshar, J. (1991) 'Taxation with Costly Administration', *Scandinavian Journal of Economics*, vol. 93 (1), pp. 75–88.

Rutherford, T. F. (1989) *General Equilibrium Modelling with MPS/GE*, University of Western Ontario.

Santiere, J. J. (1989) *Asignación de la Carga Tributaria por Sectores de Actividad Económica*, Programa de Asistencia Técnica para la Gestión del Sector Público Argentino, Buenos Aires.

Santiere, J. J. (1989) *Asignación de la Carga Tributaria por Niveles de Ingreso*, Programa de Asistencia Técnica para la Gestión del Sector Público Argentino, Buenos Aires.

Schenone, O. H. (1990) 'The VAT in Argentina', in M. Gillis, C. S. Shoup and G. P. Sicat (eds), *Value Added Taxation in Developing Countries*, a World Bank symposium, Washington.

Secretaría de Hacienda (1989) *Sector Público: Esquema de Ahorro-Inversión-Financiamiento 1961–1986*, Buenos Aires.

Secretaría de Industria-PNUD (1989) *Matriz de insumo-producto de los sectores productores de bienes, 1984*, Buenos Aires.

Shoup, C. S. (1990) 'Choosing Among Types of VATs', in M. Gillis, C. S. Shoup and G. P. Sicat, *Value Added Taxation in Developing Countries*, a World Bank symposium, Washington.

Shoven, J. B. and J. Whalley (1977) 'Equal Yield Tax Alternatives', *Journal of Public Economics*, vol. 8, pp. 211–24.

Vargas de Flood, M. C. and M. M. Harriague (1992) *El gasto público consolidado*, Ministerio de Economía, Secretaría de Programación Económica, Doc. de Trabajo Nro. GP-01, Buenos Aires.

3
Fiscal Reform and Macroeconomic Stabilization in Argentina

Guillermo Rozenwurcel[1]

Ōll E62 H50
823 H25

Introduction

The two hyperinflationary episodes of 1989 and 1990 left the Argentine economy in a critical situation. In a context of huge fiscal imbalances, massive capital flights and swift demonetization, prices rose almost 50 times in 1989 and another 13 in 1990, while real investment collapsed and output dropped 6.6 per cent in 1989 to remain constant the following year.

At the end of March 1991 the government announced a new stabilization policy based on the full convertibility of the domestic currency at a fixed exchange rate established by law, and a 100 per cent backing of the money base with foreign reserves. A sharp fiscal adjustment was the other key component of the programme. At the same time, the government hastened the rhythm of privatizations, trade liberalization and other market-oriented structural reforms already underway since the beginning of Menem's administration.

The Convertibility Plan was considerably effective in stabilizing the economy. The fiscal balance showed a remarkable improvement, whereas optimistic expectations and a favourable international background triggered an impressive inflow of private capital and a rapid process of remonetization. As a result, inflation dropped dramatically and economic activity began a fast recovery. However, given the introduction of a fixed nominal exchange rate regime, the convergence of domestic inflation towards international rates was not fast enough to prevent a substantial appreciation of the domestic currency in real terms.

Furthermore, against the background of a falling real exchange rate, trade liberalization caused an abrupt rise in imports. As exports remained stagnant, the trade balance sharply deteriorated and the current account, which ran a surplus in 1990, turned into a growing deficit from 1991.

The other source of potential trouble for the prospects of stabilization was the fragility still displayed by the public sector. No matter how important the achievements in tax revenues had been so far, non-financial current expenditures had also shown a significant growing trend, basically because of both the heavy burden of the social security system and the lack of fiscal adjustment in the provinces. In such a context, investment cuts, the decline in international interest rates, the real appreciation of the exchange rate, and once-and-for-all privatization revenues played a key role in keeping the public sector borrowing requirements under control. Nevertheless, this was clearly not a permanent solution.

Taking all this into account, this chapter discusses the relationship between stabilization and fiscal reform in the context of the Convertibility Plan implemented in Argentina, mainly focusing on tax reform and privatizations. The first two sections summarize the performance of the Argentine economy and the fiscal accounts respectively. Then the evolution of the tax system is traced throughout the 1980s, and the main components of the process of tax reform are examined, as well as its first results. The chief reasons underlying the improvement in tax performance are then analysed, followed by a discussion of the role played by privatizations. Finally, a preliminary assessment of the process of fiscal reform is presented and the still unsettled issues of this process are pointed out.

Recent macroeconomic trends

The Convertibility Plan announced in March 1991 achieved considerable success in overcoming hyperinflation and stabilizing the Argentine economy. As a result, annual inflation (measured in terms of the consumer price index, CPI) was cut to only 7.4 per cent in 1993, an exceptionally low rate according to Argentine historic standards, and it is expected to be even lower in 1994 (see Table 3.1). A fixed rate of exchange, a swift trade liberalization and a sharp fiscal adjustment were the key factors explaining this outcome, but legal deindexation of nominal contracts, price agreements in some strategic industries, and other incomes policy measures were also important at the initial stages of stabilization.

Regarding the fiscal stance, in particular, the improvement has been remarkable, even allowing the government to begin producing surpluses in the overall fiscal balance since 1992 – 0.7 per cent that year and 1.4 per cent in 1993 (see Table 3.1).

The success of stabilization also brought about a large increase in all monetary aggregates. The sharp reduction in macroeconomic uncertainty, the abrupt fall in inflation and economic recovery caused the demand for money to rise steadily, and the expanding money needs of the public were matched by massive capital inflows. Privatization of public concerns and some other structural reforms launched by the government were major determinants underlying this trend, and the repatriation of flight capital was equally important. However, the significance of the sudden reversal experienced by international financial conditions since the early 1990s,

Table 3.1   Key economic indicators, 1988–93

	1988	1989	1990	1991	1992	1993
Real GDP (% chg.)	−1.9	−6.2	0.1	8.9	8.7	6.0
Ind. production (% chg.)	−4.9	−7.1	2.0	11.9	7.3	4.5
CPI (% chg, end-period)	387.7	4923.3	1343.9	84.0	17.5	7.4
Real exch. rate (CPI USA/CPI Arg., 1983=100)	103.1	127.3	82.6	56.2	49.6	47.9
Ind. real wages (1983=100)	101.4	82.0	85.8	87.0	88.1	86.7
PSBR (% of GDP)	3.3	4.8	1.8	0.8	−0.7	−1.4
Total money resources (% of GDP)[a]	17.8	11.5	5.0	7.5	11.4	18.2
Investment rate (% of GDP)[b]	18.6	15.5	14.0	14.6	16.7	17.9
National savings rate (% of GDP)[b]	19.5	17.8	17.7	14.9	13.9	15.8
Export coefficient (% of GDP)[b]	9.5	13.1	10.4	7.7	6.6	6.3
Import coefficient (% of GDP)[b]	6.2	6.6	4.6	6.1	8.1	7.9
External accounts (US$ billion)						
Trade balance	3.81	5.37	8.28	3.70	−2.64	−3.70
Real services	−0.26	−0.26	−0.32	−0.93	−1.05	−1.22
Financial services	−5.13	−6.42	−6.12	−5.63	−4.59	−3.97
Current account	−1.57	−1.29	1.90	−2.83	−8.55	−8.97
External debt	58.5	63.3	61.0	63.7	65.0	68.0

[a]Including dollar deposits in the Financial System.
[b]Current prices.
Source: ECLA (various issues), DNIAF (various issues) and own estimates.

which also benefited most of the other Latin American countries, can hardly be downplayed.[2] As a result, private capital inflows amounted to nearly US$26 billion in 1991–3, while total monetary resources (M2 in pesos and dollars) rose from 5 per cent of GDP in 1990 to 18.2 per cent three years later (see Table 3.1).

Economic activity also underwent an outstanding expansionary phase from the beginning of the programme. Indeed, the GDP growth rate stood at 8.9 per cent in 1991, 8.7 per cent in 1992 and 6.0 per cent in 1993. The performance of industrial output was also impressive: its average growth rate was 7.9 per cent for those same years (Table 3.1). The huge capital inflow induced by both domestic stabilization and a positive external environment was essential in determining this trend.

Economic recovery was led by consumption which experienced a boom as a consequence of the repatriation of capital from abroad and of the increased availability of private sector credit. The consumption boom was so strong that, somewhat paradoxically, it deepened the decline in the national savings rate brought about during the past decade by the debt crisis first, and by the hyperinflation episodes afterwards. As a result, the level of national savings dropped to only 3.9 per cent of GDP in 1992, and while it recovered to 15.8 per cent of GDP in 1993 it was still far below the 1988 rate of 19.5 per cent.

Aggregate investment also showed a significant improvement. According to official data gross fixed capital formation grew from 14 per cent of GDP in 1990 to 17.9 per cent of GDP in 1993 (Table 3.1). So far, this improvement has only enabled the economy to recover the investment rates prevailing in the mid-1980s, before the hyperinflationary outburst but after the debt crisis. Nevertheless, these rates are substantially lower than the ones observed in the 1970s. Meanwhile, the substantial growth in private sector money demand allowed the central bank to accumulate a considerable sum of foreign currency over 1990–1993. As a result, the stock of international reserves (excluding gold) added up to over US$15 billion by the end of 1993. This amount is equivalent to almost one year of imports, but represents about one-third of total monetary resources.

Other foreign sector indicators also evolved favourably. For one thing, privatizations and debt–equity swaps contributed to cutting down the stock of foreign debt by more than 8 per cent between 1989 and 1992. Moreover, as a proportion of GDP, foreign debt fell from 38 per cent in 1989 to 27 per cent in 1993, even though the appreciation of the domestic currency was largely responsible for this result. Interest-due payments, in nominal terms and also as a percentage of both total exports and GDP, also diminished because of both the reduction in foreign debt and the fall in international interest rates. Additionally, after complex negotiations, a final agreement with creditor banks was signed in December 1992 under the auspices of the Brady Programme, thereby normalizing Argentina's relations with the international financial community.

The Convertibility Plan, however, despite all its achievements, did not perform that well regarding other indicators. In the first place, and in spite of the impressive growth rates of 1990–1993 in aggregate output, economic activity during that period was extremely uneven. As a result of a sharp trade liberalization and a negative evolution of relative prices, the level of activity in the economic sectors and regions more exposed to foreign competition notoriously lagged behind the average trend, and in some cases contracted in absolute terms. Even more striking, output expansion was accompanied by a steady rise in unemployment rates, which jumped from 6.9 per cent in May 1991 to 10.8 per cent in May 1994.

The evolution of relative prices, in turn, had much to do with the dynamics of inflation. In fact, the rapid growth in nominal aggregate demand, and the persistence of implicit defensive pricing rules inherited from the high-inflation period, especially in the sectors supplying services, made the convergence of domestic inflation towards international rates a rather slow process. Under convertibility rules, and with an absolutely passive policy regarding capital inflows, this caused a sizeable appreciation of the domestic currency, impairing the competitiveness of the tradable sectors. Indeed, the real exchange rate, which at the beginning of the plan was almost 34 per cent below its average level in the second quarter of 1990 (generally accepted, even in the government's view, as a reasonable reference for this variable), fell another 15 per cent from April 1991 to the end of 1992.

Real appreciation, coupled with trade liberalization and a booming domestic absorption induced a sudden worsening of the trade balance. On the one hand, total imports grew rapidly in both volume and value during the last two years: they rose from an extremely low level of US$4.1 billion in 1990 to US$8 billion in 1991, and on to almost US$16.8 billion in 1993. Total exports, in turn, remained stagnant around the peak attained in 1990 in the aftermath of hyperinflation, when they reached US$12.4 billion. As a result, the huge US$8 billion trade surplus achieved in 1990 was more than halved in 1991, and it has turned into a growing deficit since 1992 – US$2.6 billion that year and US$3.7 billion in 1993 (Table 3.1). Meanwhile, the deficit in real services sharply worsened as well, with tourism expenditures abroad largely accounting for this outcome.

In spite of a sizeable reduction in financial services, which went down from US$6.1 billion in 1990 to less than US$4 billion in 1993, the deterioration in foreign trade and real services caused the current-account balance to revert from a US$1.9 billion surplus in 1990 to a US$2.8 billion deficit in 1991, which soared to almost US$9 billion in 1993 (Table 3.1). The rapidly growing deficit in the current account since 1991 has been totally financed through the capital account. In fact, the impressive amount of capital inflows even made a considerable increase in foreign reserves possible. As has already been said, private sector capital movements were mainly responsible for this outcome, accounting for a US$26 billion inflow throughout the same period.

As can be concluded from this analysis, economic prospects are simultaneously influenced by conflicting factors. On the positive side, inflation has roughly converged to international rates, foreign reserves look high enough to sustain the credibility of the economic policy, and the agreement reached with foreign creditors under the Brady initiative has eased Argentina's access to voluntary lending in the world's financial markets. Nevertheless, many difficulties still lie ahead. From a long-term perspective the rate of investment is still low, and its current growth is being geared primarily towards production for domestic markets and non-tradable services, the recently privatized public utilities leading the process. Moreover, practically all the recent expansion in aggregate investment has been financed by foreign savings. National savings, on the contrary, has not yet reacted to ongoing structural reforms and still remains at quite low levels.

From a shorter-term perspective, the rise in unemployment and the deep crisis underway in many regional economies are having obvious negative repercussions on income distribution and social cohesion, thereby threatening the sustainability of the programme on political economy grounds. Additionally, the rigidity imposed on the exchange rate policy by the

Convertibility Law will make it hard to reverse the real appreciation of the domestic currency and will probably aggravate the problems of the tradable sectors, as well as the current-account deficit.

As a result, the external balance will remain highly dependent on the continuity of substantial capital inflows at a time when international financial markets begin to show clear symptoms that their future evolution will not be as favourable to the country as it has been in the recent past. This trend, coupled with the growing disparity between the monetary liabilities of the domestic financial system and central banks' foreign reserves, is making the overall economic environment increasingly fragile before potentially destabilizing shocks, either external or domestic.

The other source of potential trouble for the prospects of stabilization is the fragility still displayed by the public sector. We will consider fiscal performance more carefully in the following section.

Fiscal performance after convertibility

The debt crisis that emerged at the beginning of the 1980s dramatically worsened the already chronic budgetary imbalances of the Argentine public sector. In fact, the credit rationing which arose in the world's financial markets as a consequence of the crisis made it necessary for the country to produce a permanent trade surplus to meet, at least partially, the large interest payments due on the previously accumulated foreign debt. The required adjustment had long-lasting negative implications on the overall functioning of the economy, constituting the well-known 'external transfer' problem.

But that was not all. Given that almost all the foreign debt had become public by the time of the crisis, the transfer problem simultaneously had a fiscal dimension: on the one hand, the only way the government could obtain the necessary foreign currency to face its enlarged foreign payments, since Argentina's foreign trade business is mostly in private hands, was by 'buying' the trade surplus from the private sector; but on the other hand, the magnitude of the trade surplus to be transferred from the private to the public sector was extremely large when compared with either the revenue-generating capacity of the tax system or the availability of domestic credit.[3]

This internal-transfer problem also had serious macroeconomic repercussions throughout the 1980s. Because of the government's failure to induce a permanent increase in the tax burden, the repeated attempts to adjust the fiscal accounts so as to create the primary surplus required by interest payments were concentrated primarily on the expenditure side, and mostly in investment, with obvious consequences on the economy's growth performance. Nevertheless, expenditure cuts were not enough either, so the government had no choice but to rely heavily on central bank financing and domestic indebtedness. Given the prevailing low levels of monetization, this move exerted enormous pressure on both inflation and real interest rates, exacerbating the adverse economic effects brought about by the external transfer problem.

By the end of the 1980s, the failure to close both the external and fiscal gaps simultaneously led the economy to hyperinflation. Notwithstanding, this traumatic experience had one positive outcome: it created a widespread demand for economic stability and made a sustainable fiscal adjustment feasible. The Administration, in office since 1989, took advantage of this opportunity to promote several ambitious reforms in the sphere of the state, which at first focused primarily on the tax system and the privatization of public enterprises. These reforms, together with the implementation of the Convertibility Plan and the positive change experienced by the external environment, produced a remarkable fiscal improvement.

In the first place, tax receipts have experienced a dramatic increase over the period 1990–1993. The impressive recovery in tax performance, which represented about five points of GDP including both federal and provincial taxes, was due to several reasons. First, the stabilization was very successful in sharply reducing inflation while rapidly expanding output. Second, the impact of stabilization was greatly amplified by the decision to concentrate the tax effort on a broadened VAT and a few other taxes, and by the outstanding improvement achieved in tax administration, particularly regarding collection and control procedures. Last but not least, the private sector showed an increasing disposition to pay conventional taxes.[4]

As a result, tax pressure at the federal level jumped to an unprecedented 16.6 per cent of GDP in 1992, four points higher than in 1990 and remaining roughly constant the following year. At the same time, current income (which also includes the public firms' surpluses and other non-tax revenues) reached 17.5 per cent of GDP in 1992, and stayed practically at the same level in 1993 (see Table 3.2). However, non-financial current expenditures also displayed a growing trend, climbing to about 15 per cent of GDP in 1992–3, mainly as a consequence of an adverse evolution of transfers to both the social security system and the provinces. The resulting primary savings were about 2.5 per cent of GDP in the same period; this level, though much higher than the one attained in 1991, was roughly similar to that of 1989 and even lower than that of 1990 (Table 3.2).

The evolution of current savings, in contrast, proved to be much more favourable, reverting from a negative 2.7 per cent of GDP in 1989 to a positive 1.4 per cent in 1993. An unexpectedly swift decrease in foreign debt interest payments, which went down from 4.4 per cent of GDP in 1989 to 1.0 per cent in 1993, helped explain this outcome (Table 3.2). Indeed, the lower interest payments were the consequence of three different factors. First, through privatizations and debt–equity swaps, the government achieved a modest reduction in its overall foreign indebtedness. Second, and more important, the government benefited from the exogenous change in world financial markets which brought about a sharp decline in international interest rates.

Table 3.2 National public sector accounts, 1988–93 (percentage of GDP)

	1988	1989	1990	1991	1992	1993
Current income	13.8	14.7	14.0	15.5	17.5	17.3
tax revenue	11.9	12.9	12.5	14.2	16.6	16.1
non-tax revenue[a]	1.9	1.8	1.5	1.3	0.9	1.2
Non-financial current exp.	12.4	12.6	11.1	14.4	15.0	14.9
Personnel	2.9	2.6	2.2	2.9	2.4	2.5
Transfers to social sec. system	3.7	3.3	4.0	5.0	5.3	5.7
Transfers to provinces	4.2	5.0	3.7	5.0	5.6	5.4
Other expenditures	1.6	1.7	1.2	1.5	1.7	1.3
Primary savings	1.4	2.1	2.9	1.1	2.5	2.4
Interest payments	2.6	4.8	3.2	1.6	1.7	1.2
foreign debt	2.4	4.4	2.9	1.3	1.4	1.0
domestic debt	0.2	0.4	0.3	0.3	0.3	0.2
Current savings	−1.2	−2.7	−0.3	−0.5	0.8	1.2
Capital income	0.3	0.5	0.4	1.2	1.4	1.0
Privatizations (cash)	0.0	0.0	0.3	1.2	1.3	0.9
others	0.3	0.5	0.1	0.0	0.1	0.1
Capital expenditures	2.5	2.0	1.3	1.2	1.5	0.8
P.S. borrowing requirements	3.4	4.2	1.2	0.5	−0.7	−1.4

[a]Non-tax revenue includes the public firms' surplus.
Source: ECLA (various issues), DNIAF (various issues) and own estimates.

Finally, the real appreciation of the exchange rate induced by stabilization had, from a fiscal perspective, the positive side-effect of reducing the burden of foreign interest when measured as a proportion of GDP.[5]

Cash revenues arising from privatizations, which were especially necessary at the beginning of the stabilization process, extremely low levels of public investment, and an almost balanced consolidated budget of public firms also contributed to the impressive fiscal adjustment of the early 1990s. Considering the evolution of the national government's overall balance, the turn-around in the fiscal stance indeed looks so impressive that it is difficult to think that a permanent solution to the domestic transfer problem of the 1980s had not, by 1993 been finally reached. A closer scrutiny reveals, however, that the fiscal position was still quite fragile.

There are several reasons which support this assessment. First, there is the role played by privatizations during 1990–93. As already mentioned, their cash proceeds which averaged over one point of GDP in 1991–3 helped close the fiscal gap, especially in the early stages of stabilization, but their importance in strengthening the financial position of the government was much greater because they also contributed to reducing public debt through the implementation of debt–equity swap schemes. Privatizations are, nonetheless, a temporary instrument. In order for the current fiscal equilibrium to be sustainable they will eventually have to be replaced by revenues arising from other sources or by expenditure cuts.

Second, current trends in world financial markets suggest that Latin American countries as a whole are likely to face higher interest rates and lower capital inflows in the near future. Besides the direct impact of higher rates on interest-due payments, the fiscal balance could also be affected by the negative effects of a tightened external constraint on domestic economic performance. When it finally becomes necessary, external adjustment will inevitably mean a slowing down of economic activity and, consequently, lower tax revenues. Likewise, if the adjustment also requires an exchange rate devaluation, the real burden of interest payments will additionally be heightened through this channel.[6]

The fragility still displayed by fiscal accounts is also explained by domestic factors. For one thing, economic policy will have to face enormous pressure to raise non-financial current expenditures. In fact, overall current public expenditure at both the federal and provincial levels had already increased from 25.3 per cent in 1990 to 27.5 per cent in 1993. Maintaining fiscal balance will also be difficult for two other reasons. One is the ongoing crisis in the regional economies. So far, regional difficulties have prevented the provinces from replicating the fiscal adjustment attained at the federal level despite the national government's many attempts to persuade provincial administrations to do so, through either financial benefits or threats with severe penalties in the distribution of federal tax revenues.

The second reason is that public investment has almost vanished and cannot go anywhere but up. As a matter of fact, and leaving aside investments made by public firms (because they are obviously much lower than in the past after privatizations), overall capital expenditures in the public sector have experienced a dramatic decrease, even when compared to the already meagre levels in the late 1980s. Consequently, if a collapse in the economic and social infrastructure is to be avoided, they will no doubt have to be raised substantially.

There is still the impact of the social security reform implemented in 1993 to be considered. No matter how relevant this structural reform is to enhancing national savings and fostering the development of domestic financial markets, the transition from the old regime to the new will certainly have significant and enduring fiscal costs.

Indeed, social security reform has established that a restructured public pay-as-you-go system will coexist with a new capitalization scheme to be operated by private pension funds. The problem is that the transition to the new regime will inevitably produce a financial imbalance in the remaining public system: while outlays will stay basically unaffected by the reform, as long as they depend on the number of passive workers retired under the old regime, revenues will suffer a sudden fall as the active workers who now choose the capitalization scheme shift their payments to the private pension funds. First estimates suggest that the initial loss in revenues will be about one percentage point of GDP.[7]

We have already advanced a number of reasons why the sustainability of the present fiscal equilibrium cannot be taken for granted. If anything, they all stress the vital importance that future tax performance will have in preserving the fiscal balance. However, symptoms had already appeared suggesting that at some point during the first half of 1994 tax revenues might have reached a plateau, which would not be easy to surpass in the near future. In fact, for the first time since Convertibility, the June 1994 federal tax collection was lower than it had been a year earlier, and the same happened in July. A gradual cooling down of economic activity and an incipient fatigue in tax compliance on the part of the private sector might explain this trend.

Moreover, fiscal revenue prospects are further endangered by a complex policy dilemma regarding the targets of tax policy. In fact, while convertibility rules have extremely reduced the feasibility of active monetary policy, and the government's commitment to trade liberalization precludes the systematic use of import restrictions (though there have been some exceptions), fiscal policy is practically the only remaining instrument for macroeconomic management. But fiscal policy, which given the prevailing constraints on public expenditure management basically means tax policy, is subject to conflicting demands. On the one hand, as we have already emphasized, it is of critical importance to prevent the emergence of fiscal imbalances from jeopardizing economic stability. On the other hand, it is the only instrument available to counteract the most negative side effect of the ongoing stabilization process, namely the impact of exchange rate appreciation on competitiveness and unemployment.

In fact, the need to deal with an overvalued domestic currency explains the recurrent attempts to produce a so-called 'fiscal devaluation', in other words to improve *effective* exchange rates by resorting to tax policy. Along this line, a first policy package was announced in October 1992, including export rebates, fuel tax cuts and the elimination of tax stamps and other minor taxes. Since then, other comparable measures have followed, the most important being a selective reduction of employers' contributions to the social security system in tradable sectors. Furthermore, out of concern over trends in unemployment, the government announced that this last measure would be extended to non-tradable sectors as of 1995.

Preliminary estimates suggest that, all measures included, the improvement in nominal effective rates brought about by this fiscal devaluation did not exceed 5 per cent, quite a modest figure considering the actual level of real appreciation. However, preliminary calculations also estimate the fiscal cost of these measures to have been substantial, ranging between 1.0 per cent and 1.5 per cent of GDP.[8]

In sum, the sustainability of fiscal equilibrium depends largely on how successfully the government handles the tax policy dilemmas we have just discussed. With this in mind, we will now examine the tax reforms undertaken in greater detail, and we start by considering the initial conditions.

The evolution of the tax system throughout the 1980s

During the 1980s the tax structure was hit by an extremely unstable macro-economic scenario. Sharp fluctuations in tax revenues were much more the result of macroeconomic factors, such as high inflation, relative price volatility and wide output swings, than the consequence of changes within the tax system.

As we have already seen in the previous section, the external adjustment imposed by the debt crisis had strong negative repercussions on the fiscal accounts. Since the foreign debt was mainly concentrated in the public sector and the foreign exchange generated by the trade surplus was in private hands, fiscal imbalances worsened sharply and became one of the dominant features of the economy.

Recurrent attempts to cut the fiscal deficit were made throughout the period. Each of those attempts included a tax package aimed at sharply increasing the tax effort, but their design, primarily guided by short-run revenue considerations, fell short of what a comprehensive tax reform should have been. In fact, they heavily relied on temporary emergency taxes, and could not properly take into account either efficiency or equity matters. As a result, the fiscal accounts usually showed an ephemeral recovery after every adjustment, but the achievements did not last long. The chronic fiscal gap and the volatility of the macroeconomic environment exposed the tax system to permanent pressure and prevented it from consolidating a definite pattern. Consequently, regarding its tax structure, Argentina's performance during the 1980s seems to have followed a hybrid path.[9]

The behaviour of both direct taxes and VAT, in particular, was rather unsatisfactory. On the one hand, revenues arising from income and wealth taxes were too low – 1.6 per cent of GDP on average over the whole decade, representing about 13 per cent of federal tax revenues.[10] It should be mentioned, though, that Argentina had already shown a poor record on direct taxation in the 1970s when economic conditions were much better.

On the other hand, the country adopted the value added tax in the mid-1970s, earlier than most Latin American economies. Until very recently, however, experience with this tax has also been disappointing. From the beginning its base was not comprehensive, and a multiple rate scheme was implemented. By 1980 the tax base was broadened, and in 1981 the tax rate was increased to 20 per cent. This enabled VAT collection to reach 3.8 per cent of GDP that year, but the attempt proved to be short-lived. Between 1982 and 1984 new exemptions were granted for public services, foodstuffs and medicines. Moreover, the tax rate was progressively reduced to only 14 per cent in 1990. These changes, coupled with deteriorating economic activity and declining imports, led to a fall in VAT revenues which on average amounted to slightly more than 2 per cent of GDP (16.5 per cent of total federal collection) from 1984 to 1990.

Due to the meagre performance of both direct and value added taxes, the share of excise taxes in total collection gained enormous relevance during the 1980s. In fact, excise taxes represented on average one-third of the federal tax burden over that period. Fuel tax revenues, in particular, were roughly equivalent to those stemming from VAT.[11]

Wage income was the other significant source of federal taxation. Funds coming from this source, representing almost 25 per cent of the total, are earmarked for the social security system. However, despite the fact that wage taxes were quite high, and at the same time pensions were still kept well below legal standards, the structural crisis of the system constantly demanded additional funds.

Finally, federal taxation was completed by trade taxes. On average they comprised around 14 per cent of the total but were subject to sharp fluctuations owing to the instability of trade policies throughout the period, particularly regarding import tariffs and export tax rates.

As has already been noted, neither efficiency nor equity implications of the tax system were a major issue during the 1980s. The inflationary environment and the volatility in tax revenues help to explain this fact. However, during the first half of the 1980s, while the economy was plunging into deep stagflation, the government authorized massive tax expenditures. Though phrased in terms of regional and sectoral targets of industrial policy, the social costs and benefits of the decision were not duly taken into account. Indeed, tax expenditures were appropriated by a small number of firms, while there was hardly any impact on aggregate employment or investment. And, despite temporary improvements the evolution of the overall tax burden (considering both federal and provincial taxes) showed a declining trend over the decade. Starting from over 17.5 per cent of GDP in 1980, total collection dropped steadily until 1983 when it reached 11.7 per cent of GDP, remaining at about the same level in 1984. Partly as a consequence of the tax package implemented during 1984 and 1985, but largely as a result of the temporary stabilization achieved by the Austral Plan, the tax burden recovered its 1980 level in 1985–6.

This significant improvement, however, was basically brought about by increases in both export taxes, which later proved politically unsustainable, and wage taxes. To a lesser extent, other equally distortive taxes such as the fuel tax and that imposed on bank drafts (which reached 0.7 per cent of GDP in 1988) also contributed to the same end. Additionally, a compulsory savings regime was established from 1985 to 1989 which, in practice, worked as an 'emergency' tax. Instead, other measures aimed at changing the tax structure in a deeper and more permanent way did not produce the expected outcome. That was the case, in particular, of the measures taken to improve the performance of direct taxes and the VAT, which failed to induce any relevant rise in revenues. To a great extent, that was because they were heavily contingent on administrative resources which were simply unavailable.

Be that as it may, the recovery did not last long. In 1987, the Austral Plan began to weaken and inflation accelerated, leading to a renewed fall in tax revenues. As a result, the average total tax burden for 1988–90 stayed below 15 per cent of GDP. Moreover, the deterioration in tax collection attained unprecedented levels during the two hyperinflationary outbursts, in the second quarter of 1989 and the first quarter of 1990. In both periods the federal tax burden fell beneath 10 per cent of GDP, reaching its lowest levels in the decade.

The process of tax reform: 1990–3

After the failure of a first stabilization attempt, which gave rise to the second hyperinflationary outburst in late 1989 and early 1990, President Menem's administration firmly adopted the market-friendly approach to structural reforms advocated by the World Bank and the Washington Consensus. The public sector thus became one of the chief reform targets and, as a consequence, both tax reform and privatizations were placed at the top of the government's agenda.

Regarding tax reform, it is possible to distinguish two different stages. First, priority was given to increasing revenues by any means in order to overcome the effects of hyperinflation on the fiscal accounts. Second, more attention was paid to allocative and distributive issues. As a result, the tax structure acquired a new profile, quite different from the one it had in the 1980s.

In the midst of hyperinflation, as already mentioned, tax collection reached extremely low levels. In the first half of 1989, total tax revenues in real terms were 22 per cent lower than those in the same period of 1988. The Olivera–Tanzi effect was the basic underlying factor: according to official estimates, during the second quarter of 1989 the loss due to this effect amounted to 31.5 per cent of earned revenues (equivalent to 3.2 per cent of GDP) at the federal level.[12] Moreover, the lack of private credit and high real interest rates motivated long delays in tax payments.

The performance of taxes linked to domestic activity was also affected by a deep recession and the virtual interruption of economic transactions: revenues arising from VAT, excises and income tax were reduced to about one-half of their level in the second quarter of 1988. The extreme instability of the exchange rate regime, in turn, impaired the performance of trade taxes. The sudden fall in inflation brought about by the first policy announcements of President Menem's administration fueled a rapid recovery in tax collection from July to November 1989. The reverse Olivera–Tanzi effect was responsible for about 40 per cent of the recovery, but several emergency measures were also adopted – a major contribution being higher taxation on exports, which tried to capture at least part of the windfall gains arising from the steep devaluation of the domestic currency.

Despite the above-mentioned second hyperinflationary episode in late 1989 and early 1990, a second stage in the tax policy developed over 1991–3, particularly since the 1991 stabilization programme. In this new stage, a series of successive reforms attained a permanent improvement in tax collection, whilst also shaping a new tax structure. The core of the reform strategy was a simpler system, eliminating all minor distortive taxes, and placing VAT at the centre of the new scheme.[13] Indeed, the VAT base was broadened to unprecedented levels (including agriculture and all major service activities), while multiple rates were eliminated and the remaining general rate strongly raised from 14 per cent in 1990 to 18 per cent 1992. At the same time, VAT compliance was enhanced through several administrative mechanisms such as widespread withholding and standardized billing, in order to diminish evasion, particularly by small businesses and informal trading.

In 1992 important steps were taken concerning the reform of the income tax. First, Congress failed to enact the administration's extremely innovative proposal of a tax on the net surpluses of firms. This tax was intended to replace both the traditional income tax and employer's contributions to social security, altering tax incentives in the right direction, while radically simplifying tax administration because of the close connection between its base and that of VAT. In the end a more conventional reform was passed. With regard to corporate income tax, besides increasing the tax rate from 20 per cent to 30 per cent in April 1992, restrictions applied to deductions of past losses arising from business declarations were the most important aspect of the reform.

Deductions of past losses were a major drag on corporate income-tax collection throughout the 1980s, due to abuses with tax-expenditure schemes perpetrated by discretionary industrial policies, and also because of the negative impact of inflation-adjustment accounting mechanisms on taxable profits. Owing to the sharp reduction in inflation and the drastic cut in tax expenditures, it is unlikely that this issue will represent a serious problem in the future. However, something had to be done with the declared losses accumulated in previous years but not yet deducted in subsequent declarations. The solution adopted in 1993 was to transform those losses into fiscal credits at a uniform rate of 20 per cent, and to pay the credits with long-term public bonds (*Bonos de Consolidación de Deudas*).

Regarding personal income tax, the marginal rate was cut from 45 per cent to 30 per cent, and the number of income brackets was reduced to six. The major innovation, however, was the suppression of the non-taxable minimum income. Instead, taxpayers incorporated into the social security system will be allowed to partially compute their monthly contributions to the system as payments in advance in their annual income tax declarations. It is expected that this measure will help diminish evasion in the social security system, especially among self-employed workers and professionals.

Other important reforms comprised the elimination of virtually all tax-expenditure schemes (measures included in the Economic Emergency Law of 1990), the suppression of export taxes and over 20 other distortive taxes (such as tax stamps, a tax on bank drafts, and so on.), and a simplified collection and distribution mechanism for the fuel tax. It is also worth mentioning the 1993 administrative decision to assign the Federal Tax Bureau (*Dirección General Impositiva*) the responsibility for collecting social security contributions, previously under the Ministry of Labour's competence, in order to enhance tax compliance in this area.

In contrast, the institution of a corporate gross asset tax, similar to the one applied in Mexico and other Latin American countries in 1990, did not produce the expected outcome. Despite increasing the tax rate from the initial level of 1 per cent to 2 per cent, the proceeds remained negligible (less than one-quarter of a percentage point of GDP), so in 1993 the government finally decided to eliminate it.

Additionally, a much more rigorous legal framework was established in 1990, when the *Ley Penal Tributaria* (No. 23771) was passed by Congress, intending to foster tax compliance by imposing severe penalties (including imprisonment) on evasion. By the end of 1993 over 1700 cases had been opened under this new law.

Nevertheless, it is highly probable that the impact of all these reforms in actual tax collection would not have been so positive had it not been for the impressive improvement observed in the design and functioning of the *Dirección General Impositiva* (DGI). Indeed, the improvements in tax administration and the consequent reduction in evasion were especially relevant for two reasons: (1) they enabled the government to increase revenues without resorting to emergency taxes, and (2) they improved horizontal equity, in particular regarding VAT collection.

As can be seen in Table 3.3, the restructuring of the Tax Bureau involved higher wages and a swift increase in personnel. In fact, the number of employees jumped from 10 500 to 16 000 in just three years (from November 1989 to November 1992), and according to the 1994 Federal Budget it was expected to reach 26 500 that year, with average wages rising from US$1100 to 1800. The restructuring also involved major changes in working routines, the adoption of wage incentives associated with performance, and a new wage scale encompassing greater pay differentials.

Administrative efficiency was further pursued through technological upgrading: personal computers in use numbered only 20 in 1989 but rose to 1164 in 1992; more powerful equipment was also incorporated. Meanwhile, a much larger share of the Tax Bureau staff was assigned to monitoring

Table 3.3 Tax bureau performance indicators, 1989–92

	November 1989	November 1992
Monthly tax collection (US$ millions)	1000	2000
Total employees	10500	16000
Monthly average wage (US$)	1100	1800
Cost of tax collection (as a per cent of the total)	3.2	2.7
Employees per PC	480	14
Employees in controlling and monitoring activities	1400	6500
Monthly inspections	360	1800
Number of 'major' taxpayers	1500	7500

Source: Dirección General Impositiva and Durán and Gomez Sabaini (1994).

and controlling tax compliance (6500 employees in 1992 as compared to 1400 in 1989). As a result, the number of monthly inspections rose from 360 to 1800 during the period considered. Likewise, temporary closing down of establishments responsible for tax offences jumped from 751 in 1990 to over 16000 in 1993.

The reforms in tax administration were truly effective.[14] While nominal revenues doubled from November 1989 to November 1992 (in fact they grew another 75 per cent from then to mid-1994), collection costs lagged far behind: they represented 3.2 per cent of total revenues in November 1989, but dropped to only 2.7 per cent in November 1992.[15] Altogether, the reform process was quite successful so far. As a matter of fact, tax collection at the federal level increased by more than 50 per cent in real terms from its yearly average in 1988–90 to 1992. As a consequence, the federal tax burden climbed from an average 12.4 per cent of GDP in the former period to a historic peak of 16.6 per cent in the latter. Adding to that figure the 3.2 per cent of GDP collected at the provincial level, the total tax burden amounted to almost 20 per cent of GDP in 1992, about 36 per cent higher than in 1988–90, and it remained around that level in 1993.

As can be inferred from Table 3.4, the federal tax structure also changed dramatically, and basically in the right direction regarding economic incentives. The most relevant feature of this change was the central role won by the VAT. In 1989 the value added tax collected 1.6 per cent of GDP, representing 12.4 per cent of the federal tax burden. In 1993 it collected 6.1 per cent of GDP, or almost 38 per cent of that burden.

At the same time, revenues arising from social security contributions (wage taxes) increased sharply as well. They climbed from 2.7 per cent of GDP in 1989 to 4.9 per cent in 1993, while their share in the federal burden rose from nearly 21 per cent to over 30 per cent during the same period. Nonetheless, as already explained, the initial impact of the ongoing social security reform will be the reduction of the funds going to the public segment of the system.

Table 3.4 Tax structure, 1988–93 (percentage of GDP)

	1988	1989	1990	1991	1992	1993
Federal taxes						
income	1.3	1.7	0.6	0.6	1.2	1.7
Wealth	0.5	0.7	0.7	0.6	0.4	0.3
VAT	1.9	1.6	2.2	3.5	5.9	6.1
Excises and fuel	2.4	1.7	2.3	2.3	2.1	1.5
Foreign trade	1.1	2.8	1.8	0.9	0.9	0.9
Social security	3.3	2.7	3.6	4.3	4.8	4.9
Others	1.4	1.7	1.3	2.0	1.3	0.7
Total	11.9	12.9	12.5	14.2	16.6	16.1
Provincial taxes	2.2	1.9	2.3	2.6	3.2	3.3
Total tax burden	14.1	14.8	14.8	16.8	19.8	19.4

Source: ECLA (various issues), DNIAF (various issues) and own estimates.

Income and wealth taxes, however, did not perform that well. Indeed, their joint revenues dropped slightly from 2.4 per cent of GDP in 1989 to 2 per cent in 1993. As a result, their share in the federal burden also diminished, falling from 18 per cent to 12.4 per cent of the total.

Nevertheless, the fact is that both VAT and social security contributions produced a huge increase in fiscal revenues: contrasting 1993 to 1989, this increase represented 6.7 per cent of GDP. About half that total was due to the overall growth experienced by federal tax collection between those years, while the balance made it possible to sharply reduce the burden of trade and other highly distortive minor taxes in GDP. As a consequence of the virtual elimination of export taxes and the significant reduction in import tariffs, foreign trade taxes dropped from 2.8 per cent of GDP (almost 22% of the federal burden) in 1989 to 0.9 per cent of GDP (5.5 per cent of federal collection) in 1993. In turn, minor taxes which jointly totalled 1.7 per cent of GDP (13 per cent of the federal total) in 1989, fell to 0.7 per cent of GDP (4% of that total) in 1993.

Finally, excise taxes (including fuel) grew only slightly from 1989 to 1992 but dropped again in 1993, reaching only 1.5 per cent of GDP and a share of less than 10 per cent in the total tax burden that year.

Reasons behind the improvement in tax performance[16]

The previous section has shown the significant increase in fiscal revenues which took place over 1990–3. In fact, the federal tax effort reached 16.1 per cent of GDP in 1993, almost 1.5 points higher than the preceding historic maximum attained in 1986, and about 3.5 points higher than the 1980–91 average (Table 3.5). The purpose of this section is to identify and quantify the

Table 3.5 Changes in federal tax collection (percentage of GDP)

	1993 compared to		
	1981	1986	1989
Income	0.4	0.6	0.0
Wealth	−0.3	−0.3	−0.4
VAT	2.3	3.6	4.5
Domestic transactions	2.1	3.1	3.8
Imports	0.2	0.5	0.7
Excises and fuel	−1.2	−1.8	−0.2
Foreign trade	−0.4	−1.1	−1.9
Social security	3.0	1.0	2.2
Others	−0.2	−0.6	−1.0
Federal tax burden	3.6	1.4	3.2

Source: ECLA (various issues), DNIAF (various issues) and own estimates.

main factors explaining that outcome. Of course, this is just a preliminary analysis intended to establish approximate orders of magnitude among those factors. A deeper appraisal would demand a much more disaggregated analysis and a database which is currently unavailable in the Argentine case.

For our purpose, we have compared the performance of tax receipts in 1993 with their performance in some selected years of the 1980s: 1981, 1986 and 1989. This choice was not arbitrary. Indeed, given the extreme economic instability which characterized the 1980s, it enabled us to make a coverage of different macroeconomic and fiscal contexts. 1981 marked the commencement of the debt crisis, and both aggregate economic indicators and tax performance began a fast-worsening process. Owing to a broad legal base and a high rate, however, VAT collection was quite important in 1981. The Austral Plan launched in mid-1985 temporarily interrupted the declining trend of the Argentine economy. As a result, tax performance reached the already-mentioned historic maximum of 1986. In 1989, instead, the country was in the midst of hyperinflation and tax revenues fell again to a low level.

From Table 3.5 it is immediately apparent that VAT and social security contributions were practically the only factors responsible for the improvement in tax performance. In effect, as a percentage of GDP, revenues originating in both taxes were 5.3, 4.6 and 6.7 points higher than those of 1981, 1986 and 1989 respectively. In all three cases, indeed, this rise was even greater than the change in the overall tax burden, while the contribution of income and wealth taxes stayed roughly constant, and that of the remaining taxes actually declined.

Therefore, in order to explain the current positive changes in overall tax collection, it is both necessary and sufficient to identify the main factors behind the good performance in VAT and social security contributions.[17] Let us first discuss the VAT case, which was responsible for the largest revenue increases since the beginning of the current process of tax reforms. This tax is levied on both domestic transactions ('VAT-national') and imports ('VAT-imports'). Revenues arising from the latter are obviously much smaller than those coming from the former. Consequently, according to the reference year, the growth in VAT-imports explains only 10 to 15 per cent of the growth in total VAT receipts, the remaining proportion being explained by VAT-national.

As can be seen in Table 3.6, regardless of the base year considered, almost the entire increase in VAT-imports comes from changes in the tax base, while changes in both the tax rate and 'other' factors were of minor importance. The main determinants of the tax base are the dollar value of imports, the effective import exchange rate, and legal exemptions.

The recent growth in this variable, which reached its highest level in 1993 (Table 3.7), is to be fully credited to the behaviour of import volumes. As a matter of fact, a swift trade liberalization compounded with a sizeable appreciation of the exchange rate to produce an import boom over 1990–3. As a result, purchases abroad nearly tripled in dollar terms from 1989 to 1993, more than compensating for the appreciation of the domestic currency.

In the case of VAT-imports, collection procedures are simple and well-established, and tax evasion, then, is not a major issue here. This is the reason

Table 3.6 VAT on imports: determinants of changes in effective performance (percentage of GDP)

	1993 compared to		
	1981	1986	1989
Effective revenues	0.22	0.53	0.64
Tax base	0.20	0.48	0.44
Tax rate	−0.08	0.00	0.13
Others	0.10	0.05	0.07

Source: ECLA (various issues), DNIAF (various issues) and own estimates.

Table 3.7 VAT on Imports, 1981–1993 (selected years)

	1981	1986	1989	1993
Effective revenues (% of GDP)	0.9	0.6	0.5	1.1
Tax base (% of GDP)	5.4	3.7	3.7	6.6
Tax rate (%)	20.0	18.0	15.0	18.0
Theoretical revenues (% of GDP)	1.1	0.7	0.6	1.2
Effective/theoretical revenues (%)	86.7	90.9	87.5	95.0

Source: ECLA (various issues), DNIAF (various issues) and own estimates.

why effective revenues are not very different from the theoretical ones in Table 3.7, and 'other' determinants of VAT-imports performance are almost negligible in Table 3.6.

Estimating the determinants of the changes in the VAT-national is a more complex task, basically because of the difficulties in rigorously calculating its tax base. In the first place, in order to identify properly all legal exemptions, it would be necessary to work with a disaggregation of GDP of more than four digits. In the second place, given that the sectoral disaggregation of final consumption is also inaccessible, a recent estimation of the input–output matrix would be needed. Finally, a sectoral disaggregation of investment and exports would also be required. Since all these elements are unavailable in the Argentine case, a different approach had to be chosen. Based on previous calculations for 1981, 1986 and 1989, and estimates for 1993, the taxable sectoral products at a two-digit disaggregation level were determined. Deducting export and investment fiscal credits, provisional estimations of the net tax base and the theoretical tax collection were obtained. At the same time, based on effective revenues and legal lags, a series of earned revenues was constructed.[18]

As can be seen in Table 3.8, the tax base (after deductions) was over 30 per cent in 1981, dropped to less than 20 per cent in the late 1980s, and strongly recovered in the early 1990s reaching 41 per cent in 1993. In fact, taxable GDP (before deductions) in the case of VAT-national was estimated at about 65 per cent of total GDP for that year, which is quite high according to international standards. Meanwhile, the tax rate fell from 20 per cent in 1981 to 18 per cent in 1986, and to a further 15 per cent in 1989, only to recover its 1986 level as of 1992.

As a result of the evolution of both the tax base and rate, theoretical collection reached 7.4 per cent in 1993, a level that more than doubled the figures for 1986 and 1989 and was even higher than the previous 1981 peak. The other remarkable fact in Table 3.8 is the improvement evidenced by the effective/theoretical revenue ratio: after reaching 50 per cent in 1981 and 1986, it dropped to less than 40 per cent in 1989, and then recovered to almost 70 per cent in 1993.

Table 3.8   VAT on domestic transactions, 1981–93 (selected years)

	1981	1986	1989	1993
Effective revenues (% of GDP)	2.9	1.9	1.1	5.0
Tax base (% of GDP)	31.5	18.4	19.1	41.0
Tax rate (%)	20.0	18.0	15.0	18.0
Theoretical revenues (% of GDP)	6.0	3.3	2.9	7.4
Effective/theoretical revenues (%)	48.3	57.6	37.9	67.6

Source: ECLA (various issues), DNIAF (various issues) and own estimates.

From the evolution of theoretical collections it is rather simple to calculate the contribution of changes in the tax base and rate to the evolution of VAT-national revenues. The difference between theoretical and earned receipts, in turn, was attributed to 'other' determinants, the effects of changes in tax administration being included in this category. Finally, a 'lag' effect, encompassing but not identical to the Olivera–Tanzi effect, was included to account for the difference between earned and effective revenues. Results are reported in Table 3.9, which shows that changes in the tax base, mainly due to legal revisions, are the most important factor explaining the 1993 improvement in VAT-national revenues, particularly when compared with 1986 and 1989. This factor is somewhat less relevant when compared to 1981 because the VAT-national also had quite a broad base that year.

The significance of 'other' determinants, especially when the reference years are 1981 and 1989, at least partially reflects recent improvements in tax compliance.[19] Instead, tax rate changes and the 'lag' effect seem to have played a less important role as determinants of the VAT-national growth.[20] With regard to the performance of social security contributions, revenues arising from salaried workers represent more than 80 per cent of the system's total receipts. Therefore, the evolution of aggregate wages was taken as a proxy for the evolution of the system's tax base.

As can be seen in Table 3.10, changes in the tax base have played a negative role in the behaviour of social security contributions in 1993, particularly when compared with their performance in 1981 and 1986. This can basically be attributed to the fall experienced by real wages over the previous decade. To some extent, the recent increase in output per worker has also strengthened the negative trend in the tax base. Therefore, the significant improvement in social security contributions is essentially explained by two factors:tax rate hikes, most relevant in the comparisons with 1981 and 1986, and a positive 'lag' effect, crucially important in the comparison with 1989. Unlike   the importance shown by 'other' determinants in the case of VAT-national, results regarding their contribution are not conclusive in this case.

Table 3.9   VAT on domestic transactions: determinants of changes in effective performance (percentage of GDP)

	1993 compared to		
	1981	1986	1989
Effective revenues	2.10	3.10	3.85
Tax base	1.51	2.74	2.43
Tax rate	−0.60	0.00	0.40
Others	0.97	0.26	0.62
Lag effect	0.22	0.10	0.40

Source: ECLA (various issues), DNIAF (various issues) and own estimates.

Table 3.10 Social security contributions: determinants of changes in effective performance (percentage of GDP)

	1993 compared to		
	1981	1986	1989
Effective revenues	2.88	0.90	2.12
Tax base	−1.12	−1.47	0.06
Tax rate	3.62	1.35	0.70
Others	0.33	0.73	−0.16
Lag effect	0.71	0.28	1.52

Source: ECLA (various issues), DNIAF (various issues) and own estimates.

The role played by privatizations[21]

As already mentioned, the privatizing of public firms was one of the major goals of President Menem's administration. Beginning in 1990, this process evolved at an extremely fast pace, and the calls for bids attracted offers from a large number of local and international companies. By the end of 1992 most public utilities and oil-fields had already been sold. In 1993, moreover, the government undertook the privatization of YPF, the state-owned oil company and Argentina's largest concern. As a first step in that process, 40 per cent of the company's shares were sold to domestic and international investors in June that year. Once the privatization programme is completed, very few companies will remain in the hands of the public sector.

The immediate beneficiary has been the national government. Including the sale of YPF shares, it has collected around US$17.3 billion since the beginning of privatizations: US$9.5 billion in cash, the rest being the market value of all other payments involved (see Table 3.11). So far, these funds have been an important factor in explaining the fiscal improvement, as well as the government's ability to service the public debt without resorting to inflationary financing.

In both the market-friendly literature and the current rhetoric employed by governments in many developing countries, privatizations, together with deregulation, are considered basic tools for enhancing both the productivity of existing resources and the efficiency of investment decisions. Indeed, they are expected to produce such effects through their incentives on private initiative and creativity. They are thus supposed to work mainly through microeconomic channels.

Nevertheless, in most actual cases privatizations seem to have served other purposes as well. Argentina is a good example. With an outstanding performance regarding both the relative magnitude of the privatized assets and the speed exhibited in completing the process, Argentina's privatizations have

Table 3.11 Financial results of the privatization process, 1990–5 (US$ millions)

Sector	Form of transfer	Cash	Amortization of foreign debt (market value)	Transferred liabilities	Total	Amortization of foreign debt (nominal value)
Telecommunications	Sale of stocks	2 279.0	1 264.3	–	3 543.3	5 029.0
Airlines	Direct sale	190.1	394.1	–	584.2	1 313.8
Railways	Concession	–	–	–	–	–
Electricity	Direct sale	1 283.1	1 258.5	1 003.0	3 544.6	2 516.9
Harbours	Concession / direct sale	12.3	–	–	12.3	–
Roads	Concession	–	–	–	–	–
TV and radio	Concession	–	–	–	–	–
Petroleum	Sale of stocks	1 806.8	–	–	1 806.8	–
YPF (petroleum comp.)	Concession	3 040.0	953.3	–	3 993.3	1 271.1
Gas	Direct sale	658.0	1 498.9	1 110.1	3 267.0	2 997.9
Water and sewage	Concession	–	–	–	–	–
Industry						
petrochemical	Sale of stocks	53.5	26.8	–	80.3	132.0
ships	Direct sale	59.8	–	–	59.8	–
steel	Direct sale	143.3	15.9	250.0	409.2	30.0
Public real estate	Direct sale	3.2	5.8	–	9.0	13.0
Others	Direct sale / concession	4.5	0.7	–	5.2	3.3
Total amount		9 533.6	5 418.3	2 363.1	17 315.0	13 307.0

Source: Own calculations based on Secretaria de Programación Económica (1994).

fulfilled some crucial functions which were very different from those advocated by the standard approach. Moreover, given the way they were implemented, and even though it is still too early to assess their long-run impact on productivity, there seem to be justified doubts on their final contribution to overall efficiency and growth.

As was also the case with tax policy, two different stages can be identified regarding the privatization process. The first covered 1990 and the first quarter of 1991, while the second can be associated with the Convertibilty Plan launched in April 1991. During the first stage, the economic situation was very bad. Even though the government had managed to curb the second hyperinflationary outburst in March 1990, inflation remained very high (fluctuating around a 10 per cent monthly rate) and a recessionary trend persisted throughout the rest of the year.

In such a context, one of the main functions of the privatization program responded to political economy considerations. Given that the credibility of the administration was questioned for the persistency of the economic crisis, the continuity of the privatization process was meant to regain support from the business community, attesting that the government was sticking to its original commitments. At the same time, privatizations were presented to public opinion as the only way out of the economic crisis. In order to meet the administration's political needs, then, the first major privatizations were submitted to tight deadlines. A thorough assessment of truly important economic issues, such as the pricing policy of the privatized firms, or the establishment of regulatory frameworks according to the new realities, was dismissed or postponed when it threatened to delay the process.

The second relevant role played by privatizations was related to macroeconomic stabilization. In fact, the narrowness of the domestic financial markets, aggravated by two hyperinflationary episodes and the compulsory rescheduling of short-term bank deposits and public bonds in January 1990, made it compelling to find a temporary way to finance the remaining fiscal gap so that the intended adjustment could have enough time to produce its full effects. As had previously been the case with the bridge loans provided by multilateral institutions, privatization revenues served that purpose too.

Taking into account the political and financial constraints faced by the government in 1990, the public firms chosen to start the process were those which could more easily attract the interest of the private sector – Entel (the public phone company), and Aerolíneas Argentinas (the state-owned airline). In both cases the new owners were granted extremely high real tariffs, as well as the preservation of quasi-monopolistic conditions in their respective markets. At the same time, the government initiated the concession of oil fields to the private sector.

The Convertibility Plan marked the second stage in the privatization process. The success of stabilization helped the government recover credibility, and political considerations became somewhat less prominent in orienting that process. However, given the clear aversion still evidenced by domestic financial markets to meet government borrowing requirements, and despite a significant improvement in tax performance, privatization cash receipts together with the sharp decline in foreign debt interest payments continued to be relevant in closing the fiscal gap from 1991 to 1993. In fact, in 1991 privatization cash receipts were slightly higher than primary savings and covered almost all foreign interest payments. Primary savings more than doubled in 1992–3, but privatization cash revenues still represented over 50 per cent of those savings and almost 100 per cent of foreign interest payments in both those years (see Table 3.2).

Privatizations were also critically important in the reduction of the outstanding public debt. From the beginning of the programme to the end of 1993, the government had already rescued the equivalent of about US$3.3 billion (face value) in titles of both domestic and foreign public debt. In particular, the exchange of foreign debt titles held by the public sector for equity constituted the bulk of the first two major privatizations (Entel and Aerolíneas). These operations alone enabled the government to rescue US$6.5 billion in foreign titles (about 20 per cent of the debt with commercial banks at that moment), therefore making it possible for Argentina to join the Brady Programme.

As already mentioned, in 1993 the government undertook the privatization of YPF, the state-owned oil company, initially selling 40 per cent of the company's shares. The revenues of this operation amounted to slightly less than US$2.5 billion. Nearly half of that sum was destined to pay federal debts with the provinces, the remainder being used to diminish the government's long-standing debt with pensioners. Besides contributing to strengthening the fiscal situation, privatizations also played a key role regarding the evolution of the economy's external accounts. In fact, capital inflows have been crucial in closing the current account's growing imbalance since the beginning of the Convertibility Plan. Privatization cash revenues were an important component of these inflows: more than one-third of the private capital account surplus over 1990–3 – can be directly or indirectly attributed to privatizations.

Having discussed the short-term effects of privatizations on stabilization, what can be said about their long-term impact on efficiency and growth? It is widely acknowledged that the sustainability of the stabilization process, and the prospects of growth resumption in the Argentine economy are critically contingent on two factors: (1) the rise in both the national savings rate and the investment rate, and (2) the improvement in the competitiveness of the tradable sectors. The long-run effects of privatizations should therefore be assessed regarding these factors. Nevertheless, even though it is still too early to fully estimate such effects, the way privatizations were conducted casts some doubts on their final contribution to overall efficiency and growth.

Let us consider, in the first place, the different ways in which the domestic private sector can finance the purchase of public firms. Macroeconomically speaking, there are no more than four options (and all possible combinations of them): (1) a rise in private savings, (2) a fall in private investment, (3) an increase in the private-sector flow demand for credit, or (4) a decline in the private-sector flow demand for financial assets. The first two options imply that the private-sector financial surplus (deficit) is growing (diminishing); the third and fourth ones that, given the private-sector financial balance, its composition is changing.[22]

From this point of view, privatizations could have a positive effect on growth provided they induce a rise in private savings while keeping public savings constant, thereby enabling an increase in aggregate investment. Given that the additional private savings will be transferred to the public sector, this requires that the government not use privatization earnings to meet current expenses or debt payments. However, it is pretty obvious in the Argentine case that privatizations were not financed by higher private savings. Instead, they were basically funded by a combination of higher private foreign indebtedness (option 3) and the repatriation of flight capital (option 4). Moreover, prevailing incentives since the beginning of the Convertibility Plan have been such that the massive capital inflows helped finance not only privatizations, but also a boom in private consumption, thereby inducing a sort of crowding-out effect on private savings.[23]

Considering the evolution of the fiscal accounts (see Table 3.2), it is also evident that privatization earnings did not fund higher levels of public investment, but rather replaced other financing sources unavailable to the government during the recent period. In that sense, it could be argued that the use of privatization revenues to meet current expenses and debt payments had a somewhat crowding-out effect on aggregate investment.

There is also a different way in which privatizations could have a positive effect on growth. Most privatization contracts impose investment commitments on the new owners of the former public firms. These investments are expected to have a favourable effect on the productivity of those firms. But in order to improve overall competitiveness, it is necessary for those productivity gains to spill over the rest of the economy. To make privatizations more attractive, however, the government authorized significant rises in the prices charged by former public firms, which are now at a historic peak in real terms.[24] In fact, this event, coupled with the real appreciation of the domestic currency, has impaired the competitiveness of the economy.[25]

There is also a timing problem connected with the sustainability of stabilization because privatized firms are mainly located in nontradable sectors. Even if a proper regulatory framework could ensure that productivity gains be passed on to the rest of the economy, the positive effects of an investment spurt in non-tradable sectors on the economy's international competitiveness would be far from immediate. In the meantime, the government might well have to face the familiar trade-off between a growing external imbalance and recession, thereby jeopardizing the prospects of the stabilization effort.

Concluding remarks

The current performance of the Argentine economy provides new evidence for the ongoing debate about the proper sequencing between stabilization and fiscal reform. If anything, the initial failure of President Menem's administration to stabilize the economy, as well as its subsequent success under the Convertibility Plan, confirmed that when inflation surpasses a certain threshold, stabilization cannot wait until the structural reforms reshape the public sector according to market-oriented principles. Some kind of shock therapy is needed to first bring inflation down to less disruptive levels, say under 20 per cent. The Convertibility Plan did so mainly by establishing the exchange rate as the nominal anchor of the economy.

Of course, this does not at all mean that fiscal reform is irrelevant. It means rather that fiscal reform is less concerned with the generation of stabilization than its *sustainability*. Nevertheless, the Convertibility Plan regime imposed severe constraints on the government's ability to finance fiscal imbalances. Two different stages can be distinguished according to the way in which these constraints were met. During the first stage priority was given to increasing fiscal revenues by any means. Not only tax policy but also privatizations were chiefly devoted to that end. During the second stage, more attention was paid to allocative and distributive considerations.

The outstanding recovery in tax revenues is probably one of the most significant economic changes which took place in 1990–3. Stabilization, together with a dramatic output expansion, no doubt played a major role in the process. It would be a mistake, however, to credit exclusively that improvement to macroeconomic reasons. In fact, immediately after the government took office, political conditions created by hyperinflation enabled it to have a wholly new legal framework passed by the Congress. Unthinkable in the past, this laid the foundation for the forthcoming structural reforms. Against this background, a comprehensive tax reform process was begun, which was to a great extent the cause of the powerful response in tax revenues to output growth during the Convertibility Plan.

Regardless of its long-run effects, the sharp fiscal adjustment brought about by this rapid increase in tax receipts was decisive to the credibility and sustainability of the stabilization programme.

There were two components of the reform process responsible for that outcome: the progressive establishment of VAT as the core of the tax system, and a radical transformation in tax administration, including much more rigorous penalties for tax evasion. Thanks to these measures, the government was able to begin to overcome one of the major weaknesses of the Argentine economy: the lack of an adequate tax base. As a result, the overall tax burden almost reached an unprecedented 20 per cent of GDP in 1992–3. The figure is even more impressive considering that no 'emergency' taxes were applied.

As soon as the tax system managed to consolidate its revenue generating function, other measures followed aimed at increasing efficiency. First, highly distortive export taxes were abolished. Then, other equally distortive minor taxes were eliminated, while the fuel tax was greatly reduced. In 1993 income tax underwent important changes as well. The strategy was clearly to build a simpler tax system, placing VAT at its centre, while gradually approaching international standards in income tax performance.

At the same time, it is quite evident that horizontal equity has also been greatly improved. Implementation of widespread withholding mechanisms, standardized billing and other specific administrative controls produced a clear improvement in tax compliance. Other specific measures included in the tax reform package, such as the abrupt reduction in tax expenditures and the restrictions applied for the deduction of declared past losses in the case of corporate income taxes also contributed to that end. Likewise, legal changes made tax evasion a much riskier endeavour than in the past.

Despite all positive changes achieved by tax reform in this short period, however, several questions still remain open. First, it is too early to assess whether the tax system will be able to ensure a level of revenues consistent with public expenditures on a permanent basis. On the one hand, tax performance during 1993 and the first half of 1994 seem to suggest that future growth in federal tax collection will not be as fast as in the recent past. On the other hand, political pressure and conflicting demands for better social services have kept public expenditures on a growing path. Moreover, VAT's central role in the system has made tax revenues much more dependent on output fluctuations than in the past. In this regard, the economic authorities force a difficult dilemma: a contractionary policy is needed to reduce a dangerously growing external gap, but at the same time the fiscal balance can be seriously harmed by that very same policy. A similar dilemma applies to the exchange rate policy, because the real burden of interest payments depends on the real exchange rate.

Additionally, many of the structural reforms already in progress will also require significant public funds to finance imbalances which will inevitably arise during the transition. The social security reform is a clear case in point. In a long-run perspective, then, in order to keep the fiscal deficit under control, it will be necessary for the government to pace public sector reforms with the evolution of the revenue generating capacity of the tax system.

Regarding income distribution, there is little doubt that the government's abandonment of the inflationary tax as a way to finance its activities had positive implications on vertical equity.[26] However, the fact that the increase in tax revenues was entirely due to the behaviour of VAT and social security contributions may have had quite the opposite effect. More research on the final incidence of these taxes is needed to reach a more definite conclusion on this matter.[27] Nevertheless, according to the analysis presented in this chapter, there is still ample room to improve further the tax system's performance, not only from the point of view of tax collection but also from that of equity and efficiency.

At the federal level, three issues clearly emerge. First, income tax proceeds were still extremely low: they would have to grow about two points of GDP just to reach the average level of the other major Latin American economies (Brazil, Mexico, Colombia and Chile), which in turn is only half the average level of income tax collection in OECD countries. This fact has had quite a negative impact on both the overall tax burden and its distribution. Considering the successful experience already achieved with the VAT, it seems only reasonable to expect that better administrative procedures could also ensure much higher revenues in this case without altering current tax rates.

Second, evasion was still significant in the VAT case, despite the substantial improvements achieved in the administration of this tax. Since the estimated gap between the theoretical and effective collection was about 30 per cent in the VAT on domestic transactions, closing one-third of this gap would imply approximately one point of GDP in higher revenues at the prevailing tax rate, or it would allow a reduction of about three points in the VAT rate without meaningfully affecting collection.

Lastly, the rate established for the employer's contributions to the social security system is excessively high, impairing the competitiveness of domestic production and affecting technological choices of investment projects. In acknowledgement of this the government implemented a progressive reduction in this rate in 1994. However, a serious risk exists that this measure might cause a dangerous imbalance in the social security budget unless evasion in this area, especially in the case of self-employed workers, is greatly diminished. On the other hand, much remains to be done concerning tax reform at the provincial level, particularly regarding efficiency. The most salient problem is that of multiple taxation generated by the turnover tax, which applies to all (including intermediate) sales and constitutes the core of provincial tax systems.

In fact, the fiscal relation between the federal and provincial governments continues to be a very complex question. There is a complicated system of dividing tax collection which is legally subject to revenue-sharing between the national government and the provinces. This allocation system has undergone many changes in the past. Lately, as total tax collection has been increasing dramatically, the national government has been trying to prevent these increases from automatically being passed on to the provinces. In October 1992 the so-called 'Fiscal Pact' was signed whereby the national government was allowed to keep 15 per cent of the collection of such taxes to finance the social security system. In addition, educational and health services provided by the federal government were transferred to the provinces. A second version of that arrangement, along similar lines to those of the first, was agreed in August 1993.

At the same time, in the context of these successive 'fiscal pacts', the government has been trying to induce the provinces to adapt to budget constraints by reducing their spending, reforming their tax systems and privatizing concerns owned by the provincial governments. In return, provinces are offered a number of benefits, including access to multilateral credit. So far, however, the provinces have been most reluctant to execute a fiscal reform such as that in progress at the federal level. The growing difficulties experienced by regional economies, and particularly the current trend in unemployment, are certainly important reasons behind this attitude.

Finally, a few remarks should be made on the several roles played by privatizations. In fact, despite the standard justification on long-term efficiency grounds, so far they have basically served short-term macroeconomic purposes. In 1990, when the economy was still in a deep crisis, privatizations helped the government regain credibility. Privatization revenues have also been very important as a means to temporarily finance the remaining fiscal imbalances, as well as to reduce the outstanding public debt. Last but not least, they have played a key role in closing the external gap generated by the stabilization plan. Nevertheless, the way privatizations have been conducted raises some doubts about their final contribution to efficiency and growth. On the one hand, they do not seem to have had any positive impact on aggregate savings and investment. On the other hand, due to the lack of an appropriate regulatory framework, productivity gains in privatized firms are not spilling over the rest of the economy, thereby preventing overall competitiveness from improving.

It is still too early to appraise the long-term impact of privatizations on the Argentine economy. However, there is at least one aspect of the process which seems irreversible, and that is the dramatic change experienced by the political economy environment. New private monopolies have been created, enjoying a substantial amount of economic power. At the same time, the public sector which is supposed to control these powerful new groups has been left extremely weak as a result of the long-standing crisis of the 1980s. It is very difficult to foresee what the outcome of this new environment will turn out to be.

Notes

1 CEDES Buenos Aires, July 1994. The material in this chapter was originally prepared as a paper for the International Research Project on 'Fiscal Reform and Structural Change' sponsored by IDRC (Canada). Previous versions were presented at the Research Network Seminars held at the Indian Statistical Institute, New Delhi (August 1993) and El Colegio de México, Mexico City (April 1994). The author wishes to thank Guillermo Perry, John Whalley, Klauss Schmidt-Hebbel, Gary McMahon, Vito Tanzi, Carlos Urzua, Nelson Dias and participants in the Network Seminars at the Indian Statistical Institute (New Delhi) and El Colegio

de México (Mexico City) for their useful comments and discussions. I am also very grateful for Viviana Durán's contribution in preparing the section dealing with the reasons for the improvement in tax performance, as well as for her insightful comments on the rest of the material.

2 Calvo *et al.* (1993) convincingly stresses the importance of supply factors in the current process of capital inflows into Latin America.

3 For a more detailed discussion of the 'domestic transfer' problem, see Fanelli *et al.* (1992a).

4 Having recently experienced the hardships of hyperinflation, most people realized that substituting conventional taxes for the inflation tax would certainly be a Pareto-improving move in the Argentine economic context and adjusted their behavior accordingly. Of course, the significant improvement in horizontal equity achieved through a much more severe legal framework and a more efficient tax administration, as well as a massive publicity campaign implemented by the tax authorities, greatly contributed to coordinate private decisions and make that move possible. However, comparing the success of this reform to the failure of previous well-designed reform attempts, we believe that the private sector's change in attitude was a major factor underlying the sustained increase observed in tax revenues during the last three years.

5 Using a CGE model for Argentina, Chisari (1994) shows that reductions in the interest payments on the public foreign debt also have substantial long-term effects on social welfare. Indeed, assuming that the interest rate on the public debt has to equal the productive capital rate of return, Chisari obtains an improvement of about 2.5 per cent in the public sector utility level, while maintaining the utility levels of private economic agents roughly constant.

6 For a more detailed discussion of this trade-off, see Perry and Herrera (1994).

7 Significant fiscal costs during the transition are a well-established fact of this kind of social security reform. In fact, Chile implemented a similar reform in 1981, and in this case the remaining public system has registered an average financial imbalance of about 6 per cent of GDP over the first ten years under the new regime, much higher than the one experienced before the reform (see Budnevich, 1993).

8 On this issue, see Gerchunoff and Machinea (1994).

9 For a comprehensive analysis of tax performance throughout this period, see Carciofi *et al.* (1994).

10 Federal taxes constitute roughly 80 per cent to 85 per cent of the total tax burden, the remaining fraction corresponding to the provincial level. Federal taxes, however, are subject to a sharing scheme which has been a permanent source of conflict between central and local authorities.

11 However, the impact of higher fuel tax revenues on the overall fiscal balance was to a great extent counterbalanced by the worsening in the operational results of YPF, the state-owned oil company. This was the consequence of the government's recurrent attempts to manipulate gasoline prices to curb inflation.

12 Dirección Nacional de Investigaciones y Análisis Fiscal (1989).

13 For a discussion of the welfare and allocative effects of this strategy from a general equilibrium perspective, see Chisari (1994).

14 On this issue, see Durán and Gomez Sabaini (1994).

15 Besides its positive short-term implications, the reduction in collection costs is extremely relevant for its long-term repercussions as well. In fact, as Chisari (1994) points out, given that in a general equilibrium setting the welfare consequences for the private sector as a whole of an increased VAT compliance are ambiguous, it is

necessary that collection costs be significantly reduced for a VAT-based tax reform to become acceptable for all economic agents.

16 This section was prepared together with Viviana Durán.

17 As was already said, 1993 was chosen as the base year for the comparisons made in this section. Federal tax collection was slightly lower in 1993 than in 1992. However, for our purpose this is irrelevant because the analysis is focused on the evolution of VAT and social security revenues, which were almost identical in both years. In fact, the difference in overall performance was basically explained by the fall induced by the government's policy in the burden of excises (including fuel) and other minor taxes, which could not be fully offset by the rise in income tax proceeds.

18 For a more thorough methodological discussion and previous estimations see Durán (1989a).

19 Calculations were made under the simplifying assumption of a proportional impact of legal base changes on collection. Previous econometric estimates seemed to justify this assumption (see Durán, 1989b). Owing to the recent extension of VAT in 1991 to economic sectors where control of tax evasion is rather complex, however, this assumption may no longer be valid, thereby contributing to an underestimation of the actual impact of current improvements on tax administration.

20 For an analysis of the welfare implications of changes in the VAT base, rates and compliance, see Chisari (1994).

21 For a detailed description of the privatization process, see Alexander and Corti (1993). Canavese and Rozenwurcel (1992), Gerchunoff and Canovas (1993) and Frenkel and Rozenwurcel (1994) analyse some of its micro and macroeconomic implications. An assessment of its impact on the external sector can be found in Fanelli and Machinea (1994), and in Chudnovsky *et al.* (1994).

22 This point is also discussed in Fanelli *et al.* (1992b).

23 In fact, the increase in foreign savings was so impressive that national private savings dropped not only as a proportion of GDP but also in absolute terms. Measured at constant (1986) prices, in 1992 private savings were about 15 per cent lower than in 1990. Despite a recovery in the following year they still remained 3 per cent below the 1990 level.

24 The prices of recently privatized public services are also well above international levels. For an international comparison in the cases of electricity and telecommunications, see ECLA (1994).

25 A discussion of this policy dilemma appears in Canavese and Rozenwurcel (1993).

26 See Ahumada *et al.* (1993) for a quantitative estimation of this effect.

27 Chisari (1994) presents a first important attempt to discuss rigorously this issue in a CGE framework for the case of VAT.

References

Alexander, M. and C. Corti (1993) 'Argentina's Privatization Program', Washington, DC: World Bank, CFS Discussion Paper 103.

Ahumada, H., A. Canavese, P. Sanguinetti and W. Escudero (1993) 'Efectos Distributivos del Impuesto Inflacionario: una estimación para el caso argentino', Buenos Aires: Instituto Di Tella.

Budnevich, C. (1993) 'Implicancias Financieras de las Privatizaciones en chile: lecciones del periodo 1985–1990', in O. Muñoz (ed.), *Después de las Privatizaciones. Hacia el Estado Regulador*, Santiago de Chile, CIEPLAN.

Calvo, G., L. Leiderman and C. Reinhart (1993) 'The Capital Inflows Problem. Concepts and Issues', Washington, DC: International Monetary Fund.

Canavese, A. and G. Rozenwurcel (1992) 'Privatizaciones, Crecimiento y Distribución del Ingreso', in P. Gerchunoff (ed.), *Las Privatizaciones en la Argentina*, Buenos Aires: Instituto T. Di Tella.

Carciofi, R., G. Barris and O. Cetrangolo (1994) *Reformas Tributarias en America Latina. Análisis de la experiencia durante la decada de los años ochenta*, Santiago de Chile, ECLA.

Chisari, O. (1994) 'Tax Reform, Tax Compliance and Factor Mobility. A CGE Model for Argentina', Buenos Aires, mimeo.

Chudnovsky, D., A. Lopez and F. Porta (1994) 'La Nueva Inversión Extranjera Directa en la Argentina. Privatizaciones, Mercado Interno e Integración Regional', Buenos Aires: CENIT, Documento de Trabajo/15.

Direccion Nacional de Investigaciones y Analisis Fiscal, 'Evolución de la Recaudación Tributaria', various issues, Buenos Aires: Secretaria de Ingresos Públicos.

Durán, V. (1989a) 'Estimación de la función de recaudación del Impuesto al Valor Agregado', Buenos Aires: Programa de Estudios sobre Politica Tributaria–PNUD.

Durán, V. (1989b) 'Una exploración econometrica del Impuesto al Valor Agregado', Buenos Aires: Programa de Estudios sobre Política Tributaria–PNUD.

Durán, V. and J. C. Gomez Sabaini (1994) 'Lecciones sobre Reformas Fiscales en Argentina: 1990–1993', Buenos Aires: ECLA–PNUD.

Economic Commission for Latin America (ECLA) 'Indicadores Macroeconómicos de la Argentina', various issues, Buenos Aires.

Economic Commission for Latin America and the Caribbean – ECLA (1994) 'La Crisis de la Empresa Pública, las Privatizaciones y la Equidad Social', Santiago de Chile: *Serie Reformas* de Política Pública 26.

Fanelli, J. M. and J. L. Machinea (1994), 'Capital Movements in Argentina', Buenos Aires: Documento CEDES/99.

Fanelli, J. M., R. Frenkel and G. Rozenwurcel (1992a) 'Growth and Structural Reform in Latin America. Where We Stand', in A. Zini Jr. (ed.), *The Market and the State in Economic Development in the 1990s*, Amsterdam: North Holland.

Fanelli, J. M., R. Frenkel and G. Rozenwurcel (1992b) 'Transformación Estructural, Estabilización y Reforma del Estado en Argentina', Buenos Aires: Documento CEDES/82.

Frenkel, R. and G. Rozenwurcel (1994), 'The Multiple Roles of Privatizations in Argentina', paper presented at a Conference on 'Institutional Design and Democratization', CILAS, University of California, San Diego.

Gerchunoff, P. and J. L. Machinea (1994) 'El teorema de la doble imposibilidad. Un ensayo sobre la política económica después de la estabilización', Buenos Aires, mimeo.

Gerchunoff, P. and G. Canovas (1993) 'Las Privatizaciones en la Argentina: impactos micro y macroeconómicos', Buenos Aires: Instituto T. Di Tella.

Perry, G. and A. M. Herrera (1994) *Finanzas Publicas. Estabilización y Reforma Estructural en America Latina*, Washington D.C.: Banco Interamericano de Desarrollo.

Secretaria de Programación Económica (1994) *Informe Económico Año 1993*, Buenos Aires: Ministerio de Economía.

4

Interactions between Trade and Tax Reform in Mexico: Some General Equilibrium Results

Horacio Sobarzo[1]

Introduction

Applied general equilibrium (AGE) models have become a widely used instrument to evaluate the resource allocation effects of different policy options. In particular, these models have been used to evaluate the effects produced by tax reform and trade liberalization (see Shoven and Whalley, 1984). More recently, some applied work has also been developed in the areas of environmental and regional economics (see Shoven and Whalley [1992]).

It has been a common practice that these models focus their attention on a single issue. Models designed to analyse tax reform often do not emphasize foreign trade whereas, at the opposite extreme, models built to evaluate trade liberalization do not explore in detail the interactions with the domestic tax structure. Thus, there has been relatively little analysis on the interactions between tax reform and the structure and composition of trade. This is the purpose of the present model and, indeed, exploring this aspect constitutes the first motivation of the exercise presented here.

The second motivation arises from the lack of studies of this type for the Mexican economy. Although there has been some recent work on AGE modelling of Mexico to evaluate the effects of trade liberalization and, more particularly, the effects of a North American Free Trade Agreement (NAFTA) (see USITC, 1992), nothing has been done to evaluate the tax reform process that took place in Mexico after 1985.[2] While the present model says something about tax reform, its purpose is not to evaluate the whole process but to look at the interactions (or lack of) between some aspects of tax reform and trade performance.[3] Therefore, the model built here has two important features: (a) the tax structure is incorporated and most taxes are explicitly identified, and (b) the model is trade-oriented.

The general conclusion that emerges from the study is that the changes in VAT and public pricing policy do not have strong effects on trade performance and, more generally, on reallocation of resources. Government revenues do increase, however, mainly as a result of increasing tax compliance.

The chapter is organized as follows. The next section contains a brief description of the database of the model. Then the structure of the model is described, its parameters explored and an analysis of the main results given. The final section contains concluding remarks and comments on some limitations.

The database

This section presents a very brief description of the database for the year 1985. This data was organized in a social accounting matrix (SAM) framework, and therefore the discussion refers to the main components of the SAM.

Supply side

The SAM identifies 27 sectors of production, 21 of which are tradeable whereas the remaining 6 are non-tradeable. Of these 27 sectors, two, petroleum and electricity, are operated by the government as public monopolies and therefore, for modelling purposes they will be treated differently.

Within the cost structure of production activities, three main components are identified: (a) intermediate costs, which consist of purchases of domestic and imported commodities, (b) production taxes and subsidies, wherever they exist, and (c) payments to factors of production, which consist of capital and three types of labour – unskilled, skilled and highly skilled.[4] Each activity is assumed to produce only one commodity; part of the production is sold to domestic markets while the remaining production is exported to the rest of the world.

The total supply of commodities is obtained by adding imports to the production sold in domestic markets. The total supply of commodities, destined for domestic markets, is divided into intermediate and final demand. Consumption taxes (VAT) are then charged on that portion of production devoted to final demand. In other words the VAT is modelled as a sales tax. This is a desirable property due to the potential complexities of modelling the crediting mechanism of the tax for producers.[5]

The part of production that is not sold to domestic markets is exported to the rest of the world, with export taxes being charged where they exist.

Income generation and institutions

As stated earlier, production activities use three types of labour. Payments to capital, however, are divided into private and public. Petroleum and electricity pay to public capital while the remaining 25 of the 27 sectors make payments to private capital.

The income from private capital is disbursed across formal and informal sectors. The formal sector divides its capital income between companies and households. The income received by companies is split into payments of dividends to domestic shareholders, corporate taxes and savings. Household capital income is distributed across three household income levels, which are referred to as poor, medium and rich.[6] Each household category has several sources of income: income from labour, income from the ownership of capital, dividends, transfers from the government and transfers from abroad (on a net basis). Household income is in turn spent on consumption, payment of taxes[7] and savings.

Demand side

There are three components of demand: intermediate demand, final domestic demand and demand for exports. Intermediate demand comes from the 27 sectors of production. Final domestic demand consists of consumption demand from the three households, government consumption, demand for investment goods from the 27 sectors, and changes in inventories. Export demands originate from the rest of the world. The sum of all these different demands must equal the total supply.

A description of the model

Production functions

With the exception of petroleum and electricity, all production sectors are modelled with nested production functions. First, they combine intermediate inputs (made of composite goods) in fixed proportions (Leontief technology). In the factor markets we have capital and three kinds of labour: the three different types of labour combine themselves through a Cobb–Douglas function. In turn, the resulting aggregate of labour combines in a Cobb–Douglas manner with capital. It is important to mention that all factors of

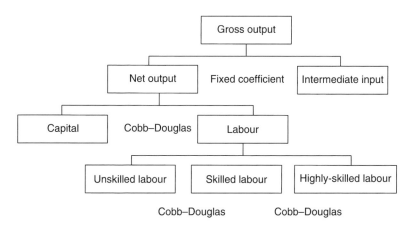

Figure 4.1 Nesting structure of production functions

production are perfectly mobile between sectors[8] and fixed in total quantities. Prices adjust to clear factor markets. Finally, the resulting value added combines in fixed proportions with the aggregate of raw materials (see Figure 4.1).

Pricing behaviour

Two types of assumptions are used in regard to industry behaviour, perfectly competitive and regulated. Perfectly competitive industries (25 sectors) follow the marginal cost-pricing rule. In the case of regulated industries we have two different forms of behaviour. First, in the petroleum sector, we shall assume that the government controls both the level of production as well as the price. Since the level of production is exogenous we need to assume that there is enough capacity to produce this exogenous level. This explains why capital in this sector is not treated as a factor but, instead, as a residual account that receives a rent (difference between income and expenditures). The quantity consumed domestically is determined by domestic demand. Once this demand has been satisfied, the residual is sold to foreign markets as exports. Notice, however, that the price fixed by the government would normally be different from the world market price. Therefore, the difference between the domestic price and the world market price constitutes a rent that goes to the government as revenue.

Second, we model electricity as a typical public utility. That is, it will be assumed that the price is fixed by the government and the level of output will always adjust to satisfy demand. In this context, the marginal cost curve will not determine the level of production. Nonetheless, it will determine production costs. Therefore, the difference between production costs (which are determined by the marginal cost and the level of demand) and revenues (which are determined by the fixed price), will constitute a subsidy to domestic consumers. This subsidy is in fact modelled as a rent going from the government to consumers.

Supply of commodities

The supply of commodities from domestic production and from imports are combined using a CES function in order to form a composite good. In other words, we adopt the Armington assumption of differentiating goods by region of origin (see Armington, 1969).[9]

In the case of four commodities (agriculture, petroleum, wearing apparel, and transport equipment), there exists quantity restrictions or quotas on imports.

Income generation

Factors of production collect their income from various activities and then distribute their income in fixed shares in the following manner. Private capital disburses its income across formal and informal sectors in fixed shares. The formal sector, in turn, divides its income in fixed shares between companies and households. Public capital is one source of government income; the other sources include existing income and commodity taxes. These three sources of government income are disbursed in fixed shares between consumption, savings and transfers to households. The three types of labour distribute their income in fixed shares among the three household income levels.

The amount of savings collected in the system is disbursed across investment and changes in inventories. In turn, investment is allocated across sectors in fixed value shares.

Demand for commodities

The three components of demand include intermediate demand, final domestic demand, and demand for exports. Intermediate demand is modelled in fixed proportions (Leontief technology). Final domestic demand consists of private consumption from the three types of households, government consumption, investment, and changes in inventories. Households and the government demand composite commodities according to a Cobb–Douglas specification. Investment, already allocated to the sectors of production, translates into demand for commodities in fixed quantity ratios. Changes in inventories are modelled as a consumption system in which the quantity is pre-specified. That is, the quantity is independent of the price of the good.

The last component of final demand is demand for exports. Here, we will assume that the rest of the world demands domestically produced commodities according to a demand function of the form

$$E_i = E_0(\P_j/PWE_i)^n$$

where n is the price elasticity of demand, $\P_j$ is a world price of an aggregation of commodities of type j, E_0 is a constant that reflects the level of demand when $\P_j$ equals the world price, PWE_i. In turn, the world price of commodity i is defined as

$$PWE_i = (Pd_i/[1 + te_i]ER)$$

where PD_i is the domestic price of commodity i, te_i is the rate of tax or subsidy on exports of commodity i, and ER is the exchange rate (price of a 'dollar' in local currency).

Notice that the small country assumption is being used here in that changes in PWE_i will not affect $\P_j$. Nonetheless, changes in PWE_i will affect the rest of the world's demand for our exports. Our *numéraire* is the domestic consumer price index, given by the consumption basket of 'poor' households.

Closure of the system

Choosing a closure rule is a strategic issue that, to a great extent, will determine the results. We adopt the so-called neoclassical closure rule, also known as the savings-driven rule. The current account is specified exogenously and therefore investment adjusts to the available savings. In other words, we have chosen a scenario in which the economy is constrained in its foreign borrowing.

Some results

The main results of several policy experiments are presented in this section. Before defining these policy experiments, however, something needs to be said about the value of the parameters as well as the level of effective VAT rates of the benchmark equilibrium.

Parameter values and effective VAT rates

Many of the parameters, as is the case of share parameters in the CES functions, are defined in the calibration process of the SAM. Some of them, however, need to be specified exogenously. All the CES aggregates used in the labour market were specified as Cobb–Douglas. However, export demand and elasticities of substitution between domestic and imported commodities have different values. Table 4.1 reports the elasticity values used in the policy experiments, and also the level of effective VAT rates as they appear in the benchmark equilibrium. This is important since, as we shall see, some simulations move VAT rates from their effective to their statutory level.

Policy experiments

Several simulations were carried out, all concerning changes in indirect taxes and prices of energy (petroleum and electricity). We report three of them, and make some comments on others. The three reported scenarios are described as follows:

Scenario A: Move from effective to statutory 10 per cent VAT rates.
Scenario B: Increase in prices of energy (petroleum and electricity).
Scenario C: A and B simultaneously.

Scenario A

This simulation attempts to provide a measure of tax evasion and the potential effects of increasing tax compliance. Column one of Table 4.2 describes the main aggregate effects. Aggregate welfare shows a reduction of 3.0 per cent.[10] The welfare effects by income groups are as follows: a 2.7 per cent reduction for the group classified as poor and a 3.3 per cent reduction of welfare for the other two groups (medium and rich). Imports increase by

27 per cent, which is a result of substitution away from domestic consumer goods in favour of imported ones. Exports also increase by 1.9 per cent.

Table 4.1 Elasticity values

Commodities	Elasticity of substitution (dom. and imp. goods)	Export demand elasticity	Effective[1] VAT rate (%)
Agriculture	3.0	2.0	
Mining	0.5	2.0	
Petroleum	0.5	2.0	
Food	1.125	2.0	
Beverages	1.125	2.0	0.8
Tobacco[2]	–	2.0	
Textiles	1.125	2.0	8.2
Wearing apparel	1.125	3.0	0.9
Leather	1.125	3.0	2.3
Wood	0.5	3.0	7.9
Paper	0.5	3.0	7.7
Chemicals	0.5	3.0	4.5
Rubber	0.5	3.0	10.0
Non-metallic products	0.5	3.0	6.7
Iron and steel	0.5	3.0	
Non-ferrous metals	0.5	3.0	5.0
Metallic products	0.5	3.0	9.6
Non-electrical machinery	0.375	3.0	9.3
Electrical machinery	0.375	3.0	8.5
Transport equipment	0.375	3.0	9.2
Other manufactures	0.375	3.0	5.1
Commerce			7.0
Transport and communications			0.5
Financial services			4.0
Other services			3.7

Notes: [1] refers to benchmark equilibrium VAT rates;
[2] There are no imports of tobacco.

Table 4.2 Main aggregate effects (per cent change)

	Scenario A	Scenario B	Scenario C
Welfare (total)	−3.0	−1.4	−4.5
Welfare of poor	−2.7	−1.4	−4.1
Welfare of medium	−3.3	−1.7	−5.0
Welfare of rich	−3.3	−1.2	−4.5
Imports	2.7	3.6	6.4
Exports	1.9	1.5	3.5

The effects on government revenue are of a significant magnitude (see Table 4.3). Indirect tax revenues rise 20.9 per cent with total government revenues increasing by 13.4 per cent.

The sectoral effects are described in Table 4.4. As can be seen, although the global effect on exports is not very large, the effect on individual exports is in the range of 3 to 6 per cent. The exception is petroleum, whose drop contributes to the difference between sectorial and global export performance. Commodity imports, on the other hand, show differing results; some of them fall whereas some others rise. In general, however, with the exceptions of metallic products and non-electrical machinery, the effects do not seem to be very significant.

Turning now to commodity prices the effects are not very large, especially in the case of producer prices. Consumer prices, however, perform rather differently; some of them decrease while some others increase. This is obviously explained by the experiment itself since consumer prices rose as a result of higher tax rates. The last thing to note about sectorial effects concerns factor reallocations. It can be seen that with the exception of metallic products and non-electrical machinery, both labour and capital register moderate changes.[11]

In summary, this first scenario suggests that increasing tax compliance was successful in raising government revenues, whereas the effects on the structure and composition of trade as well as resource reallocation were less important.

Scenario B

The purpose of the second experiment was to simulate a 40 per cent increase in the price of petroleum together with a 15 per cent increase in the price of electricity.[12] The aggregate effects are presented in column two of Table 4.2. As can be seen, welfare registers a 1.4 per cent reduction and, unlike the previous experiment in which the group referred to as poor was relatively less affected, in this second experiment the relatively less affected was the high income group (rich). Imports grow 3.6 per cent whereas exports increase by 1.5 per cent. In general, it can be said that the adjustment of public prices also has a strong impact in the main aggregates of the economy.

Table 4.3   Government revenue (per cent change)

	Scenario A	Scenario B	Scenario C
Indirect taxes	20.9	9.0	30.4
Direct taxes	−0.2	−0.6	−0.9
Production subsidies	−2.4	0.4	−1.9
Government revenue	13.4	7.2	20.9

Table 4.4 Scenario A: sectorial effects of a change from an effective to a 10% statutory VAT rate (per cent change)

Sectors	Export	Import	Producer prices	Consumer prices	Capital	Labour
Agriculture	3.8		−2.9	−2.9	0.6	−0.06
Mining	3.6	2.8	−2.8	−2.6	3.8	3.3
Petroleum	−0.3		0.0	0.03	0.0	0.0
Food	3.9	−2.0	−2.9	−2.9	0.4	−0.04
Beverages	3.9	−5.2	−2.9	0.5	−2.8	−3.3
Tobacco	3.9		−2.9	−2.9	0.5	0.0
Textiles	3.5	2.7	−2.8	−2.0	−0.3	−0.9
Wearing apparel	5.6		−2.8	0.4	−2.3	−2.9
Leather	5.7	−5.4	−2.9	1.2	−2.9	−3.5
Wood	5.9	−0.5	−2.9	−1.7	2.0	1.4
Paper	5.5	−0.4	−2.8	−1.5	0.6	0.1
Chemicals	3.9	−1.6	−2.3	3.1	−0.6	−1.1
Rubber	5.1	−0.8	−2.7	−2.6	0.2	−0.2
Non-metallic products	5.4	1.4	−2.8	−0.1	2.7	2.1
Iron and steel	4.7	4.2	−2.6	−2.3	5.3	4.8
Non-ferrous metals	5.1	2.8	−2.7	3.1	3.9	3.3
Metallic products	5.4	10.0	−2.8	−19.9	11.0	10.5
Non-electrical machinery	5.0	12.3	−2.6	−1.7	12.3	11.8
Electrical machinery	5.5	5.3	−2.8	−0.7	6.1	5.6
Transport equipment	3.4		−2.1	0.2	3.2	2.7
Other manufactures	4.9	−1.9	−2.6	−0.3	0.6	0.2
Construction			−2.7	−2.7	5.5	4.8
Electricity			0.0	0.0	0.0	1.4
Commerce			−3.0	0.2	−0.5	−1.0
Transport and communications			−2.8	7.0	−4.2	−4.7
Financial services			−3.1	2.1	−2.5	−2.9
Other services			−2.9	2.8	0.0	−0.4

The impact on government revenue is shown in column two of Table 4.3. Government revenue increases by 7.2 per cent, which, although not as strong as in the previous experiment, is significant. It would thus appear that public pricing policy plays a relatively important role in the tax reform process.

Moving now to the sectoral effects, and focusing in particular on trade performance, two aspects deserve to be mentioned (see Table 4.5). First, on the import side it can be seen that for all commodities imports grow, although not in a very significant magnitude. Second, in examining exports with the exception of petroleum, all of them fall and the reductions are in several cases relatively important. Therefore, compared to scenario A it would appear that the adjustment of public prices tends to reverse the effects on exports.

Table 4.5   Scenario B: sectorial effects of an increase in energy prices (per cent changes)

Sectors	Export	Import	Producer prices	Consumer prices	Capital	Labour
Agriculture	−6.9		−0.8	−0.8	−0.7	−1.2
Mining	−7.5	2.5	−0.8	−0.9	−1.2	−1.8
Petroleum	13.0		40.0	38.1	0.0	0.0
Food	−6.6	3.3	−0.9	−1.1	−0.6	−1.1
Beverages	−6.6	3.5	−0.9	−1.0	−0.3	−0.8
Tobacco	−7.2		−0.6	−0.6	−0.6	−1.1
Textiles	−8.7	3.9	0.1	0.0	−1.4	−1.9
Wearing apparel	−11.4		−0.3	−0.4	−0.9	−1.4
Leather	−10.5	3.7	−0.7	−0.7	−0.4	−0.9
Wood	−9.7	5.0	−1.0	−1.0	0.8	0.4
Paper	−11.1	1.5	−0.4	−0.9	−0.3	−1.0
Chemicals	−27.0	2.6	6.2	4.8	−3.6	−4.2
Rubber	−15.1	1.8	1.0	0.6	−0.8	−1.3
Non-metallic products	−12.2	3.8	−0.08	−0.2	0.9	0.3
Iron and steel	−10.3	4.1	−0.8	−1.5	2.1	1.4
Non-ferrous metals	−11.3	3.0	−0.4	−1.3	0.8	0.2
Metallic products	−9.6	8.9	−1.0	−1.5	6.8	6.2
Non-electrical machinery	−8.9	10.4	−1.2	−3.0	7.4	6.8
Electrical machinery	−9.6	6.1	−1.0	−1.8	2.2	1.7
Transport equipment	−10.7		−0.6	0.7	−0.6	−1.2
Other manufactures	−15.6	1.7	1.2	−1.3	−4.5	−5.1
Construction			−0.6	−0.6	4.2	3.6
Electricity			15.0	14.9	0.0	−9.5
Commerce			−1.1	−1.2	−0.5	−1.0
Transport and communications			0.7	0.3	−1.5	−2.0
Financial services			−1.3	−1.4	0.6	−0.05
Other services			−0.9	−0.9	2.2	1.6

Prices behave differently: some of them rise while others fall. This behaviour obeys two main effects: on the one hand, the increases in petroleum and electricity generates an upward pressure on prices as production costs increase; on the other hand, the fall in the level of economic activity pushes prices downwards. It is also interesting to note that the effects on factor reallocations, although higher than in the previous experiment, are still relatively small.

Summarizing, this second experiment suggests that the adjustment of public prices was also a relatively important instrument for raising revenue. In terms of trade performance and allocation of resources, however, with the exception of exports, the magnitudes involved were to some extent less important, especially if we keep in mind the magnitudes involved in the simulation itself.

Scenario C

The last simulation performs experiments A and B simultaneously, and the aggregate effects are shown in column three of Table 4.2. As expected, the compound effects of the two previous scenarios in terms of welfare is now stronger (−4.5 per cent), and the same can be said in terms of foreign trade aggregates. Notice that in this last scenario it is the medium income level group which is the most affected in terms of welfare.

The impact on public finances is also significant. Government revenue increases by 20.9 per cent with revenue from indirect taxes growing by 30.4 per cent. As expected, this scenario registers the largest increase in government revenue.

Table 4.6 Scenario C: sectorial effects of a change from an effective to a 10 per cent statutory VAT rate and an increase in energy prices (per cent change)

Sectors	Export	Import	Producer prices	Consumer prices	Capital	Labour
Agriculture	−3.2		−3.7	−3.7	−0.08	−1.2
Mining	−4.0	5.3	−3.5	−3.5	2.6	1.4
Petroleum	12.9		38.1	38.1	0.0	0.0
Food	−2.8	1.1	−4.0	−4.0	−0.2	−1.2
Beverages	−2.8	−1.9	−3.9	−0.4	−3.2	−4.1
Tobacco	−3.4		−3.6	−3.6	−0.2	−1.2
Textiles	−5.4	1.0	−2.7	−2.0	−1.8	−2.8
Wearing apparel	−6.2		−3.3	−0.01	−3.3	−4.3
Leather	−5.1	−1.9	−3.6	0.4	−3.4	−4.4
Wood	−4.1	4.4	−3.9	−2.8	2.9	1.8
Paper	−6.0	1.0	−3.5	−2.4	0.3	−0.8
Chemicals	−24.4	0.9	2.6	8.3	−4.3	−5.3
Rubber	−10.6	0.9	−1.9	−1.9	−0.6	−1.6
Non-metallic products	−7.3	5.3	−2.9	−0.4	3.7	2.5
Iron and steel	−5.8	8.5	−3.7	−3.7	7.4	6.3
Non-ferrous metals	−6.5	5.8	−3.6	1.8	4.7	3.5
Metallic products	−4.4	19.1	−4.0	−21.1	18.0	16.9
Non-electrical machinery	−4.1	22.9	−4.7	−4.7	19.9	18.7
Electrical machinery	−4.4	11.5	−4.2	−2.6	8.5	7.4
Transport equipment	−7.5		0.9	1.0	2.5	1.5
Other manufactures	−11.4	−0.3	−3.1	−1.5	−4.0	−5.1
Construction			−3.3	−3.3	9.8	8.5
Electricity			14.9	14.9	0.0	−8.2
Commerce			−4.1	−1.0	−1.1	−2.1
Transport and communications			−2.3	7.4	−5.7	−6.7
Financial services			−4.5	0.6	−2.0	−3.0
Other services			−3.8	1.8	2.2	1.1

The sectoral effects are described in Table 4.6. It can be seen that with the exception of wearing apparel, leather, non-metallic products, iron and steel, non-ferrous metals, metallic products and non-electrical machinery, the effects on resource allocation do not change much if compared with scenarios A and B.

Perhaps the most interesting point to note about this last experiment concerns the effect on trade performance, as described by Table 4.6. On the import side all categories increase by relatively small amounts with three exceptions. On the export side it would appear that with the exception of petroleum the additional effect of adjusting public prices is to reverse the trend in exports. This is explained by the fact that the adjustment of public prices has the effect of increasing producers' prices leading to a fall in exports, whereas in the experiment of increasing VAT rates alone, the impact is felt mainly in consumer prices. This point is reinforced if we consider an additional simulation (scenario D) that consists of calibrating the model to a 15 per cent VAT rate and then performing a reduction of this rate to a 10 per cent level together with an increase in energy prices, as actually happened in the 1991 reform.[13] The results of this experiment are shown in Tables A.1 and A.3 in the Appendix. These results suggest that, to some extent, public pricing policy adjustments swamped changes in VAT rates both in terms of revenue, and also in terms of exports.

Furthermore, in addition to scenario C we simulated a simultaneous removal of tariffs (scenario E). The additional effects, particularly in terms of reallocation of resources were very small (see Tables A.2 and A.4 in the Appendix).

Overall, considering the magnitudes involved in scenario C, it seems that tax reform, that is VAT modifications, did not have important effects on trade performance.

Concluding remarks

Several conclusions can be drawn from the previous analysis, which can be outlined as follows:

1 Although we did not explicitly model tax evasion, our estimates suggest that increasing tax compliance was successful in raising additional revenue. In terms of the structure and composition of trade, however, the effects were relatively less significant.

2 Pricing policy of energy also seemed to play an important role in raising revenue. Taken together, VAT changes and pricing policy of energy, it would appear that the latter tends to swamp the former, at least in their price and export effects. This last point emerges very clearly in the experiment in which VAT rates moved from 15 to 10 per cent and energy

prices increased, and is less evident when VAT rates moved from their effective to their statutory levels.

3 The resource allocation implications of trade liberalization are relatively unimportant.

The general conclusion emerging from the results of the model is that the most important part of the reform, in terms of revenue, came from increasing tax compliance, whereas in terms of trade structure and allocation of resources the effects were not very important.

These conclusions, however, have to be interpreted within the limitations of the model. Three of them deserve to be mentioned. First, we did not model changes in direct taxes nor in government expenditures, which were both important instruments of fiscal reform. Second, the data on the composition of value added as reported in the Mexican National Accounts (and therefore in our model) is heavily in favour of capital; in principle, this is not evident in an economy like the Mexican. While this could be a data problem arising from a wrong classification of self-employed labour, it nevertheless raises the question of whether or not market structure is playing some important role. If this is so, we would require to incorporate market imperfections within the model, and the conclusions might be different. Third, we did not carry sensitivity analysis with the parameters, and therefore, the question of the extent to which these values are driving the results remains open.

Appendix

Table A.1 Main aggregate effects (per cent change)

	Scenario D	Scenario E
Welfare (total)	−1.9	−2.7
Welfare of poor	−1.2	−2.7
Welfare of medium	−1.7	−3.4
Welfare of rich	−2.9	−2.2
Imports	1.2	7.1
Exports	−0.1	4.6

Table A.2 Government revenue (per cent change)

	Scenario D	Scenario E
Indirect taxes	−9.6	15.5
Direct taxes	−0.4	−0.9
Production subsidies	1.6	−1.6
Government revenue	−5.8	11.8

Table A.3 Scenario D: sectoral effects of a change from 15 per cent to 10 per cent VAT rates and an increase in energy prices (per cent change)

Sectors	Export	Import	Producer prices	Consumer prices	Capital	Labour
Agriculture	−10.2		2.1	2.1	−1.3	−1.1
Mining	−10.6	0.02	2.4	1.8	−4.6	−4.6
Petroleum	13.3		40.0	38.1	0.0	0.0
Food	−10.0	5.3	2.0	1.8	−1.1	−1.1
Beverages	−9.9	9.9	2.0	−2.5	3.3	3.3
Tobacco	−10.4		2.3	2.3	−1.2	−1.2
Textiles	−11.6	9.2	2.9	−1.6	1.1	1.2
Wearing apparel	−15.8		2.5	−1.8	2.5	2.5
Leather	−15.1	9.7	2.2	−2.2	2.7	2.8
Wood	−14.5	7.3	2.0	−2.5	0.6	0.7
Paper	−15.5	3.1	2.3	−2.6	0.06	−0.04
Chemicals	−29.2	4.3	8.6	2.3	−2.8	−2.9
Rubber	−18.9	3.5	3.8	−1.1	−0.1	−0.2
Non-metallic products	−16.4	2.8	2.7	−1.8	−1.2	−1.2
Iron and steel	−14.1	0.1	1.8	0.8	−2.7	−2.8
Non-ferrous metals	−15.4	0.7	2.3	−3.3	−2.4	−2.4
Metallic products	−14.0	−0.03	1.8	−3.2	−2.8	−2.8
Non-electrical machinery	−13.1	−1.5	1.4	−5.4	−4.3	−4.3
Electrical machinery	−14.1	1.7	1.8	−3.7	−2.7	−2.8
Transport equipment	−14.2		1.8	−2.6	−2.9	−3.0
Other manufactures	−19.1	5.8	3.9	−3.7	−3.1	−3.2
Construction			2.1	2.1	−1.1	−1.0
Electricity			15.0	14.9	0.0	−10.1
Commerce			1.9	−2.6	0.8	0.8
Transport and communications			3.6	−1.3	0.1	0.2
Financial services			1.8	−2.6	2.7	2.5
Other services			1.9	−2.5	1.2	1.1

Table A.4 Scenario E: sectorial effects of a change from an effective to a 10 per cent statutory VAT rate, increase in energy prices and removal of tariffs (per cent change)

Sectors	Export	Import	Producer prices	Consumer prices	Capital	Labour
Agriculture	−1.8		−2.3	−2.3	−0.2	−0.9
Mining	−2.4	5.4	−2.0	−2.6	1.5	0.8
Petroleum	13.2		40.0	38.1	0.0	0.0
Food	−1.4	9.7	−2.5	−2.9	−0.3	−0.9
Beverages	−1.3	21.5	−2.6	0.2	−2.9	−3.5
Tobacco	−1.9		−2.3	−2.3	−0.1	−0.8
Textiles	−3.4	12.9	−1.5	−1.9	−1.3	−2.0
Wearing apparel	−3.5		−2.1	0.9	−3.0	−3.6
Leather	−2.8	10.1	−2.3	1.2	−3.1	−3.7
Wood	−2.0	15.3	−2.6	−2.8	2.2	1.5
Paper	−3.2	3.8	−2.2	−4.8	0.6	0.0
Chemicals	−21.4	5.0	4.8	6.3	−3.9	−4.6
Rubber	−7.6	9.2	−0.6	−14.1	2.8	2.1
Non-metallic products	−4.8	9.4	−1.6	−3.9	3.1	2.3
Iron and steel	−1.8	7.6	−2.6	−3.8	4.5	3.8
Non-ferrous metals	−3.4	6.7	−2.1	−0.9	2.8	2.0
Metallic products	−1.2	18.7	−2.8	−31.1	12.7	12.0
Non-electrical machinery	−0.1	17.3	−3.2	−8.2	12.7	12.0
Electrical machinery	−1.1	12.2	−2.9	−5.3	6.4	5.7
Transport equipment	−4.1		−1.9	−0.1	2.2	1.5
Other manufactures	−7.9	7.6	−0.5	−6.2	−1.9	−2.5
Construction			−2.3	−2.3	6.6	5.8
Electricity			15.0	14.9	0.0	−8.3
Commerce			−2.7	−2.0	0.2	−0.4
Transport and communications			−0.7	6.9	−4.9	−5.5
Financial services			−3.0	0.9	−1.6	−2.2
Other services			−2.5	1.5	0.9	0.2

Notes

1 Centro de Estudios Económicos, El Colegio de México, Camino al Ajusco 20, Col. Pedregal de Sta. Teresa, C.P. 10740, México D.F., México, Tel: (5) 645–5955 ext. 4163; Fax: (5) 645–0464. The author wants to thank John Whalley for very helpful guidance and comments. Financing by the International Development Research Centre of Canada is gratefully acknowledged. The author alone is responsible for any errors or omissions.

2 The work by Kehoe and Serra (1983) looks at the introduction of VAT in Mexico in 1980.

3 Urzúa (1994) provides a detailed description of the recent tax reform process in Mexico.

4 The criteria for this three-way labour classification were based on levels of education, as given in the 1989 income and expenditure survey.

5　In a model in which factors of production are freely mobile (as exists here), sales taxes to final consumers is equivalent to VAT.
6　This classification was also based on the 1989 income and expenditure survey.
7　Regarding payment of personal income taxes, a simplifying assumption of proportionality was adopted, given the lack of information. Thus, the amount of tax revenue from personal income taxes was distributed between the three households according to their income level. While there is no empirical support for doing this, the only rationale is that one can think that tax evasion grows with income levels.
8　Except for petroleum and electricity. In these two sectors capital (public) is sector-specific.
9　It should be noticed that, on the import side, the small country assumption is adopted; that is, it is assumed that the supply of imports from the rest of the world is perfectly elastic so that demand for imports will not influence world commodity prices.
10　The so-called equivalent variation is used as a measure of welfare.
11　The details of reallocation of the different categories of labour are available on request.
12　As it actually occurred with the so-called solidarity pact (PECE).
13　See Urzúa (1994).

References

Armington, P. (1969) 'A Theory of Demand for Products Distinguished by Place of Production', *IMF Staff Papers*, vol. 16, pp. 159–78.

Kehoe, T. and J. Serra (1983) 'A Computational General Equilibrium Model with Endogenous Unemployment: An Analysis of the 1980 Fiscal Reform in Mexico', *Journal of Public Economics*, vol. 22, pp. 1–26.

Shoven, J. and J. Whalley (1984) 'Applied General Equilibrium Models of Taxation and International Trade: An Introduction and Survey', *Journal of Economic Literature*, vol. 22, pp. 1007–51.

Shoven, J. and J. Whalley (1992) *Applying General Equilibrium*, Cambridge: Cambridge University Press.

United States International Trade Commission (1992) 'Economy-wide Modeling of the Economic Implications of a FTA with Mexico and a NAFTA with Canada and Mexico', Publication 2508, May, Washington, DC.

Urzúa, C. (1994) 'An Appraisal of Recent Tax Reforms in Mexico', paper presented at the Workshop on Tax Reform in Developing Countries, held in Mexico City.

5

An Appraisal of Recent Tax Reforms in Mexico

Carlos M. Urzúa

Ō∂3 H∂5
Ō16 E62
H50 L33

Introduction

Mexico experienced dramatic economic changes in the late 1980s and the beginning of the 1990s. These changes, most of which now seem irreversible, have turned Mexico from an inward-looking country to a very open one; from a country with significant state participation in the economy, to one in which state intervention keeps shrinking; from an economy with a high inflation rate and a sizable government deficit to one in which both macro-economic variables have been controlled. Although several serious problems remain (such as an extremely unequal distribution of income, very low savings and a sizable current account deficit), the Mexican economy is growing moderately, on what seems to be a stable path.

The purpose of this chapter is to make an appraisal of the tax reforms in Mexico in the late 1980s and early 1990s putting emphasis on their macro-economic consequences. The chapter also examines the pattern of government expenditures during the three presidential regimes between 1977 and 1994 and issues such as the privatization of public enterprises. The plan is as follows: the next section provides a brief account of the recent evolution of the Mexican economy. Then a closer look is taken at tax reforms from 1989 to 1993 on the main categories of corporate income tax, personal income tax, value added tax, excise taxes, tariffs and other sources of revenue, and present an international comparison of the tax effort, with some comments on three other fiscal issues – privatization, fiscal federalism and tax enforcement. Then, in contrast, changes in the composition of government expenditures are examined, and an international comparison of expenditures by function is given. The last section presents conclusions.

A brief account of the Mexican economy

This section provides a quick overview of the most important economic events that took place in Mexico from 1977 to 1994, paying particular attention to fiscal reforms. This period covers the regimes of the three presidents: López Portillo, De la Madrid, and Salinas. The review is divided into three parts, each corresponding to one presidential regime. This division is useful since, as is well known, the executive in Mexico has enough control over the legislative branch to make the important economic decisions almost entirely its own responsibility. The review will not be complete, however, without mentioning, at least in passing, two other key periods in the development of the Mexican economy. The first one is known as the 'stabilizing development' (*desarrollo estabilizador*) period and covers the 1950s and 1960s. During these years Mexico experienced a very high rate of growth (the average real growth rate from 1950 to 1970 was greater than 6 per cent), and a remarkable stability of prices. It is worth noting that government revenue was then, as one would expect given the stage of development of Mexico, mostly dependent on indirect taxes. The tax burden of direct taxes was quite low compared to other countries at roughly the same stage of development, although it rose as a result of increases in income tax schedules over the years. In any case, government revenue did not have to grow very fast to match the relatively minor rate of growth of expenditures that Mexico experienced in the 1950s and 1960s.

The second period is sometimes called the 'shared development' (*desarrollo compartido*) period, and corresponds to the years in which President Echeverría was in power (1970–6). Under his mandate, the Mexican government suddenly changed the direction of some economic and social policies. It was felt by the new group in power that the success of the old strategy was made at the expense of a worsening income distribution, a deterioration of living standards, and a low employment rate. Although only the first of these indictments was clearly true, the political climate then prevailing in Mexico was conducive to changes.

Thus, as was also common at that time in other Latin American countries, the government decided to promote better income distribution and a higher employment rate by increasing the role taken by the public sector. On the revenue side, there were plans of making comprehensive changes in the tax system. The plans, as recounted by Gil Díaz (1987 and 1990), called for a more progressive tax system, an increase in excise taxes, an effort to improve tax compliance and, above all, an attempt to globalize income taxation as much as possible. However, very strong opposition from the private sector forced the government to stop its tax reform as early as December 1972. This confrontation is now a textbook case on the political economy of Mexican tax reforms (see Solís, 1981).

Expenditures, on the other hand, grew quickly during this period and, furthermore, the number of state-owned enterprises increased tenfold (from 84 in 1970 to 845 in 1976). In order to finance this increase in expenditures, given the constraint on tax revenue, the government had to rely on foreign borrowing (which increased more than four times during the period), domestic borrowing, and an inflation tax. In the end, the Mexican economy had to endure a high (for Mexican standards) inflation rate, significant budget and trade deficits, and an overvalued fixed exchange rate. After two decades of fixed parity the peso had to be devalued in 1976.

The López Portillo period: 1977–82

These years can be usefully divided into three sub-periods. The first, from the end of 1976 to the end of 1977, was a time of stabilization under a stand-by agreement with the IMF. The second lasted until 1981 when oil discoveries and easy foreign credit helped to break all the constraints to growth. The final period is the year from the end of 1981 to the end of 1982, when the drop in oil prices, the increase in world interest rates, and the rising trade deficit forced Mexico to stop interest payments on its foreign debt.

During the stabilization period, the government simply reduced expenditures. Very soon, however, the constraint on expenditures was not binding since the oil revenues of Petroleos Mexicunos (PEMEX), the state-owned monopoly, increased very fast in the second half of the 1970s, and Mexico was again allowed to borrow in the Eurocurrency market. From 1978 on, the economy grew again and at an increasing pace. This is shown in Figure 5.1. As

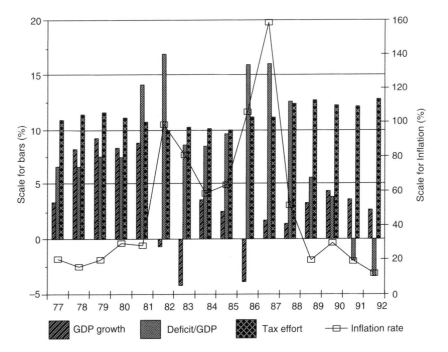

Figure 5.1 Evolution of the Mexican economy

can also be appreciated from the figure, in the first years of the recovery inflation was moderate and the increase in the public deficit was not unduly high.

With a booming economy, tax authorities found themselves in a very comfortable situation during that period. Tax reforms were initiated in 1978 primarily to make the tax system more progressive and simplify tax collection. Furthermore, at the beginning of 1980 the treasury was able to introduce a value added tax (to be reviewed in the next section), a tax that had been strenuously opposed by the private sector in the 1960s. Once the federal government was able to borrow from abroad again, it did so with zest. During 1981 alone, Mexico managed to borrow more than US$ 19 billion. This money was used to finance the rapidly increasing trade deficit and to counteract the burgeoning capital flight that developed after the domestic currency was allowed to appreciate and private agents were speculating that twin deficits were unsustainable in the long run. It also paid the interest on foreign debts that were increasing as the world interest rates climbed.

Public expenditures grew very fast in the early 1980s. The federal government was engaged in a very ambitious public investment programme, and was also required to finance the deficit of the rest of the public sector. (It even had to rescue a large private conglomerate in 1981.) There were also many public enterprises. During President López Portillo's mandate, the number of federally-owned enterprises grew from 845 to 1155. These included the phone monopoly, two main airlines, most of the steel companies and all the commercial banks. The latter were nationalized the day of the last presidential address in 1982.

As can be appreciated from Figure 5.1, the public deficit was already at very worrisome levels at the end of 1980. Curiously enough, the more the economy grew, the more the government seemed to need to increase expenditures (these outright procyclical policies have been examined in Urzúa, 1991). The final outcome is well known. Due to these domestic factors and two key external factors, the drop in oil prices and the increase in world real interest rates, the Mexican economy was almost bankrupt in 1982.

The De la Madrid period: 1983–8

During this period there were several attempts to stabilize the economy. Tax reforms and the control of government expenditures were seen as key ingredients in all stabilization programmes. The government deficit had to be controlled through an increase in tax collection, a realignment in the prices of government-produced goods, and a cut in government spending.

In 1983 the basic rate for the VAT was increased together with the personal income tax (see the next section). Excise taxes were also increased. With an increase in taxes, a sharp reduction in government expenditures (especially capital expenditures) and a devaluation, Mexico soon started reaping benefits (see Figure 5.1). After a considerable decrease in GDP in 1983, the economy rebounded in 1984 while the inflation rate was lowered, the public deficit was halved and the current account balance was turned around.

In 1986, however, the Mexican economy suffered a large external shock when world oil prices collapsed. The drop in oil revenue and the increase in expenditures during an election year had an immediate effect on the public deficit (see Figure 5.1). By 1987, Mexico was experiencing a record annual inflation rate of 159 per cent, and the peso was suffering speculative attacks. These factors impelled the government to implement a somewhat heterodox stabilization programme called the Economic Solidarity Pact (*Pacto de Solidaridad Económica*) in December 1987. After reaching a consensus among the government, the private sector and the workers, the pact was implemented along the following lines: a freeze of prices and wages, a sharp devaluation of the peso which was used afterwards as a nominal anchor, a reduction of tariffs (which continued the trend of current-account liberalization initiated in the mid-1980s), a very restrictive fiscal policy,[1] and a somewhat restrictive monetary policy. As shown in Figure 5.1, the pact was quite successful in bringing down both the inflation rate and the public deficit without going into a recession at the end of De la Madrid's period.

The Salinas period: 1988–94

During his mandate, President Salinas implemented major economic reforms that would have been unthinkable only a few years before: stringent fiscal and monetary policies were sustained during the period; there was a continuation of a privatization programme that ranks as the largest (in terms of enterprises sold) in the Western world; a free trade agreement with the United States and Canada was signed in 1993; and, finally, there was an agrarian reform that disposed of the *ejidos* system, the communal land regime that resulted from the Mexican Revolution (1910–21).

The macroeconomic indicators shown in Figure 5.1 for this period are positive.[2] The economy grew at a moderate pace while the inflation rate was kept at a reasonable level. The tax effort increased with the application of some reforms, so that the public deficit was finally controlled and, in 1992 and 1993, the government was able to run surpluses. The tax system was frequently revised by the Salinas administration. One of the purported goals pursued by the reforms was to lower income tax rates to make them comparable to those in the United States, while at the same time keeping tax revenue constant. As reviewed in the next section, this was accomplished to some extent by widening the tax base and devising new mechanisms to increase tax compliance. Another two reforms that deserve special mention are the reduction of the basic VAT rate, accompanied by an increase in fuel and electricity prices at the end of 1991, and the fiscal stimulus to the economy at the end of 1993 that was achieved by lowering income tax rates.

There was a definite push towards privatization during this period. Among those enterprises that were privatized were the profitable commercial banks and the phone monopoly. The only big enterprises that apparently will remain in the hands of the state are the oil company PEMEX, the electric utilities and the train system. It should be mentioned that although the government originally meant to put most of the revenue from privatization in a 'contingency fund', in the end the money was used primarily to reduce the debt overhang (to be discussed later).

On the other side of the balance sheet, the Salinas administration continued to pursue stringent expenditure policies during the entire period. Government capital investment continued to be low (although increasing), and the administration actively pursued a decrease in current expenditures by reducing the number of employees in the federal government. The only expenditure items that increased significantly over the years were those corresponding to social expenditures. In particular, as will be reviewed later, the so-called National Solidarity Programme, which was created in 1990 with the main objective of attacking extreme poverty, received an increasing level of funds over the period.

Fiscal reforms in Mexico

This section is an examination of the most recent reforms in corporate income tax, personal income tax, value added tax, and other taxes (such as excise and trade taxes). It will also make tax burden comparisons with other countries. It will be evident in the review that the tax reforms in Mexico have been made gradually, a piecemeal approach which contrasts with the reforms adopted in other Latin American countries. As Bird (1992, p. 25) has written, 'Mexico's tax reform is thus best seen not as a "response to crisis" but as an ongoing process of adjustment to changing circumstances and, to some extent, to changing intellectual fashions'.

As a general reference on the structure of federal taxes in Mexico, part A of Table 5.1 presents the contribution of each of the taxes since 1977. Aside from the notes to the table, it is worth noting three other points. First, the table does not follow exactly the format of presentation regularly used by the government. Second, the income taxes paid by the state oil company PEMEX are separated from the rest of the corporate income tax to avoid spurious comparisons over the years. And, third, the reader should pay special attention to the item labelled 'capital income' (*aprovechamientos*), since it includes the income accruing from the sale of state enterprises.

The table also presents figures on social security payments in part B, together with figures for state and local revenue in part C. The latter have recently gained importance since in 1993 the main social security institution, IMSS, began having financial problems, mostly due to bad management. As a result, the rate of social security contributions has already been adjusted twice during the 1990s. The figures on state and local taxes show that the tax effort at state and local levels is quite meagre by international standards,

Table 5.1 Total revenue at the federal and state levels, 1977–93 (per cent of GDP)

	1977	1978	1979	1980	1981	1982	1983	1984	1985	1986	1987	1988	1989	1990	1991	1992	1993
A. FEDERAL REVENUE	12.46	13.01	13.47	14.98	14.77	15.30	17.68	16.99	16.66	15.76	16.96	16.19	17.94	17.33	20.72	20.85	n.a.
INCOME TAXES PAID BY PEMEX[1]	0.99	1.15	1.48	3.66	3.82	4.67	6.49	5.75	5.89	3.65	5.09	3.42	3.49	3.78	3.58	3.35	3.13
NON-OIL TAX REVENUE	10.68	11.11	11.33	10.54	10.06	9.54	10.17	10.46	9.90	11.14	10.79	11.55	12.22	11.73	11.99	12.43	12.21
Income tax[2]	5.07	5.72	5.65	5.15	4.96	4.30	3.86	4.12	4.01	4.22	4.03	4.71	5.09	4.81	4.97	5.52	5.56
Personal income tax	2.54	2.85	2.64	2.33	2.48	2.54	1.95	1.92	1.91	1.91	2.16	2.16	2.35	2.13	2.30	2.56	2.56
Corporate income tax[3]	2.02	2.30	2.47	2.38	2.04	1.29	1.29	1.63	1.54	1.77	1.44	2.14	2.38	2.38	2.43	2.74	2.78
Foreign remittances & other	0.51	0.57	0.54	0.44	0.44	0.47	0.62	0.57	0.56	0.54	0.43	0.41	0.36	0.30	0.24	0.22	0.22
Value added tax[4]	2.11	2.07	2.39	2.68	2.59	2.21	2.98	3.20	2.88	2.89	3.05	3.25	3.35	3.88	3.76	2.99	2.94
From imports	n.a.	n.a.	n.a.	0.67	0.72	0.54	0.46	0.55	0.37	0.53	0.79	0.97	1.08	1.22	1.35	1.01	0.96
Excise taxes	1.69	1.65	1.52	1.07	1.02	1.81	2.39	2.24	2.10	2.77	2.50	2.66	2.49	1.63	1.49	1.96	1.84
From gasoline	0.57	0.53	0.47	0.38	0.34	1.18	1.55	1.53	1.38	1.90	1.68	1.74	1.57	0.75	0.81	1.24	1.12
Import taxes	0.58	0.65	0.89	0.99	1.09	0.84	0.52	0.52	0.62	0.81	0.81	0.43	0.79	0.93	1.15	1.26	1.14
Export taxes	0.29	0.11	0.07	0.04	0.00	0.02	0.02	0.01	0.01	0.06	0.01	0.01	0.02	0.01	0.00	0.00	0.00
Other taxes	0.94	0.91	0.81	0.61	0.40	0.36	0.40	0.37	0.28	0.39	0.39	0.49	0.48	0.47	0.62	0.70	0.73
NON-TAX REVENUE	0.79	0.75	0.66	0.78	0.89	1.09	1.02	0.78	0.87	0.97	1.08	1.22	2.23	1.82	5.15	5.07	n.a.
Capital income[5]	0.29	0.21	0.16	0.16	0.16	0.46	0.24	0.10	0.20	0.24	0.35	0.35	1.50	0.81	4.13	4.20	n.a.
Others	0.50	0.54	0.50	0.62	0.72	0.64	0.79	0.69	0.67	0.73	0.73	0.86	0.74	1.02	1.03	0.87	n.a.
B. SOCIAL SECURITY	2.58	2.64	2.58	2.38	2.46	2.63	2.30	2.16	2.17	2.32	2.23	2.44	2.48	2.61	2.82	2.96	n.a.
C. STATE AND LOCAL REVENUE	1.96	2.02	2.02	1.53	1.38	1.33	1.11	1.16	1.25	1.44	1.25	1.05	1.20	1.41	n.a.	n.a.	n.a.
TOTAL REVENUE (A + B + C)	17.00	17.67	18.07	18.89	18.61	19.26	21.09	20.31	20.08	19.52	20.44	19.68	21.62	21.35	n.a.	n.a.	n.a.

Notes:
[1] Excludes VAT, import taxes and excises, which are entered in part B.
[2] To avoid spurious comparisons, the tax on phone services from 1990 on is added (as in the 1980s) to the excise taxes.
[3] Includes a tax on gross assets from 1989 on.
[4] During 1977–9 it was a turnover tax instead of a value added tax.
[5] Includes income from the sale of state enterprises.

Sources: Constructed by the author using information from Dirección General de Política de Ingresos, SHCP, Quinto Informe de Gobierno (1993), INEGI, and Urzúa (1991).

mostly due to low taxes on land property. Curiously enough, this seems to be the first time that state and local taxes have been consolidated with the federal tax figures. This omission on the part of even the federal authorities (and the academic community) sadly exemplifies the highly centralized political structure that still prevails in Mexico.

The corporate income tax and the tax on gross assets

As already noted, the tax revenue from the corporate income tax (the *impuesto al ingreso de las personas morales*) was low during the 1950s compared even with other developing countries. However, in the 1960s the tax base rose steadily and the mechanisms for tax collection were improved. In the early 1970s the ambitious tax reforms planned at the beginning of the Echeverría administration ended up in simple measures such as an increase in corporate income tax rates up to 42 per cent and an increase in the withholding tax on interest income. The next big tax reform was in 1978, but it centred on personal income taxes and preparation for the introduction of a value added tax in 1980. Corporate income tax received renewed attention only after the crisis of 1982. Corporate taxes were partially reformed to take into account some inflation distortions,[3] and to try to incorporate sectors that until then had enjoyed special treatment (for example, the construction industry).

Nevertheless, as shown in Table 5.1, corporate income tax continued to be very low during the mid-1980s. High inflation rates and widespread tax evasion accounted for this phenomenon. For instance, firms were able to decrease tax payments through the deduction of interest payments that had a high inflationary component,[4] and the Olivera–Tanzi effect was also at work with monthly inflation rates exceeding 10 per cent. These factors prompted the government to initiate a more comprehensive reform of corporate income tax in 1986. The first change involved shortening tax collection lags by requiring monthly payments, and a second important change was adjustments to index fully corporate income tax (firms were allowed to adopt this in a gradual fashion). This indexation scheme involved, 'inflation-proof' depreciation of assets (Auerbach and Jorgenson, 1980). Finally, the flat corporate income tax rate was lowered to 35 per cent on the new tax base.

In 1989 the new Salinas administration introduced a new tax of 2 per cent on firms' gross assets (the *impuesto al activo*). In 1994, the tax had the following features: first, it could be used as a credit on the corporate tax, so it functioned as a minimum income tax; and a complete carry-back and forward between the two taxes was allowed for up to ten years. Second, it taxed gross assets. Third, it avoided cascade effects by not taxing the assets of other enterprises held by the firm. Fourth, new enterprises were exempted for the first two years, and firms that were liquidating were also exempted. Finally, the financial sector was exempted – presumably because most of the assets of financial firms are liabilities of other firms.

It should be noted that this tax on assets is far from a novelty. As described by Sadka and Tanzi (1992), a variant of this tax was used in Milan in the seventeenth century. A similar tax was also put into practice in 1988 by the Bolivians, albeit with some problems since by taxing net worth instead of gross worth the authorities lost revenue with firms which disguised bad debt.[5]

As shown in Table 5.1, the true fiscal effectiveness of this tax on assets can be a matter of dispute.[6] The increase in 1989 of the corporate income tax effort was not large, and even that change cannot be attributed entirely to the new tax, for several formerly privileged tax regimes were eliminated at the same time. In fact, the biggest gain in the corporate income tax effort was obtained earlier, in 1988, mostly due to the substantial drop in inflation achieved that year (as reviewed earlier).

What then explains the gain, shown in Table 5.1, of around half of a point of GDP in the corporate income tax effort from 1989 to 1993? There are two main factors. First, the tax base was dramatically increased by incorporating small and medium-sized enterprises that were previously untaxed or enjoyed special treatment. According to the government, the number of firms incorporated to the tax system grew from 1 929 194 in 1989 to 5 602 486 in 1993. And, second, tax authorities increased the number of fiscal audits sharply during the period to around 5.8 per cent of the total number of taxpayers. The effectiveness of the audits was also increased so that the government has claimed that each peso spent on audits translated into a collection of an extra 46 pesos in 1993.

The last reform on corporate income tax was made at the end of 1993. Alarmed by a lethargic growth, the government tried to stimulate the economy by decreasing direct taxes. This led to a one-point decrease in the corporate income tax rate. With this change, the flat corporate income tax rate in Mexico in 1994 was lower than in the United States, where the top rate at the federal level was one point higher than in Mexico (35 per cent versus 34 per cent). State and local taxes have always been higher in the United States.

Before closing this sub-section, it is worth drawing attention to the federal government revenue accruing from PEMEX, the oil monopoly owned by the state. As can be appreciated from Table 5.1, its tax burden was at a peak in 1983 and, although it has decreased since then to half of its value, it is still larger than the corporate income tax burden. This is so because PEMEX is heavily taxed (by means of an 'extraordinary tax'), to the extent that the monopoly has to depend on foreign oil sales to obtain operating profits. It is interesting to note that the ups and downs in oil tax collection shown in Table 5.1 are not only related to changes in world oil prices over the years, but also to variations in the real exchange rate. Given that PEMEX is a net exporter, the devaluations that took place during the stabilization processes of the 1980s had a positive impact on tax revenue. Urzúa (1991) provides a detailed discussion of the fiscal importance for Mexico of the real exchange rate (and of other non-traditional variables that affect fiscal revenue).

The personal income tax

The maximum rate for personal income tax (*impuesto sobre la renta de las personas físicas*) was 35 per cent at the beginning of the 1970s. For reasons already mentioned, the top rate was increased to 42 per cent in 1972, and three years later to 50 per cent. This last reform also included, for the first time, rental income from housing as part of the income tax base.

During the tax reforms of 1978–82, the maximum personal income tax rate was further increased to 55 per cent in 1979, but at the same time the tax schedule was made more progressive. The net effect was a reduction in the tax effort (see Table 5.1). Furthermore, a deduction equal to an annual minimum wage was implemented instead of some itemized deductions. This measure was actually quite progressive, since, as noted by Gil Díaz (1987, p. 337), it increased by 'as much as 200 percent the amount of deductions for lower-income individuals', while reducing the amount for higher-income classes. Moreover, during the same period a crude attempt was made to 'globalize' the income tax base by including capital gains, rents and dividends. However, items such as gains from transactions made by individuals in the stockmarket, authorship rights and fringe benefits were exempt.

After the crisis in 1982, revenue from personal income tax dropped sharply (see Table 5.1). This happened even though a surtax of 10 per cent was implemented in 1983, and there were constant inflation adjustments in the tax schedule. Widespread tax avoidance and evasion, and especially a growing underground economy, seem to have been the most important causes of the fall in revenue. This deterioration persisted during the entire De la Madrid period. As a result, the Salinas administration focused its efforts on devising better mechanisms of tax collection, on establishing harsher penalties in the case of tax avoidance and evasion, and on trying to increase the tax base. The authorities prosecuted, with some publicity, several high-profile tax evaders. They also tried to widen the income tax base by simplifying the tax regime for small contributors, and eliminating existing exemptions.[7]

As shown in Table 5.1, the personal income tax effort did increase in the late 1980s and early 1990s due to those measures. Nevertheless, the tax effort level in 1993 was still below the one prevailing in the late 1970s, partly because of the much publicized reduction of personal income tax rates during the Salinas administration. It should be noted that it primarily benefited individuals in high-income brackets, rather than the 'captive' wage-earners that constitute the bulk of individual taxpayers. In fact, Urzúa (1994b) shows that the distributional tax progressivity indices corresponding to the Salinas period (prior to the tax reform in 1993) do *not* compare favourably with the ones for the 1980s.

As in the case of the corporate income tax rates, personal income tax rates were also lowered at the end of 1993 in on attempt to stimulate the economy. The biggest beneficiaries of this reform were low-income wage-earners, since for them there could be, for the first time in Mexico, a negative income tax.[8]

The value added tax

A value added tax (VAT) on consumption of domestic goods and imports was introduced in 1980. It substituted the *impuesto sobre ingresos mercantiles* which was a turnover tax on each stage of production. Its introduction simplified the tax system, which was its main purpose, rendering over 25 federal taxes and 300 local excises obsolete. The basic VAT rate was set at 10 per cent, with exceptions of a zero rate for some basic agricultural products and a basket of foodstuffs (enlarged in 1991), and a 6 per cent rate on goods along the northern border (to be competitive with US sales taxes). Although the basic rate was too low to have a revenue-neutral reform (note the drop in part C of Table 5.1), the government chose it to make the introduction of the VAT more palatable to the private sector. As mentioned earlier, there had been strong opposition to the introduction of a VAT in the mid-1960s, with the private sector arguing that it was inflationary. Interestingly enough, Tait (1990) has reported that Mexico was one of the few countries in his sample where the introduction of a VAT led to a change in the inflation rate, rather than a shift in the price level.[9]

After the crisis in 1982, the need for revenue made the new De la Madrid administration increase the basic VAT rate to 15 per cent in 1983. The tax authorities added a 6 per cent rate on previously exempt medicines and most food items, and a 20 per cent rate for some luxury goods. This explains the jump of VAT revenue in that year (see Table 5.1). During the Salinas administration there were two additional changes in the VAT. In 1990, its collection passed from the hands of the states to the federal government, which had argued all along that the states were not putting enough effort into tax collection. Judging from the numbers in Table 5.1, the federal government was probably right.

A second change took place in November 1991, when the VAT basic rate was decreased from 15 per cent to 10 per cent, a rate that now applies to all luxuries and transactions along the border. At the same time, the government increased, among other things, the price of gasoline and electricity by 55 per cent and 15.3 per cent respectively, and established a mechanism of monthly price adjustments. As a consequence, VAT collection fell in 1992 compared to 1991. This drop represented about 0.77 points of GDP, and was not completely offset by the increase in energy prices (see Table 5.1). As is suggested in a CGE (computable general equilibrium) exercise by Sobarzo (1994), not only were there no large (static) effects on tax revenue from this reform, there were also no important allocation effects on the production side. However, the impact of this reform on social welfare is also questionable, and it is shown in Urzúa (1994a) by means of an estimated complete demand system using survey data for 11 531 households that the welfare impact was slightly favourable for high-income groups.

Before concluding this sub-section, it can be noted that the VAT effort did not improve significantly during the years 1980 to 1993. In fact, as shown in Table 5.1, the VAT collection from consumption of domestic (not imported) goods was lower in 1993 than in 1980, the year of its introduction.

Other taxes

Even since the 1950s and 1960s, the revenue from taxes on imports has been relatively unimportant in Mexico when compared to other Latin American countries. The reason has been the high degree of protection that the Mexican economy had until the mid-1980s, coupled with the sudden trade liberalization that ensued. As shown in Table 5.1, except for an outlier in 1980, it is only in the 1990s that taxes on imports account for more than 1 per cent of GDP (due to a sharp deterioration in the balance of trade). It is also worth noting that the process of trade liberalization that started in the mid-1980s did not have a significant impact on tax revenue from imports. Although this liberalization represented a direct fiscal loss due to the reduction in tariffs, the effect was not very large because most of the liberalization entailed the conversion from non-tariff barriers to low tariffs.

Excise taxes, on the other hand, have played a more active role. As shown in Table 5.1, and as one would have surmised, excise taxes tend to lag behind in good times and tend to be used heavily in bad times. It should be noted that, together with the introduction of the VAT, these taxes were changed to an ad valorem basis in 1980, so that the high inflation during the 1980s does not explain the variations in revenue from excises. Rather, the cause lies in government behaviour: since the 1970s, the government has tended to use the prices of goods produced by the public sector as anchors to control inflation. The price of gasoline constitutes perhaps the most dramatic example of this (see Table 5.1).

Low public tariffs are also a consequence of the perennial industrial policy that calls for subsidizing domestic use of hydrocarbons and electricity. That behaviour has brought, of course, some negative consequences. One is the weak financial position of PEMEX (as mentioned earlier), and the financial problems of the electric utilities and the train system are also exacerbated by their low public tariffs. Furthermore, energy subsidies obviously encourage the use of energy. In particular, low gasoline prices have encouraged the intensive use of automobiles, which is one of the main causes for the heavy pollution in Mexico City and other large cities. During the early 1990s, many Mexican economists, and others (see, for example, World Bank, 1992), called for a sharp increase in gasoline prices as the only immediate way to curb the ever increasing use of automobiles. However, the Salinas administration, mesmerized by its goal of reaching a single-digit inflation rate, never followed this advice.

An international comparison of the tax burden

It is always a sobering exercise to make comparisons between countries. Figure 5.2 compares the tax burden in six Latin American countries, as well as two Asian and one African.[10] Rather than presenting the multivariate data in table form, the figure uses face features (following Chernoff, 1973) to represent the effort of six different taxes (including social security). Although we have never seen the use of Chernoff's faces in this context, or in any other economic context, they seem to be tailor-made for our purpose.

We invite the reader to take a close look at the figure. Among the most outstanding features, one can cite the remarkable turnaround in the tax structure of Argentina during the last years; the large value added tax burden in Chile (and Argentina today); the notably regular face features in the case of Côte d'Ivoire; and the large excise taxes in the case of India. The three faces

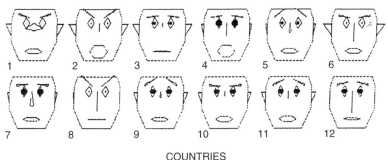

COUNTRIES

1. Argentina (1988)	7. Côte d' Ivoire (1990)
2. Argentina (1992)	8. India (1990)
3. Brazil (1989)	9. Mexico (1980)
4. Chile (1988)	10. Mexico (1988)
5. Colombia (1990)	11. Mexico (1991)
6. Costa Rica (1991)	12. Philippines (1991)

TYPE OF TAX	FACE FEATURE
Income tax	Iris size
Social security	Ear width
VAT or Sales tax	Mouth open amount
Excises	Brow slant
Import taxes	Nose length
Export taxes	Nose width

Figure 5.2 Tax burden for selected countries (proportion of GDP)
Source: Constructed by the author using information provided by participants in the IDRC project, and, for the case of non-participants, consolidated central government data in IMF (1992).

portraying Mexico show quite regular features, except for the low trade tax effort explained earlier. Furthermore, the three faces are quite similar, even though there have been several supposedly significant tax reforms from 1983 to 1993.

Other fiscal issues

Three fiscal issues have recently gained importance in Mexico: the privatization of public enterprises, fiscal federalism (or the lack of it), and tax compliance. The first is perhaps the most interesting. At the onset of the debt crisis in 1982 the Mexican federal government owned 1155 enterprises (see Table 5.2), but by mid-1993 this number had been decreased to 259, of which 50 were in the process of being sold. What were the reasons behind this privatization drive? Efficiency goals and/or ideological reasons are the typical answers that are given to explain the privatization wave that has swept the world since the 1980s, yet it seems that the most important explanation in the case of Mexico is fiscal. In the 1980s the economy was burdened by a huge domestic debt, for which the nation in 1988 had to make interest payments that were five times larger than the ones paid for the foreign debt (see next section). Thus, although the government had claimed that the sales revenue as shown in Table 5.1 was going to be put into a 'contingency fund', the largest part of it has gone to retire domestic debt.

Given the number of enterprises that were sold, it is a daunting task to examine in depth the privatization process in Mexico.[11] As a general comment one can say that, with some exceptions (for example, the sale of Teléfonos de México, TELMEX) and some instances of 'gift-seeking' (to use the happy expression coined by Spraos, 1992), the process of selling was

Table 5.2 Number of state-owned enterprises (at the end of each year)

1982	1155
1983	1090
1984	1044
1985	955
1986	807
1987	661
1988	618
1989	549
1990	418
1991	328
1992	270
1993*	259

Note: The table includes only federal enterprises; * Middle of 1993.
Source: *Quinto Informe de Gobierno* (1993).

accomplished quite well, and with a minimum of bureaucracy. However, generally speaking the same good marks cannot be given to the privatization outcomes. (See Urzúa (1997), pp. 90–94.)

Turning to the second fiscal issue, we can start noting that 'decentralization' has become a sexy, all-purpose word in Mexican politics since the 1980s. Since Mexico is *de jure* a federal republic, it would seem unnecessary in foreign eyes even to talk about decentralization. Yet, the central government in Mexico has *de facto* great influence on the states and municipalities. Many reasons have been given to explain this phenomenon. For instance, Mexico's colonial heritage, its dominant catholic religion, and its semi-authoritarian and corporativist political structures. The fact is that, as noted by Gershberg (1990), the share of public spending that is controlled by the federal government is out of line when compared with the shares in other federal republics such as the United States and Germany (and, one can surmise, Brazil and Argentina).

Local governments are granted as sources of revenue the property tax, federal 'participations', and income from public services. They are, in turn, responsible for providing local public goods such as streets, water supply, public security, and so on. The most important revenue sources, however, are federal participations,[12] which mostly include sharing revenue from federal taxation, except for the oil revenue that comes from the application of the 'extraordinary' oil tax and which is reserved for the federal government. Funds are not given directly to the municipalities, but rather to their states which then distribute them. State governments are also the ones that, in effect, administer local taxes. Thus, the centralization features that dominate at the federal level also appear at the state level.

What is more worrying, however, is the fact that public expenditure is also tightly controlled by the federal and state governments, leaving the municipalities with little to say on issues such as social spending. To give the reader an idea of the degree of centralization, it should be noted that by 1992 the federal government's National Solidarity Programme, mentioned above had already surpassed more resources to spend than all the municipalities put together.

The last fiscal issue is tax compliance. As noted earlier, during the Salinas administration, in contrast to the mild stand taken by former administrations, the tax authorities decided to attack tax evasion. This was reflected by a sharp increase in the number of fiscal audits, and of tax evasion cases brought to court during the early 1990s. Another mechanism that seems to have been effective was the enforcement of government-approved cash registers (the *máquinas registradoras de comprobación fiscal*) in 1992, much the same as are required in some European countries.

One further comment must be made before concluding with the tax compliance issue. It has been said repeatedly that one of the reasons for the recent increase in personal income tax collection in Mexico is the perception by the general public of a more efficient and honest bureaucracy. This, I am afraid, may be disputed. Corruption among some government officials, at all levels, is alive and well. In April 1992, the private sector organized a National Convention of Taxpayers at which some groups planned to request an amendment to the Constitution to protect the rights of taxpayers. Although the proposal never prospered, it is worth extracting among their nine basic petitions the first of them: that any private person or organization should be able to audit any public office or enterprise.

Changes in the composition of government expenditures

In the analysis of government expenditures, Table 5.3 presents the most important spending items of the federal government. During the 1980s, the greatest spending shares corresponded to interest payments on domestic debt, although the importance of this item has been greatly reduced in the 1990s for reasons given in the last section.[13] The second greatest share corresponded to current transfers, payments from the federal government to public enterprises to cover their operating costs (these payments include those to Mexico City, which is a federal district, and those to the social security institutions). Given the privatization process of the 1980s and early 1990s, this item has also lost some of its importance (see Table 5.3). Finally, the third largest spending share corresponded, and still does, to wages and salaries paid to bureaucrats in the federal government. This last item is also the most important expenditure at state and municipal levels.

Public capital investment

The composition of government spending on capital goods has changed considerably in Mexico over the years. During the López Portillo administration, public investment reached a record high (see Table 5.3), since it was seen as a key ingredient for long-term growth, and the government had money to pay for it. During the De la Madrid administration, however, public investment fell drastically as stabilization adjustments took place. At the end of 1988, capital investment by the federal government was four times smaller as a percentage of GDP than in 1981 (admittedly a year of high spending). It is only since 1990 that public investment has started to grow again, although not at a rate that many would wish.

The reason for such variations in public capital spending is, of course, that in Mexico, as in many other countries, the least politically damaging budget cuts can be made precisely in public investment. This fact, however, has not deterred some countries from leaving public investment untouched, and even using it as a counter-cyclical tool. The successful stabilization policies followed in Chile during the early 1980s constitute an example.

Table 5.3 Total expenditures of the federal government 1977–92 (per cent of GDP)

	1977	1978	1979	1980	1981	1982	1983	1984	1985	1986	1987	1988	1989	1990	1991	1992
TOTAL EXPENDITURES	15.80	15.87	16.77	18.29	21.79	27.55	25.95	24.11	24.42	29.06	31.27	26.47	22.81	19.98	17.27	15.87
CURRENT EXPENDITURES	12.34	12.41	12.59	13.58	15.30	22.23	22.13	21.11	20.76	25.35	28.03	25.30	21.17	17.29	14.56	13.62
Wages and salaries	4.12	3.97	3.90	3.55	3.67	4.07	3.24	3.39	3.27	3.14	3.26	2.85	3.03	2.71	2.90	3.25
Interest payments	1.85	1.92	1.87	1.72	2.84	5.26	8.53	8.01	8.45	13.58	17.57	15.19	11.30	8.36	4.90	3.45
Domestic	1.12	1.09	1.15	1.23	2.29	4.14	6.36	6.15	6.57	10.93	14.49	12.62	8.89	6.68	3.11	2.11
External	0.73	0.83	0.72	0.49	0.55	1.12	2.17	1.86	1.88	2.65	3.08	2.58	2.41	1.69	1.79	1.34
Participations to states	1.44	1.51	1.60	2.28	2.50	2.23	2.79	2.86	2.69	2.58	2.66	2.85	2.83	3.02	3.09	3.19
Current transfers	4.19	4.19	4.37	5.04	4.71	5.14	5.58	4.48	4.52	4.15	3.30	2.83	2.50	1.99	2.42	2.47
Others[1]	0.74	0.82	0.85	0.99	1.58	5.52	1.98	2.37	1.83	1.89	1.24	1.57	1.51	1.21	1.25	1.25
CAPITAL EXPENDITURES	3.93	3.94	4.28	4.53	6.22	4.85	3.81	3.23	3.78	3.55	3.21	1.93	1.96	2.66	2.27	2.25
Public investment	1.32	1.22	1.24	1.52	1.46	1.48	0.78	0.85	0.91	1.00	0.90	0.53	0.51	0.84	1.04	1.04
Capital transfers	0.76	0.62	0.91	2.28	3.93	2.52	2.28	1.83	2.27	1.92	2.17	1.26	1.28	1.66	1.09	1.08
Others[2]	1.85	2.09	2.14	0.73	0.82	0.86	0.75	0.54	0.60	0.63	0.13	0.14	0.16	0.16	0.14	0.14
ADJUSTMENT[3]	0.47	0.47	0.10	−0.17	−0.27	−0.47	−0.02	0.22	0.13	−0.15	−0.03	0.76	0.32	−0.03	−0.44	−0.03
MEMORANDA:																
SOCIAL EXPENDITURES	7.84	7.91	8.37	8.06	9.19	9.13	6.66	6.70	6.94	6.66	6.21	6.08	6.17	6.47	7.71	8.52
ANNUAL CHANGE IN THE STOCK OF REAL DOMESTIC PUBLIC DEBT (%)	−7.27	8.21	22.86	11.57	20.10	103.18	−36.04	−13.15	16.98	35.96	26.81	−36.06	−6.34	−2.96	−27.88	−30.24
ANNUAL CHANGE IN THE STOCK OF REAL EXTERNAL PUBLIC DEBT (%)	9.88	6.44	1.77	0.15	41.77	4.88	2.86	6.42	0.38	2.59	4.15	−4.41	−10.41	−2.91	−1.36	−7.76

Notes:
[1] Includes acquisition of goods, expenditures carried over from the last fiscal year, etc.
[2] Includes capital expenditures carried over from the last fiscal year, and other transactions.
[3] Net deficit with other public entities.
Sources: Constructed by the author using information in Indicadores Económicos, Banco de México.

The National Solidarity Programme

According to the 1989 Income and Expenditure Survey (INEGI, 1992), one out of four Mexican households is below the poverty line (defined by an income of less than two minimum wages). Furthermore, the distribution of income worsened sharply from 1984 to 1989, a period where very stringent stabilization adjustments took place. To give the reader an idea of the magnitude of the redistribution, one can note that the income share of the highest decile rose from 33 to 38 per cent during that five-year period (a 1 per cent gain per year!).

The Programa Nacional de Solidaridad (PRONASOL), the National Solidarity Programme, was created by President Salinas with the main objective of attacking extreme poverty. One of the novel features of this social programme was that it took great pains, at least on paper, to identify the neediest, and to make the recipients active participants in the social projects. At the beginning of 1994 an armed upheaval in Chiapas, a very poor southern state where half of the population is Indian, reminded all Mexicans that several serious social problems remained unresolved. These include an extremely unequal income distribution and blatant race discrimination. The upheaval also brought into question the true effectiveness of PRONASOL. Although, in absolute terms, Chiapas had been one of the largest beneficiaries of the programme among all Mexican states, the meagre results obtained so far have made most observers question its success. Some critics

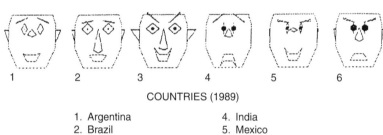

COUNTRIES (1989)

1. Argentina
2. Brazil
3. Costa Rica

4. India
5. Mexico
6. Philippines

TYPE OF EXPENDITURE	FACE FEATURE
General Public Services	Nose length
Defence	Mouth smile (if low)
Public order & safety	Ear width
Education	Brow Slant
Health. soc. sec. & welfare	Eye vertical width
Economic affairs & services	Iris size

Figure 5.3   Expenditure by function for selected countries (proportion of GDP)
Source: Constructed by the author using consolidated central government data in IMF (1992).

have argued that PRONASOL has been just a clever programme to attract more voters for the dominating party, while others have blamed its partial failure on bad administration.[14]

An international comparison of government expenditures

Before concluding this review, and in order to have some points of reference for the future, Figure 5.3 presents a comparison of central government expenditures among six countries (once again using Chernoff's faces). There are many interesting features to note in the figure, among which we can mention that the eyes of the Mexican face in Figure 5.3 (as opposed to Figure 5.2) are not as bright as one would like them to be when compared to other countries.[15]

Conclusions and directions for further work

It would seem fair to draw the general conclusion that recent tax reforms in Mexico have had varying success. On the one hand we have noted an increase in the corporate income tax effort, mostly as a result of low inflation, a much wider tax base and better tax enforcement. On the other hand we have also pointed out that VAT collections still remined low in the 1990s.

Although it is true that tax authorities were able to achieve a reduction in tax rates during 1991–3 without eroding tax collection, we can also make two qualifications. First, although at first sight the lowering of most rates would seem to imply that the Mexican tax system became much more efficient and progressive (as Altimir and Barbera, 1991, argue), the work by Sobarzo (1994) shows that the allocative effects of the reforms were not significant, and my work (Urzúa 1994a,b), mentioned earlier, suggests that the welfare effects have not been as progressive as they seem. Secondly, most of the tax reductions do not seem sustainable in the long-run. The tax effort in Mexico in the 1990s has not only been low by international standards, but also seems to be insufficient given the current political events in Mexico. Current political thinking points toward more social expenditures in the future, more public investment (given the low current level of private investment), and less executive control of spending decisions (as the legislative branch and state and local governments gain more power). Needless to say, this topic needs urgent study.

A number of less traditional fiscal issues also deserve study. First, as noted earlier, a good tax system at state and local levels is still lacking. States and municipalities have not learned to tax land and price public services. Second, a reform in the procedures of federal–state transfers and federal–state expenditures is overdue, particularly now that the country will have to become more open and democratic. Third, the recent financial troubles of the social security system call for some drastic reforms. And, fourth, a serious and open evaluation of the successes and failures of the National Solidarity Programme is much needed.

Notes

1   The control of the fiscal deficit was made easier by the privatization of state-owned enterprises at that time. As discussed later, the number of public enterprises was almost halved during De la Madrid's regime (although most of the sales involved small- and medium-sized enterprises).

2   Although, as it was mentioned earlier and will be further commented later, other economic (and social) indicators are not quite bright.

3   The inflation adjustments were essentially allowances in the case of inventory costing, and deductions in the case of net-of-debt inflationary losses.

4   Although, as mentioned earlier, indebted firms were not allowed to use depreciation deductions, so part of the loss in tax revenue mentioned was offset by this implicit gain.

5   Another earlier instance was the tax on net wealth, for both firms and individuals, implemented in Colombia in the 1970s (now abolished). It is interesting to note that, in this case, the tax on individuals was more successful than the one on firms.

6   Furthermore, even in the late 1990s it was still an open question whether the tax will endure the constant criticism from the private sector. By early 1993, almost 16 000 firms looked for protection from the tax by invoking *amparo*, a legal scheme that can be invoked in case of possible abuse by the authority (without success, as ruled later by the Supreme Court).

7   Despite these efforts, disparity in tax treatment continued to exist. For instance, in 1993 the government tried to incorporate authorship rights in the income tax base (unsuccessfully after loud opposition by Mexican writers), yet the exemption on profits realized by individuals in the stockmarket (huge during that year) was never in question.

8   To give an example, a worker earning the monthly minimum wage in Mexico City at the end of 1993 (433.81 *nuevos pesos*) would end up receiving that month, after computing taxes and credits, around 9 per cent of his salary.

9   Since the economy was growing steadily and the inflation rate in 1981 was lower than in 1980, it is not obvious how to disqualify Tait's conclusion.

10   Except for Brazil, Chile and Costa Rica, all the other countries have chapters dedicated to them in these volumes.

11   Núñez Melgoza (1993) provides a good start. For general issues on the Latin American privatization processes see Sáez and Urzúa (1994).

12   For an excellent discussion of the issues of federal–state transfers in Mexico see Boadway (1990).

13   As can also be noted from Table 5.3, interest payments on foreign debt were never as important as those on domestic debt. The former lost part of their importance (in Mexico) due to both low world interest rates and the implementation of the Brady Plan of debt reduction at the end of the 1980s.

14   García-Rocha and Guevara (1992) show that the amount of money from PRONASOL that went to each state from 1989 to 1991 seemed to be correlated more with administrative and political factors than with the number of people living under extreme poverty.

15   Although note that, for purposes of uniformity with other countries, we have chosen 1989 as the reference year rather than later years when social expenditures did increase significantly (see Table 5.3).

References

Altimir, O. and M. Barbera (1991) 'Tributación y Equidad en América Latina. Un Ejercicio de Evaluación Cuantitativa', manuscript, CEPAL, Santiago de Chile.

Auerbach, A. J. and D. W. Jorgenson (1980) 'Inflation-Proof Depreciation of Assets', *Harvard Business Review*, vol. 58, pp.113–18.

Banco de México (1993) *Indicadores Económicos*, Banco de México, México.

Bird, R. M. (1992) 'Tax Reform in Latin America: A Review of some Recent Experiences', *Latin American Research Review*, vol. 27, pp. 7–36.

Boadway, R. (1990) 'The Reform of Federal State-Transfers in Mexico', manuscript, Queen's University, Ontario.

Chernoff, H. (1973) 'Using Faces to Represent Points in K-Dimensional Space Graphically', *Journal of the American Statistical Association*, vol. 82, pp. 424–36.

García-Rocha, A. and A. Guevara (1992) 'Impacto Socioeconómico del Programa Nacional de Solidaridad en el Estado de Zacatecas', manuscript, El Colegio de México, México.

Gershberg, A. I. (1990) 'Decentralization and Public Finance in Mexico', manuscript, Regional Science Department, University of Pennsylvania.

Gil Díaz, F. (1987) 'Some Lessons from Mexico's Tax Reform', in D. Newbery and N. Stern (eds), *The Theory of Taxation for Developing Countries*, New York: Oxford University Press.

Gil Díaz, F. (1990) 'Tax Reform Issues in Mexico', in M. J. Boskin and C. E. McLure (eds), *World Tax Reform: Case Studies of Developed and Developing Countries*, San Francisco, Cal.: ICS Press.

INEGI (1992) *Encuesta Nacional de Ingresos y Gastos de los Hogares, 1989*, INEGI, Aguascalientes, México.

International Monetary Fund (1992) *Government Finance Statistics Yearbook*, Washington, DC.: IMF.

Núñez Melgoza, F. J. (1993) 'Privatización y Desempeño de la Empresa Pública: Aspectos Conceptuales y el Caso de México', manuscript, El Colegio de México, México.

Quinto Informe de Gobierno (1993) Presidencia de la República, México.

Sadka, E., and V. Tanzi (1992) 'A Tax on Gross Assets of Enterprises as a Form of Presumptive Taxation', IMF Working Paper WP/92/16, Washington, DC.: IMF.

Sáez, R. E., and C. M. Urzúa (1994) 'Privatization and Fiscal Reform in Eastern Europe: Some Lessons from Latin America', in G. McMahon (ed.), *The Latin American Economic Adjustment: Lessons for Eastern Europe*, London: Macmillan.

Solís, L. (1981) *Economic Policy Reform in Mexico: A Case Study for Developing Countries*, New York: Pergamon Press.

Sobarzo, H. (1994) 'Interactions between Trade and Tax Reforms in Mexico: Some General Equilibrium Results', in this volume.

Spraos, J. (1992) 'A Thematic Tour of Privatization, with European Illustrations', in A. A. Zini Jr. (ed.), *The Market and the State in Economic Development in the 1990s*, Amsterdam: North-Holland.

Tait, A. A. (1990) 'VAT Revenue, Inflation, and the Foreign Trade Balance', in M. Gillis, C. S. Shoup and G. P. Sicat (eds), *Value Added Taxation in Developing Countries*, Washington, DC: World Bank.

Urzúa, C. M. (1991) *El Déficit del Sector Público y la Política Fiscal en México, 1980–1989*, CEPAL/PNUD, Santiago de Chile: United Nations.

Urzúa, C. M. (1994a) 'An Empirical Analysis of Indirect Tax Reforms in Mexico', paper presented at the Latin American Meeting of the Econometric Society, Caracas, Venezuela.

Urzúa, C. M. (1994b) 'A Distributional Tax Progressivity Index for Mexico', manuscript, El Colegio de México, México.

Urzúa, C. M. (1997) 'Five Decades of Relations Between the World Bank and Mexico', in D. Kapur, J. Lewsi and R. Webb (eds), *The World Bank: Its First Half Century*, Washington, DC: Brookings.

World Bank (1992) *World Development Report*, Washington, DC: World Bank.

6
A CGE Model of Côte d'Ivoire

Ephrem Enoh, Catherine Enoh and Edmé Koffi

Introduction: the economic situation

For twenty years, from 1960 to 1980, Côte d'Ivoire underwent a period of sustained growth. However, since 1981 the Ivorian economy has been experiencing external and internal imbalances. This was due, in part, to a permanent drop in the prices of coffee and cocoa, goods which make up 75 per cent of Ivorian exports. In addition to this shock to the price of exports, the price of imports continued to rise as a consequence of the oil crisis. These price shocks had a significant impact on public finances, which relied heavily on trade taxes. With the increase in interest rates on international financial markets during the late 1970s and early 1980s, the Ivorian government found itself in a difficult situation, adding an increase in debt-servicing to a continuous decline in fiscal revenues.

In order to respond to these successive shocks, the Ivorian government had to turn to its only option for policy response, fiscal policy reform. Being a member of the Communauté Financière Africaine (CFA) zone, monetary policy reform is strictly controlled, so devaluation was not a policy option.[1] Thus, to stabilize revenues the state proceeded to increase tariff duties, in addition to imposing a VAT. In spite of these measures, the public deficit continued to grow.

In light of these occurrences, this study is designed to identify the kind of fiscal reforms which can be implemented to realize the objectives of fiscal revenue stability and the structural adjustment of the Ivorian economy. The study is also interested in 'the social equity' of the advocated reforms in considering their incidence on the well-being of the socioeconomic groups.

The model used for the simulations is static and consists of four types of economic agents: consumers, domestic and foreign producers, and the government. The model has of 15 sectors, domestic and importable final goods, four types of labour, and specific and non-specific forms of capital. A small, open price-taking country assumption is made. The data used to run the model was drawn from the 1986 SAM for the Côte d'Ivoire. The tax reforms examined in this study examine the following taxes VAT, import taxes, export taxes and income tax. Four external shocks with significant impact on the Côte d'Ivoire economy are considered: a 20 per cent decrease in the price of traditional export products (coffee and cocoa), a 20 per cent decrease in the price of all export products, a 20 per cent increase in the price of imports, and a 100 per cent change in the parity between French and CFA francs.

For a given shock, the best tax reform is the one which maintains a constant level of utility for the government. We found that no unique tax reform can perform best when confronted with all the external shocks. When confronted with a 20 per cent decrease in the price of exports, the best reform consists in replacing all indirect taxes by a common import tax with a wider base; in the case of a 20 per cent increase in the price of imports, a common import tax rate with a wider base represents the best reform; and removing all indirect and direct taxes and replacing them with a common income tax rate on households represents the best solution when a 100 per cent change in the parity of French and CFA francs occurs. The fact that the tax reform was simulated before introducing the external shocks had a great impact on the economy structure, and the VAT does not seem to be the most appropriate tax.

The model

The model structure

As already mentioned, the model covers consumers, domestic producers, foreign producers and the government as agents, and consists of 15 sectors, domestic and importable final goods, four types of labour, and specific and non-specific forms of capital, with an open price-taking country assumption used for all traded goods.

The production structure

There are 15 sectors: eight tradable and seven non-tradable goods. The production of tradables is divided between production destined for domestic consumption and that for export using a CET (constant elasticity of transformation) function. This functional form allows us to represent the short-term technological constraints which affect the economy when there is an external shock such as a drop in world prices.

Intermediate inputs are combined using a CES (constant elasticity of substitution) function, to form an aggregate input good. Inputs are formed from both domestic and imported goods, which are assumed to be perfect substitutes. A CES function is also used to combine factors into an aggregate value-added good. In the case of the agricultural good in the model, we assume a sector-specific form of capital exists in addition to the non-specific capital used by all the sectors. These two aggregates, value-added and inputs, are then combined with a Leontief production function.

The demand structure

There are seven household categories in the model: the rural export agricultural (MEXP), rural savannah agricultural (MAGS), rural non-savannah agricultural (MVIVA), urban public sector (MADP), urban formal private sector (MFOR), urban informal private sector (MINDEP), and the unemployed (MINACT). This classification of households, according to socioeconomic status, allows us to measure the incidence of different policies on the standard of living of these groups.

Households are subject to the following budget constraint

$$Tto_h + C_h + S_h + Ttg_h + It_h = K_h + L_h + Tfo_h + Tfg_h$$

where Tto_h represents direct transfers to other households, C_h is final consumption, S_h is household savings, Ttg_h is transfers to government, It_h is income tax paid, K_h and L_h are factor rewards, Tfo_h is transfers received from other households, and Tfg_h is transfer payments from the government. Since the model is static, wealth effects are not taken into account. Thus, the shares of savings and consumption in the above equation are held constant. Savings are then used in the financing of investment in the model.

Using this budget constraint, households maximize a nested CES utility function, as represented below.

The labour market

Four types of labour are included in this model: skilled labour, unskilled labour agricultural labour, and professional labour. The skilled and unskilled labour types are perfectly mobile, whereas the other two classes are restricted to non-agricultural use and agricultural use respectively. The categories of labour are combined using CES functions to form a composite form of labour in production.

The public sector

There is no behavioural model of the public sector in this model. The government collects tax revenues and redistributes these revenues by way of lump-sum transfers to households. The specific composition of the tax structure will be described below.

The rest of the world

There is no behavioural model for the rest of the world. The level of exports in this model is determined by the relative prices between world export prices and domestic prices; a small open price-taking economy assumption. Similarly, the level of imports is assumed to match demand for imports.

Data sources

The social accounting matrix

The data used in the model were drawn from the 1986 SAM for the Côte d'Ivoire, documented in Ngee–Choon *et al.* (1991). The SAM consists of six main accounts, namely: factors, institutions, investment, production activities, commodities and the rest of the world.

- *Factors*   This account shows the receipts and disbursements of factor incomes. Receipts include revenues accruing to the factors, and disbursements consist of the allocation of those factor incomes to both domestic institutions and the rest of the world.
- *Institutions*   The account for institutions describes the sources and uses of incomes for households, enterprises and the government. Households receive income from factor endowments, transfers from other households, the government, the rest of the world, and distributed profits from enterprises. Household expenditures include consumption of domestic and imported goods, savings, taxes, transfers to other households, the government and the rest of the world. Enterprises collect capital income which is then dispersed to households as profits, to the government as taxes, and to the rest of the world as interest payments and dividends. The government collects the above mentioned transfer payments as well as receiving tax income. These revenues are then paid out in the form of transfer payments.
- *Investment/savings*   The investment account shows both the detailed breakdown of investments by sector as well as the accumulation of capital goods. Since only institutions have assets and financial resources, the sources of domestic savings come from institutions. Foreign sources of investible funds come from capital inflows, reflected in a balance of payment deficit. These investible funds are allocated as real investment in stocks and fixed assets by the branches in domestic capital goods.
- *Production activities*   Production in the economy is broken down into sectors, with price equalling total costs for each sector.
- *Commodities*   This account specifies the demand and supply of commodities. The various sources of demand for domestically produced products include intermediate demand in production and final demand by households, government, and for investment purposes. The sources of demand for imports are intermediate demand in production, and final demand by households, and for investment purposes. All values are in terms of market prices.
- *Rest of the world*   The last account shows the transactions with the rest of the world. The economy receives income from the rest of the world through export earnings, net factor payments and transfers payments. These earnings, in equilibrium, are balanced by outflows which include

purchases of imports and transfer payments. In addition, in equilibrium, the balance of payments (savings of the rest of the world) plus the savings of the domestic agents must equal total investment in the economy.

Macro consistency

General identities. Total revenue (value-added, taxes, net exports) is equal to total expenditures; for example:

Resources	Billions (CFA)	Uses	Billions (CFA)
Value added from production	+2492	Consumption (C)	+2052
Transfers to the government	+145	Investment (I)	+314
Indirect taxes	+526	Government expenditure (G)	+482
		Exports (X)	+1260
		Imports (M)	−944
GDP	3164	GDP	3164

Equilibrium conditions. The SAM is constructed such that each account must balance; therefore, total income equals total expenditures. This implies that the SAM satisfies general equilibrium conditions and all equilibrium properties, and is therefore a micro-consistent benchmark equilibrium.

The budget balances of the agents are also respected in the SAM:

- households' expenditures and savings equal disposable income
- total savings equal total investment; and there is a
- government budget balance

Market clearance. For market clearance, the aggregate supply of each domestic-import composite good is fully exhausted by the aggregate demand for that good. The following identity holds:

$$Q_j + M_i = ID_i + C_i + G_i + I_i + X_i \tag{6.1}$$

where Q_j = aggregate domestic supply and ID_i = intermediate demand M = imports, C = Consumption, G = goverment expenditure, I = investment, and X = exports, for all i goods.

Normal economic profit. The total receipts from sales equal total expenditures, and the following equations hold:

$$TS_j = ID_j + C_j + I_j + G_j + X_j - M_j \tag{6.2}$$

for total sales TS_j over all j sectors.

$$Tc_j = ID_j + VA_j + TAXE_j \tag{6.3}$$

where $TAXE_j$ = VAT + import tariff duties + export tax + other production taxes, and VA_j = value added, for all j sectors

$$TS_j = TC_j \tag{6.4}$$

Walras' Law. The sum of final demand over all industries must equal the sum of taxes and value added over all industries:

$$\sum j(VA_j + TAXE_j) = \sum j(C_j + I_j + G_j + X_j - M_j) \tag{6.5}$$

Parameters. Certain key parameters of the model were specified exogenously, leaving others to be determined by calibration. The fundamental assumption made in 'calibrating' the model is that the economy is in equilibrium in any given year. By modifying the national accounts and other data for each year, a data-set is generated in which all equilibrium conditions inherent in the model are satisfied. This is termed the 'benchmark equilibrium' data-set.

Parameter values are determined in a non-stochastic manner by solving the equations which represent the equilibrium conditions of the model. Whether the observed equilibrium alone is sufficient to uniquely determine the parameter values depends upon the functional forms used. Exogenous estimates of the elasticity of substitution are obtained from Michel and Michel (1984), Benjamin and Devarajan (1985), and Ivorian sources.

Tax system

The construction of the computable general equilibrium model is ideal for analysing fiscal reform in the context of the structural adjustment programme advocated by the World Bank. Thus, the tax reforms examined in this study attempt to make the Ivorian economy more competitive, with consideration to the simplification of the tax system.

The simulations

The tax reforms

In an economy suffering from recession, the best chance of increasing tax revenues does not lie in an increase in rates, but in an improvement in the economy or in the growth of the tax base; particularly of the informal sector. The tax reform chosen must be able to provide enough resources to finance the government budget. The preferred tax reform should reduce the number of economic distortions, promote social justice (efficiency and equity), reduce the number of exempted activities, and increase the base of the tax.

Three types of taxes are considered in the model; a domestic indirect tax, import taxes, and a direct tax.

Domestic indirect tax

The indirect tax that is analysed is the VAT, chosen because of its desirable economic and budgetary qualities. At the time of this study the VAT consisted of three rates which makes the management of this tax difficult. Experience has shown that only developed countries have been successful in efficiently administering a VAT system with multiple rates, so that one of the tax reforms is to consider a common VAT rate.

The introduction of a common VAT rate must be accompanied by an improvement in the VAT administration. A well-organized administration would enable a monthly check on claims, a fast identification of frauds, and a means of managing the credits which are a large source of irregularities and fraud. Furthermore, it could facilitate VAT reimbursements which often experience long delays because of a lack of data and details. However, it still remains very difficult to apply the VAT to the informal sector. Thus, the formal sector finds itself relatively overtaxed compared to the informal sector, and this distribution encourages taxpayers to move to the informal sector.

Import taxes

The current structure of tariffs is complex; there is great dispersion among the rates with numerous exemptions and tax allowances. A common rate import tax would create a simpler system, and would reduce administration costs and free agents from the need to systematically check their records. A single rate should be followed by a progressive elimination of exemptions and rules of exceptions, which for the most part are economically justifiable.

In order to be truly efficient, the common rate should be followed by systematic controls in determining customs values. Such control is an essential function for managing import taxes, and in fact it is the only service which can actually judge the validity of a declaration and the amount of duties payable. The SGS, a service which fights against custom fraud and tax evasion, could collaborate with the values office.

Direct tax

The administration of direct taxes suffers two serious deficiencies. First, not all taxpayers are identified since the updating of information is slow, and second, collection procedures are complicated. The lack of means of verification has led legislators to impose a system of withholding at the source, and only incomes which can be held at source are actually taxed. These incomes include salaries, dividends and interest.

Some tax reforms suggest the introduction of a common income tax on households, but such a tax would cause administrative problems. In an economy such as the Côte d'Ivoire, it is virtually impossible to determine a household's income since the administration has no means to check the accuracy of the tax returns. Furthermore, the incomes of individual entrepreneurs and incomes within the informal sector cannot be known since these activities are not declared.

While there are problems associated with a common tax rate on households, this tax is considered as a reform in the model because it promotes fiscal equity and provides significant resources to the government. The seven tax reforms considered are as follows:

Reform 1   All VAT rates are replaced by a common VAT rate with a wider base; the remaining tax structure is unaltered.

Reform 2   All VAT rates are replaced by a common VAT rate with a wider base; furthermore, all indirect taxes in the economy are suppressed.

Reform 3   This reform applies a common rate and widens the base of the import tax; all other indirect taxes are left intact.

Reform 4   This reform combines reforms 1 & 2.

Reform 5   This reform package implements a common income tax rate for all households; all direct and indirect taxes are suppressed.

Reform 6   This reform package combines the replacement of all export taxes with a common tax rate on households together with reform 4.

Reform 7   All indirect taxes are replaced by a common import tax with a wider base.

The external shocks

The fiscal impact of four external shocks are also examined by the model; these shocks have a significant impact on the Côte d'Ivoire economy.

Shock 1   A 20 per cent decrease in the price of traditional export products (coffee and cocoa).

Shock 2   A 20 per cent decrease in the price of all export products.

Shock 3   A 20 per cent increase in the price of imports.

Shock 4   A 100 per cent change in the parity between French and CFA francs.

The experiments

Criteria

For a given shock, we examine a tax reform as one which maintains a constant level of utility for the government. This reform is compared to the current tax system which serves as the benchmark case. Table 6.1 presents the equal yield tax rates used to maintain the utility level for the government.

Method of comparison

When the reform for a given shock is identified, we analyse the changes in economic variables for this reform versus the benchmark case. The economic

Table 6.1 Equal yield tax rates

Tax reform	Tax rate
Reform 1	VAT: 9.21%
Reform 2	VAT: 13.40%
Reform 3	Import tax: 32.31%
Reform 4	VAT: 9.21%
	Import tax: 35.77%
Reform 5	Income tax: 29.47%
Reform 6	Income tax: 1.88%
	VAT: 9.21%
	Import tax: 35.77%
Reform 7	Import tax: 201.85%

variables examined include: GDP, the value of import goods, the value added, labour, tax income, price index, and the welfare of households.

The results

Tax reform analyses

Table 6.2 presents the government's utility level for each tax reform corresponding to the four external shocks, and it is clear that there is no unique tax reform which performs best when confronted with all the external shocks. When confronted with a 20 per cent decrease in the price of exports (shock 1 & 2), utility levels are highest when all indirect taxes are replaced by a common import tax with a wider base (reform 7); the utility levels are 0.992 and 0.988 respectively.

Faced with a 20 per cent increase in the price of imports (shock 3), a common import tax rate with a wider base (all indirect taxes left intact) provides the greatest improvement in the level of utility for the government; the level is 1.00601.

In the last shock, a 100 per cent change in the parity of French and CFA francs, the simulations indicate that a tax policy which consists of removing

Table 6.2 Utility level of the government

Tax reform	Shock 1	Shock 2	Shock 3	Shock 4
Reform 1	0.992	0.985	1.001	1.027
Reform 2	0.990	0.984	0.988	1.026
Reform 3	0.990	0.988	1.006	1.024
Reform 4	0.991	0.984	0.984	1.028
Reform 5	0.983	0.961	0.957	1.048
Reform 6	0.989	0.981	0.998	1.030
Reform 7	0.992	0.988	0.993	1.000

all indirect and direct taxes and replacing them with a common income tax rate on households represents the best solution (reform 5). The utility level of the government is 1.048.

The impact of the external shocks

In this section we examine the impact of external shocks on various economic variables.

Shock 1: a 20 per cent decrease in the price of traditional exports

It is clear from Table 6.3 that this external shock causes the level of real income to decrease, and this fall can be attributed to the fall in export prices which results in lowered production of exports. The decrease in export prices also leads to a more general decrease in economic activity, and this can be explained by the Leontief production function in which there is a choice between producing for the local market or the export market. The Leontief hypothesis suggests that there is a short-term technological constraint which is binding in an economy faced with the external shock of falling world prices.

Table 6.4 reveals that all households experience a decrease in welfare with the exception of the rural non-savannah agricultural household (MVIVA). However, the losses are not evenly distributed. In general, non-agricultural households (MFOR, MADP, MINEP) experience a smaller drop in welfare than agricultural households (MEXP, MAGS); and the unemployed (MINACT)

Table 6.3   Percentage change in GDP after the shocks

External shock	Percentage change in GDP
Shock 1	−4.3%
Shock 2	−11.3%
Shock 3	−6.2%
Shock 4	−8.5%

Table 6.4   Percentage changes in the welfare of households after the shocks

Household categories	Shock 1	Shock 2	Shock 3	Shock 4
Rural export agricultural (MEXP)	−3.00	+5.5	+0.34	−10.00
Rural savannah agricultural (MAGS)	−13.00	−22.00	−11.00	+13.30
Rural non-savannah agricultural (MVIVA)	+4.00	+9.80	+5.00	−13.00
Urban public sector (MADP)	−2.00	−7.00	−2.73	+11.50
Urban formal private Sector (MFOR)	−1.00	−10.00	+1.00	+12.20
Urban informal private sector (MINDEP)	−9.00	−14.00	−1.00	+2.50
Unemployed (MINACT)	−29.00	−50.00	−26.00	+42.00
Household total	−53.00	−87.70	−34.39	+58.50

suffer the largest welfare loss since they receive most of their income from other households and a decrease in the welfare of most households results in a fall in the value of transfers received by the unemployed.

Shock 2: a 20 per cent decrease in the price of all exports

Tables 6.5 and 6.6 show the structure of production and tax revenues after the shocks, and Table 6.7 shows the changes in resource allocation. Compared to shock 1, the negative effects on GDP and total household welfare are much larger in this case (see tables 6.3 and 6.4). The endowment of labour in the traditional export sector decreases 2.32 per cent in the first case but increases 0.64 per cent in the second case. Furthermore, the formal manufacturing sector experiences an increase in labour of 6.83 per cent compared to 5.15 per cent in the previous case (Table 6.7.)

Table 6.5 Structure of production after the shocks

	No shock	Shock 1	Shock 2	Shock 3	Shock 4
Agriculture	24.1	46.8	21.7	27.6	27.0
Industry	25.5	5.9	26.7	24.6	26.0
Non-tradables	50.4	47.3	51.6	47.8	47.0
Total	100.0	100.0	100.0	100.0	100.0

Table 6.6 Structure of tax revenue after the shocks

Tax	No shock	Shock 1	Shock 2	Shock 3	Shock 4
Tariffs	41.2	46.8	49.1	48.0	35.8
VAT	26.3	5.9	6.3	18.2	13.7
Direct taxes	32.5	47.3	44.6	33.8	50.5
Total	100.0	100.0	100.0	100.0	100.0

Table 6.7 Percentage change in resource allocation after the shock

Economic variables	Shock 1	Shock 2	Shock 3	Shock 4
GDP				
• nominal	−4.33	−5.4	−3.6	+1.7
• real	−4.30	−11.3	−6.2	−8.5
Value of import goods				
• nominal	−4.71	−6.31	34.9	−15.3
• real	−6.01	−9.80		−23.8
Labour in				
• Traditional export	−2.32	+0.64	−9.00	−17.8
• Formal manufacturing	+5.15	+6.83	−6.00	−12.2

Table 6.8 Percentage change in resource allocation after the shocks and tax reforms

Economic variables	Shock 1 + reform 7	Shock 2 + reform 7	Shock 3 + reform 3	Shock 4 + reform 5
GDP				
• nominal	−15.13	−18.63	−13.40	30.86
• real	−13.21	−19.30	−11.45	42.12
Value of import goods				
• nominal	79.26	118.03	−0.09	−21.05
• real	0.00	2.16	−18.54	−14.26
Value added (capital & labour)				
Traditional export				
• nominal	−38.70	−32.38	−17.59	87.36
• real	−37.32	−32.94	−15.74	103.48
Non-traditional export				
• nominal	−47.30	−37.16	−37.16	24.61
• real	−46.11	−37.68	−35.75	35.33
Formal manufacturing				
• nominal	0.45	−6.90	−12.79	17.83
• real	2.72	−7.67	−10.83	27.97
Food crops				
• nominal	−26.45	−20.58	−20.58	−6.48
• real	−24.79	−21.24	−18.80	1.57
Tradable goods sector				
• nominal	−22.22	−24.77	−18.36	29.56
• real	−20.46	−25.39	−16.52	40.70
Non-tradable goods sector				
• nominal	−0.63	−8.19	−12.16	25.95
• real	1.61	−12.88	−10.18	36.79
Labour in				
• Traditional export	−38.70	−30.85	−21.97	58.10
• Non-traditional	−38.70	−28.44	−20.01	36.93
Export				
• Formal manufacturing	−0.56	−5.87	−11.62	27.51
• Food crops	−24.79	−31.53	−20.46	46.83
Tax income				
• nominal	−20.92	−19.27	−8.08	21.35
• real	−19.13	−0.20	−0.06	0.32
Price index	−0.02	0.01	−0.02	−0.08

The effect on the standard of living for households is only favourable for the rural non-savannah agricultural (MVIVA) and rural export agricultural (MEXP) households; this positive effect is induced by the fact that the marginal effect on the production of traditional agricultural goods is positive.

Shock 3: a 20 per cent increase in the price of imports

A 20 per cent increase in the price of imports causes GDP to decline by 6.2 per cent (see Table 6.3) due to the dependency of the Ivoirian economy on imports, both for inputs and final consumption. While there is increased demand for domestically produced goods, the price increases also cause bottlenecks in production.

The effects on welfare are mixed as some rural groups benefit from the shock (see Table 6.4). Even the urban formal sector receives a small welfare gain, suggesting that the movement to domstically produced goods more than compnsates for the increased input prices.

Shock 4: a 100 per cent change in the parity between the French and CFA francs

Although there is a large decrease in real GDP following the devaluation, on average households benefit from the shock. In particular, the urban households benefit as the increased demand for domestic goods more than compensate for the negative welfare effects due to the higher prices of imported final and intermediate goods.

The interaction of external shocks with tax reforms

Since we have established the best tax reform for each external shock, we are now able to analyse changes from combinations of shocks and tax reforms.

Shock 1 and reform 7: All indirect taxes are replaced by a common import tax rate of 201.85 per cent with a wider base. The economy is also confronted with a 20 per cent decrease in the price of traditional export products

The results in Table 6.8 indicate that there is a significant decrease in GDP; this is induced by the fall in the production of exports. Tax revenue also decreases by approximately 20 per cent. It is interesting to note that there is a large decline in the value added of several sectors, the exceptions being the formal manufacturing and non-tradeable goods sectors.

In terms of the welfare of households, Table 6.9 reveals an overall welfare loss of 17 per cent. Only the households MVIVA, MADP and MFOR experience a welfare gain. The unemployed (MINACT) receive less transfers from the government than any other household, and thus suffer the largest welfare loss; their welfare falls by 62 per cent.

Shock 2 and reform 7: all indirect taxes are replaced by a common import tax rate of 201.85 per cent with a wider base. Furthermore, there is a 20 per cent decrease in the price of all export products

Table 6.8 reveals that GDP decreases by 19.3 per cent. This can be explained by the decrease in the price of all exports, and the decrease is larger than the case without the tax reform. The structure of the economy is significantly affected by the combined shock and tax reform; in particular, the value added in each sector experiences a notable decrease.

The results in Table 6.9 reveal that total household welfare decreases by 22 per cent. However, the rural non-savannah agricultural (MVIVA) and urban formal private (MFOR) households experience a gain in welfare.

Table 6.9   Percentage change in welfare after the shocks and tax reforms

Household categories	Shock 1 + reform 7	Shock 2 + reform 7	Shock 3 + reform 3	Shock 4 + reform 5
Rural export agricultural (MEXP)	−29	−22	−8	0.29574
Rural savannah agricultural (MAGS)	−34	−44	−29	−0.11782
Rural non-savannah agricultural (MVIVA)	1	8	4	−0.37190
Urban public sector (MADP)	1	−6	−2	0.13667
Urban formal private sector (MFOR)	18	11	3	0.09431
Urban informal private sector (MINDEP)	−14	−21	−15	−0.05411
Unemployed (MINACT)	−62	−84	−56	0.14669
Household total	−17	−22	−15	2

Shock 3, reform 3: this widens the base of the import tax and applies a common tax rate of 32.31 per cent; all other indirect taxes remain. The economy experiences a 20 per cent increase in the price of imports

Table 6.8 indicates that real GDP decreases by 11.45 per cent. This simulation also has other negative effects on the economy as a whole, and, furthermore, the value added shows a large fall in every sector.

Like the other two reforms, this reform does not provide the necessary incentives to improve economic efficiency; the result is an overall welfare decrease of 15 per cent for households (Table 6.9). However, the rural non-savannah agricultural (MVIVA) and urban formal private sector (MFOR) households experience welfare gains of 4 per cent and 3 per cent respectively. These households are not affected by the external shock due to the nature of their activities.

Shock 4, reform 5: all indirect and direct taxes are removed and a common income tax rate of 29.47 per cent is implemented. There is a 100 per cent change in the parity between the French and CFA francs

This simulation is the only simulation where we notice an improvement in economic efficiency. Table 6.8 shows that real GDP increases by 42%; an increase induced by the fact that the suppression of all indirect and direct taxes provide an incentive to produce and consume. Furthermore, in every sector the value added rises more than 15 per cent; the exception is the food crop sector. The sectors oriented towards export activities receive more value than the others.

Table 6.9 indicates that this is also the only reform in which the total welfare of households improves. Essentially, the rural export agriculture (MEXP), the urban public sector (MADP), the urban formal private sector (MFOR) and the unemployed (MINACT) households benefit from this reform.

Conclusion

The results reported from simulations of tax reforms and external shocks which fix the level of the utility of the government have permitted us to identify, under certain hypotheses, the best and most feasible reform to make the Ivorian economy more competitive. But, it is clear that there is no unique tax reform which performs best when confronted with all the external shocks. Implementing tax reforms after external shocks have considerably disturbed the structure of the economy of Côte d'Ivoire leads to controversies about the efficiency of different taxes: the VAT seems not to be the best solution in response to the external shocks. On the contrary, tariff duties, the largest tax in the old tax system, seems to remain the appropriate tool. Concerning direct taxes, in the absence of other taxes in the economy the income tax represents an efficient tool to maintain a constant level of utility for government and to improve the welfare of households in response to a change in the parity of the French and CFA francs.

In closing, all our results are subject to strong assumptions: price flexibility and production factor mobility (except agricultural capital). These assumptions remain restrictive according to the Ivorian statutory framework which includes price control and activity licenses. Secondly, the elements of the reforms chosen (a unique rate) requires good control of the tax base. And, finally, it is assumed that tax administration is efficient and rates of recovery do not fall when taxes are raised.

Note

1   In August of 1993, the CFA zone, for the first time since its inception, did devalue relative to the french franc, by 50 per cent.

References

Benjamin, N. and S. Devarajan (1985) 'Oil Revenues and Economic Policy in Cameroon', World Bank, working paper no. 745.

Chambas, G. (1994) 'Fiscalité: Développement en Afrique Subsaharienne', Paris: Economica.

Chia, N; S. Wahba; and J. Whalley (1994) ' Poverty Reducing Targeting Programmes: A General Equilibrium Approach,' *Journal of African Economies*, vol. 3, pp. 309–38.

Devarajan, S. 'Purchasing Power Parity Equilibrium Real Exchange Rate', working paper, University of California.

Michel, G. and N. Michel (1984) 'Short Term Responses to Trade and Incentive Policies in the Ivory Coast: Comparative Static Simulations in a Computable General Equilibrium Model', World Bank, staff working paper no. 647.

Ngee-Choon, C. *et al.* (1991) 'Improving the Macroeconomic Data Base: A SAM for Côte d'Ivoire, 1986', World Bank, mimeo.

Ngueyen, T. (1992) 'Comment Construire un Modèle d'Equilibre Général Calculable', World Bank, Social Poverty Division.

Rutherford, T. F. (1989) 'General Equilibrium Modelling with MPS/GE', University of Western Ontario.

Shoven, J. and J. Whalley (1977) 'Equal Yield Taxes: A Computation Procedure and an Existence of Proof', *Journal of Public Economics*, vol. 8, pp. 211–24.

Shoven, J. and J. Whalley (1984) 'Applying General Equilibriums of Taxation and International Trade', *Journal of Economic Literature*, vol. 22, pp.1007–51.

7

Fiscal Reform and Structural Adjustment in Côte d'Ivoire

Ephrem Enoh, Catherine Enoh and Edmé Koffi

Introduction

The economic crisis which has ravaged Côte d'Ivoire (CI) since the early 1980s has entailed negative economic growth and serious external and internal disequilibriums. The different measures and the well-known structural adjustment policies advocated by international institutions have until now proven to be unsuccessful. Thus, in only a few years the CI has changed from a very prosperous economy, once known as the Ivoirian miracle, into one suffering an economic recession. (See Table 7.1 for key economic indicators.)

A country with an intermediate level of income, the CI has not been able to adapt to the worldwide depression of the prices of its principal export products, coffee and cocoa. The problem arises as the Ivoirian economy has a dual external dependence; the first is a structural dependence on export revenues, and the second is a budgetary dependence on stabilization revenues (obtained through marketing board policies). Moreover, the Ivoirian tax system is at the heart of the crisis. In fact, in the context of the franc zone, fiscality appears to be a privileged instrument of economic policies. Both monetary and exchange rate policy depend on all member countries and so the CI has relinquished both. One objective of this chapter is to precisely analyse how this evolution has happened, that is, the rupture of growth in the 1980s and early 1990s.

Although fiscal policy must be used for the neutralization of external shocks and more generally for economic growth, this does not detract from its main role in providing state revenue. The stabilization of this revenue is crucial for the maintenance of a reasonable budget balance. Faced with this dilemma (to raise revenue or to stimulate growth) the second objective is to determine what are the options. The different measures adopted have in the end not attained the desired results, and it is therefore necessary to analyse the tax system, its rigidity and peculiarities, as well as the situation under which the reforms were initiated. Devaluation and tax reform will be analysed as possible alternatives.

113

Table 7.1   Macroeconomic indicators (per cent)

GDP	1970–81	1982–90	1991
GDP growth	6.4	−0.5	−0.4
GDP (structure)			
• primary	27.3	30.7	33.4
• secondary	20.6	19.2	21.9
• services	42.1	38.7	32.2
• public	9.9	11.5	13.5
Consumption (growth)	7.5	−0.2	0.3
Investment (% GDP)	23.1	13.4	10.0
Savings (% GDP)	25.8	18.9	13.8
Export goods (growth)	5.1	0.3	−3.8
Export goods (% GDP)	34.1	33.3	28.7
Export structure			
• primary	63.3	46.6	
• secondary	27.7	43.3	
• services	9.0	10.1	
Import goods (growth)	7.2	−2.2	−1.8
Import goods (% GDP)	30.2	25.0	23.5
Import structure			
• primary	13.3	18.5	
• secondary	71.1	60.6	
• services	15.6	20.8	
Trade balance (% GDP)	3.9	8.3	5.2
Balance of current account (% GDP)	−8.7	−7.9	
Terms of trade	2.3	1.4	−4.0

A creeping fiscal crisis

The CI has undergone two economic phases in its development; a period of sustained growth between 1960 and 1981 (averaging 6.4 per cent between 1970 and 1981), and a strong economic recession from 1981 to the present (with a negative growth rate averaging −0.5 per cent). This can be partly attributable to the downward trend in the world prices of raw materials (Figure 7.1) particularly for coffee and cocoa. These commodities are CI's most important exports. Furthermore, the Ivoirian fiscal system is highly dependent on the export revenue of these two commodities through the Stabilization Marketing Board. In spite of the numerous reforms adopted, fiscal revenues have been unable to compensate for the fall in stabilization revenues and thus the budget deficit has continually worsened, reaching 11 per cent of the GDP in 1991 (Figure 7.2).

At the beginning of the 1970s, the level of stabilization revenues allowed a certain lack of strictness in the fiscal administration, but at the end of the

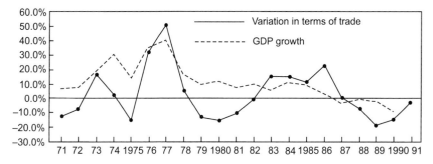

Figure 7.1 Growth and terms of trade

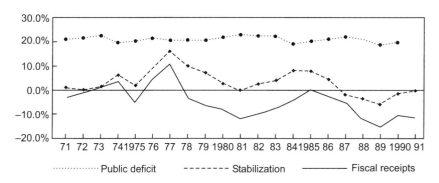

Figure 7.2 Public finances (% of GDP)

1970s measures to increase revenues and also to introduce structural changes appeared.

The fiscal system: multiple and complex taxes

It is important to review and appraise the current fiscal system in order to obtain a full understanding of the advantages and deficiencies of the Ivoirian fiscal system. Only then will it be possible to devise the reforms which will be necessary to correct the system's susceptibility to external shocks. The fiscal system is characterized by three major tax categories; direct taxes, indirect taxes and agricultural stabilization policies (see tables 7.2 to 7.4).

- The *Stabilization Fund* is responsible for maintaining stable prices to the producer, no matter what the fluctuations of world prices might be. So when the world price exceeds the guaranteed price, the mechanism acts as a tax; when the world price falls, it acts as a subsidy. Having explained the significance of agricultural export revenues in the GDP (an average of 10 per cent during the period 1975/1980), in particular those of coffee and

Table 7.2   Public finances (per cent GDP)

	1970–81	1982–90	1991
Public expenditure	34.8	37.5	40.2
• wages	9.2	11.1	
• investment	9.0	4.2	
• other	16.6	22.0	
Public revenues	33.7	30.0	27.7
• Fiscal	21.2	20.6	20.0
• *indirect taxes*	17.2	16.0	
• *direct taxes*	4.1	4.7	
• stabilization fund	5.4	1.8	−0.3
• other	7.1	7.6	8.1
Public deficit	−1.1	−7.3	−11.2
Debt service (external debt/export)	14.0	42.8	80.9

cocoa, one must note the importance of stabilization surpluses (on average CFAF 129 billion a year with a record of CFAF 254 billion in 1977). (The CFA franc is the currency of the West African Monetary Union.) However, the deterioration of world prices led to a reversal in the effect of the stabilization policy on government resources. Except for a brief revival in 1984/85, which brought the surplus back up to the 1977 level, the following years resulted predominantly in stabilization deficits, and so it was decided to abolish this mechanism of price regulation with the 1991/92 reforms. It was replaced by a mechanism which links costs of domestic production to fluctuations in world prices. In this case, if prices were to increase again (especially cocoa prices), an export tax could be introduced.

- The *Péréquation Fund* is responsible for increasing taxes on imported rice and flour in order to protect the production of local rice and other products.

- *Direct Taxes* are imposed at the point of origin of income or capital, and are paid by the agent on whom it is imposed. Generally these taxes play a distributive role since they modify the distribution of initial revenue.[1] They include taxes on revenues, profits and property, but property taxes won't be studied in detail because of their minor influence on the total (less than 7 per cent apart from in 1975). Direct taxes are complex because of the different exemptions and deductions, as well as the large number of rates.

  - *Income tax*: only the modern sector is subject to taxation. One part is collected from the source, depending uniquely on labourers in the formal sector (with salaried incomes). This tax is progressive, with rates varying from 10 per cent, to a maximum of 60 per cent for the upper income brackets.[2] The income tax base, already very small (in 1990 it amounted to 385 000 employees or 8 per cent of the active

Table 7.3 Fiscal revenues

	1975	1976	1977	1978	1979	1980	1981	1982	1983	1984	1985	1986	1987	1988	1989	1990
Fiscal revenues (CFA Franc 000s)	170 300	239 900	319 900	370 100	406 400	474 900	519 100	561 300	576 400	549 400	632 700	671 800	679 100	658 368	564 700	533 100
Indirect taxes	136 142	201 636	264 258	296 623	323 202	388 492	401 714	452 629	451 067	397 133	481 996	523 998	532 243	512 755	434 436	396 612
VAT	26 266	43 756	57 284	65 782	65 295	74 742	88 970	99 995	90 030	81 681	95 849	102 085	94 052	89 394	93 848	100 115
Tax on services	4 769	5 989	7 841	11 666	12 494	14 696	21 370	25 391	23 112	22 292	20 727	21 884	18 679	11 951	12 414	13 623
Excise taxes	8 394	9 645	12 782	15 546	18 652	23 091	16 660	24 391	29 756	8 212	46 601	65 723	102 460	98 309	87 163	92 473
Fuels	7 820	7 828	10 136	12 194	13 970	17 457	8 195	14 095	11 190	10 811	16 890	32 379	72 306	73 385	58 844	68 462
Other	574	1 817	2 646	3 352	4 682	5 634	8 465	10 111	18 566	17 401	29 711	33 344	30 154	24 924	28 319	24 011
Export duties	34 239	30 946	38 118	35 544	37 306	42 626	51 221	46 906	35 927	62 325	74 716	72 736	75 533	50 884	18 394	5 506
Tariff	40 552	72 098	96 575	103 759	111 117	129 656	141 529	139 208	138 640	132 656	147 572	162 500	155 833	150 955	144 213	119 561
Other	21 922	39 202	51 658	64 326	78 338	103 681	81 964	116 823	133 602	69 967	96 531	99 070	85 686	111 262	78 404	65 334
Direct taxes	34 158	38 264	55 642	73 477	83 198	86 408	117 386	108 771	125 733	152 267	150 704	147 802	146 857	146 613	130 264	136 488
Personal income taxes	11 707	14 025	20 193	27 101	29 313	30 823	38 945	42 122	45 413	48 163	48 707	52 676	52 433	52 678	49 396	58 728
Corporate taxes	10 930	13 763	18 223	25 132	28 724	29 213	40 142	31 892	52 035	60 599	57 941	49 157	9 053	45 059	33 451	32 586
Land	4 877	2 127	4 049	4 386	5 702	5 399	6 583	2 070	1 459	3 037	3 485	3 073	2 746	5 761	5 754	6 567
Taxes on banks	1 385	1 516	2 009	2 716	2 466	3 038	3 117	2 564	2 277	8 571	8 166	7 696	8 334	7 701	7 627	8 711
Labour taxes	5 259	6 843	11 168	14 142	16 993	17 935	28 599	30 123	24 549	31 897	32 405	35 200	34 291	34 414	34 036	29 896

Table 7.4 Fiscal structure

	1975	1976	1977	1978	1979	1980	1981	1982	1983	1984	1985	1986	1987	1988	1989	1990
Indirect taxes	0.799	0.840	0.826	0.801	0.795	0.818	0.773	0.806	0.782	0.722	0.761	0.779	0.783	0.778	0.769	0.743
VAT	0.192	0.217	0.216	0.221	0.202	0.192	0.221	0.220	0.199	0.205	0.198	0.194	0.176	0.174	0.216	0.252
Taxes on service	0.035	0.029	0.029	0.039	0.038	0.037	0.053	0.056	0.051	0.056	0.043	0.041	0.035	0.023	0.028	0.034
Excise taxes	0.061	0.017	0.018	0.052	0.057	0.059	0.041	0.053	0.065	0.071	0.096	0.125	0.192	0.191	0.200	0.233
Fuels	0.057	0.038	0.038	0.011	0.043	0.044	0.020	0.031	0.024	0.027	0.035	0.061	0.135	0.143	0.135	0.172
Other	0.001	0.009	0.010	0.011	0.014	0.014	0.021	0.022	0.041	0.043	0.061	0.063	0.056	0.018	0.065	0.060
Export duties	0.251	0.153	0.144	0.119	0.115	0.109	0.127	0.103	0.079	0.156	0.155	0.138	0.141	0.099	0.012	0.013
Tariff	0.297	0.357	0.365	0.349	0.343	0.333	0.352	0.307	0.307	0.334	0.306	0.310	0.292	0.291	0.331	0.301
Other	0.161	0.191	0.195	0.216	0.242	0.266	0.201	0.258	0.296	0.176	0.200	0.189	0.160	0.216	0.180	0.164
Direct taxes	0.200	0.159	0.173	0.198	0.204	0.181	0.226	0.193	0.217	0.277	0.238	0.220	0.216	0.221	0.230	0.256
Personal income taxes	0.312	0.366	0.362	0.368	0.352	0.356	0.331	0.387	0.361	0.316	0.323	0.356	0.357	0.361	0.379	0.430
Corporate taxes	0.319	0.359	0.327	0.342	0.345	0.338	0.341	0.293	0.413	0.397	0.384	0.332	0.334	0.309	0.256	0.238
Land	0.142	0.055	0.072	0.059	0.068	0.062	0.056	0.019	0.011	0.019	0.023	0.020	0.018	0.039	0.014	0.018
Taxes on banks	0.010	0.039	0.036	0.036	0.029	0.035	0.026	0.023	0.018	0.056	0.054	0.052	0.056	0.052	0.058	0.063
Labour taxes	0.153	0.178	0.200	0.192	0.204	0.207	0.243	0.276	0.195	0.209	0.215	0.238	0.233	0.236	0.261	0.219

population), is further reduced by the large number of available deductions or exemptions, that also diminish the progressivity of the tax.[3]

- *Corporate taxes*: individual profits are taxed at a standard rate of 35 per cent (including a 10 per cent tax for the National Investment Fund, NIF) and company profits at a standard 50 per cent (of which 10 per cent is for the NIF). Small businesses and a large number of professional and independent taxpayers are taxed by contract.

  The corporate tax base is greatly reduced by different exemptions and deductions – such as the exemption of cooperatives or agricultural credit institutions or new businesses developing in priority sectors. Having increased up to 1984, the assorted revenues of this tax began to decrease afterwards with a marked drop in 1989. This was the result of a dramatic drop in economic activity, a decrease in consumption and the subsequent closure of businesses. However, high tax rates were also a principal reason for the decrease in revenue; some businesses now refused to submit to this heavy burden and instead took shelter in the informal sector.

  Given the high current tax level, different measures were adopted to encourage a greater level of tax compliance by businesses. In 1990, the government reduced taxes on company profits from 40 per cent to 35 per cent and eliminated the additional tax on capital (10 per cent of profits).

- *Indirect Taxes* are aimed at the source of employment of income or of capital. In changing the relative price level, these taxes play an important role in the sectoral distribution of activities and thus in the structural evolution of the economy. These are several indirect taxes; the value added tax (VAT), a tax on the provision of services (TPS), export taxes, import tariffs, excise taxes (petroleum, tobacco, and so on) and various others. The strong contribution of external taxes (over 50 per cent) displays, paradoxically, both the political will for protectionism and the openness of the Ivoirian economy.

  - *VAT*: this tax is aimed at both consumers and merchants. The person taxed is the seller, except in the case of an imported product where it is the buyer who pays the tax. VAT is a deductible tax which originated as a standard 8 per cent rate on local production as well as imports. In 1978 a multiple rate structure was introduced ranging from 5 per cent to 25 per cent. In 1986 there was an increase in the rates, as well as a reduction in the number of legal rates (from four to three): a reduced legal rate of 10 per cent for articles of primary requirement, 20 per cent for regularly consumed goods and a higher rate of 26 per cent for luxury items. Certain sectors were exempted, thus strongly reducing the degree of coverage. In 1984 only 34 per cent of the value added of the modern sector was affected.

The two VAT reforms of 1978 and 1986 did not result in any great changes in the VAT revenue. The higher rates of 1986 even caused a contraction of revenues (−7 per cent). This change in revenues appears until now to have been circumstantial.

- *Tariff duties (TD)*: their goal is to control imports and to influence the demand for these goods. TDs consist of numerous rates, ranging from 0 per cent to 200 per cent, with higher rates being applied mainly to electrical appliances, cars or alcohol, and lower rates to products of primary necessity. In addition to the multitude of different rates which tend to vary from one year to the next, a variety of complicated exemptions and deductions are further imposed. The complexity of this system is largely responsible for the evasion of tariff duties.

  TD revenues increased until 1981 and then stabilized during the period 1981–9, with a slight fall in 1990. Thus all the rate increases had the sole result of maintaining the level of revenues despite the drop in the volume of imports.

- *Export Taxes:* only a few products like wood (raw and converted), coffee, cocoa and kola were taxed. In 1989, faced with the large drop in coffee and cocoa prices, the government did away with taxes on these products. With the goal of reinforcing the industrialization process, the tax on converted wood was also abolished in January 1993.

Recent tax reforms: no perceptible improvement

The different reforms applied over the course of time did not undergo spectacular changes. No perceptible improvement has taken place, either in reducing the budget deficit or in effecting structural change to disentangle fiscal revenues from world market fluctuations.[3] The increase of VAT rates in 1986 did not result in a corresponding increase in revenues. TD revenues, which have quite often been the object of change through rate changes or by widening the tax base, have suffered a drop in value since 1986; and contribution of export taxes to fiscal revenues has become marginal.

Moreover, the tax structure has remained stable. Only at the end of the period was there a slightly different distribution of fiscal revenues in favour of direct taxes. This is explained by both the fall in indirect taxes (in particular, the collapse of export taxes), and by the sustained growth of taxes on revenues. Direct taxes have represented on average 20 per cent of fiscal revenues, with a constant share between the two main taxes (on average 35 per cent of direct taxes). However, since 1985 the falloff in economic activity and the lower rates have reduced the share of profit taxes to a mere 23 per cent. The level of direct taxes remains relatively weak, at only 4.5 per cent of GDP.

Indirect taxes have represented on average 80 per cent of fiscal revenues. They played a leading role in the determination of the budget deficit since they account for 60 per cent of state revenues. Two years are of note; 1976, for the large indirect tax contribution to revenues (84 per cent) and as a part of the GDP (18 per cent), and 1984 for the opposite reason (72 per cent and 13 per cent respectively). Tariff duties have played a particularly important role, averaging 31 per cent of indirect taxes and 16 per cent of total state revenues. This tax has been the most effective (5–6 per cent of GDP) throughout the entire period. In contrast to direct taxes, the customs tax base is easily defined and controlled since the taxes are imposed at a single point. Moreover TDs are the least costly to administer. However, after having increased until 1986, the value of import taxes started to decrease in spite of the various reforms aimed at widening the tax base. It is important to note that no real effort has been made to reduce the high contribution of border taxes, as observed in other developing countries. With respect to indirect taxes, export taxes have been irregularly imposed, varying from a 25 per cent share in 1975 to only 1 per cent in 1991. The VAT has represented about 20 per cent of indirect taxes. Whereas the increase in the VAT rate in 1978 had a positive effect on the VAT share, neither the 1986 increases nor the extension of coverage in 1988 had any repercussions on the tax structure or on the VAT's efficiency. This evolution contrasts with that of the Philippines, where VAT was successfully introduced in 1986, or with Argentina's case which placed VAT as the centre of its reform.

In its complexity – that is, very broken-up tax levels, numerous exemptions, and a strong concentration of tax on a limited number of taxpayers – the fiscal system of Côte d'Ivoire is highly developed with high tax rates comparable to the fiscal systems of developed countries; but its returns do not correspond to the country's needs, in particular through the weakness of its tax base. In fact it is a very complex and inefficient system compared with other developing countries whose prime objectives of reform have often been to obtain simpler tax systems. The fiscal structure, with the privileged position of border fiscality, is just as characteristic.

It is also important to remember that for the Ivoirian example there was never a great transformation which resulted in the introduction of a brand new tax (such as the introduction of VAT in the Philippines), or in drastic changes in the share distribution between direct and indirect taxes. Rather, the reform measures were always discrete and on a small scale. Nevertheless, Ivoirian taxes have ended up being substantially higher than in other developing countries.

Reasons behind this crisis: the role played by the tax system

The rapid deterioration of the Ivoirian economic situation has had many causes which are important to consider.

The context under which the reforms were initiated

CI's growing external dependence can be effectively characterized in the contrasting summaries of the following two different time periods.

Sustained growth (1970–81)

During this period, CI's economic health can be explained by strong export growth, particularly in the export of raw materials owing to the boom in coffee and cocoa prices. Agriculture is an important facet of the Ivoirian economy, in fact much more important than in the average country of intermediate income. However, this excessive concentration on raw material exports[4] where prices are set on world markets entails an economy which is tied to the vagaries of external markets.

Up until 1978, the economy benefited substantially from the excess of stabilization revenues (5.4 per cent GDP on average); there was a positive budget balance and this enabled substantial public investment. But in 1978 the world prices of CI's agricultural exports collapsed. Thus, in spite of the implementation of austerity measures and fiscal reforms in 1978–9,[5] there was a substantial shortfall in government revenue and the government balance turned negative. The CI government turned to international borrowing to maintain its public investment programmes.

There was a trade balance surplus during the entire period thanks to the strong growth in raw material exports (63 per cent on average), but this surplus was weakened by the growing level of imports of manufactured products (an average of 71 per cent of imported goods). The demand for external financing remained weak, with a debt coverage rate of 14 per cent (or CFAF 73 billion). The disequilibrium of the balance of payments was essentially derived from private negative transfers (CFAF 200 billion) owing to the predominance of foreign workers in the CI (a consequence of this strong growth).

By the end of the 1970s, the deterioration in the terms of trade resulted in financial and structural weakness of the Ivoirian economy. This led the government to adopt the stabilization and adjustment policies advocated by the IMF and the World Bank in 1981.

Stabilization and adjustment (1982–91)

The improvement in the budget deficit in the initial years corresponded more to the improvement of the terms of trade than to the adoption of austerity measures. In fact, no lasting change was recorded and there was a relapse in the level of the deficit with the deterioration of the terms of trade after 1985. Despite government intentions, expenditure still increased, whereas revenues decreased. The different measures (for example wage freezing) were unable to stop the pressure to increase salaries. In contrast, investment expenditure was cut to a mere 4 per cent of GDP. This clearly shows the difficulty in reducing public expenditure;[6] the only alternatives being either a reduction in salaries (attempted in 1990 only to be abandoned due to serious social disruptions), or a reduction in manpower, neither one being popular.[7]

Nevertheless, these measures would be insufficient so that the level of expenditure remained a serious problem.

The drop in stabilization revenues placed stress on fiscal revenues. The government responded with an increase in international taxes, the monopolization of prices and the introduction of an export premium. At the same time, structural adjustment measures were adopted, involving both the restructuring of public companies as well as the reinforcement of budgetary discipline. These measures resulted in a drop in economic activity (a supply problem), accompanied by a growing informalization of the economy and the ensuing tax evasion.

The balance of payments, however, did not worsen. There was a slight improvement due to the drop (50 per cent) in private transfers owing to a falloff in activity and imports. Exports remained relatively stable. On the other hand, external debt became a real problem because of the large demand for external borrowing[8] to support investments, and the increase in world interest rates which increased the debt burden. Investment profitability proved itself to be quite insufficient.

All in all, by the end of the 1980s, in spite of the adopted reforms, the economic situation was very poor. Growth was negative at −0.7 per cent in 1989 and −1.6 per cent in 1990. The budget deficit represented 15.3 per cent of GDP in 1989 and 10.1 per cent in 1990. The external deficit increased from 10 per cent of GDP in 1989 to 11.1 per cent in 1990. Savings and investments slumped, while debt accumulated. Debt servicing related to exports surpassed 50 per cent and no economic indicator appeared to escape this bad situation.

A decade of structural adjustment programmes

The economic situation of the CI and especially the beginning of stabilization and structural adjustment policies (since 1981) have largely influenced the reforms adopted. The fulfilment of the conditionalities which were imposed by the Bretton Woods institutions and the CI's membership in the franc zone have greatly reduced the number of possible reforms.

The stabilization and adjustment programmes initiated consisted of a reduction of the budget deficit and also, until 1988, a reduction of the external deficit (in 1987 the trade balance was for the first time in deficit). First of all, the emphasis was on reducing expenditures, reducing credits to the economy, controlling public debt and increasing tax revenue. Pressure was therefore concentrated on the reduction of state expenditure and on increasing tax revenues, especially since one of the 1990s programme's objectives was the return to a primary surplus. Under these conditions the short term was the priority. Instead of implementing a tax reform through a real restructuring of the fiscal system, discrete measures of elevating rates were successively initiated. And because of the large contribution of indirect tax to total revenues, taxes on international trade were particularly increased. But the growth of revenue, the simple multiplication of the old tax base with the new rate, has often been overevaluated because of tax evasion. Moreover, the structural changes which were necessary, especially in order to isolate the tax system from external shocks, have been sacrificed in favour of short-term considerations.

Finally, in the context of the franc zone, devaluation as an instrument of competitiveness is not a national instrument.[9] The franc zone, which groups 13 African countries[10] and France,[11] rests on two principles; a fixed exchange rate and the convertibility of its money. The first principle implies that the CFA franc is not quoted on the exchange market. However, the parity can be modified in principle as agreed at the 1971/73 monetary council between zone members[12] if there is unanimous agreement. The second principle enables the freedom of exchange operations between the different partners and with almost all of the international community. It is important to note that certain arrangements have also regulated the movements of capital. The fixed parity has also reinforced the role of the fiscal policy.

The adverse effect of the measures

External dependence

The essential nature of Ivoirian imports, as with most developing countries, indicates it is unreasonable to expect a sizeable reduction without serious economic disturbances, the import volume being partially fixed by technical constraints. Within imported products we can see the preponderance of raw materials and semi-finished products as well as equipment goods (these two shares represent more than 50 per cent of imports). As long as local production is not sufficiently developed, so that substitution for different goods will remain impossible, the prohibitive tariff rates will have an adverse effect on the corresponding economic indicators. Although often protected by 'tariff wall and special exemption regulations', local businesses will still be heavily taxed. The actual protection,[13] calculated from the added value, is greatly reduced. The idea is that the same product, as far as final or intermediary consumption is concerned, necessitates two methods of treatment in order to answer to the objectives of the commercial policy. Moreover, exemptions are hardly going to stimulate productivity of the businesses which benefit from them and will discourage other businesses and introduce distortions.

From the point of view of exports, similar problems were encountered, but this time in terms of bottlenecks. As long as world demand is saturated, any increase in production will cause a drop in prices given the strong competition; thus, despite achieving a possible growth in market share, total revenues decrease. A double setback is thus experienced: loss of export revenues and increased state spending. Ivoirian export products are victimized by these supply constraints. There is also the example of the storage policy of 1988/89,[14] which had no effect on coffee and cocoa prices (because of the Malaysian production).

Fiscal evasion

Over the last few years, the continual increase in tax rates and the enlargement of the tax base has not always produced the desired levels of fiscal revenues. Even though the movement of fiscal revenues and GDP (or the tax base) were closely linked, they were not exactly parallel. Between 1975 and 1978, revenues decreased continuously while the growth of GDP reached a high of 10 per cent in 1978. Fiscal revenues and the growth rate for the economy were stabilized from 1989 onwards.

In 1978, the strong economic growth of the CI, especially the large surplus of the stabilization fund, permitted a certain laxity in fiscal behaviour. By the end of the decade, however, efforts to improve tax collection were made following the drop in stabilization revenues. This renewed interest helps to explain the correlation between revenues and GDP at the end of the period. Furthermore, the arrival of a new team with the nomination of a prime minister allowed significant internal changes but, more importantly, the adoption of more audacious measures. The pressure from sponsors also encouraged the team to exploit all possible budget resources to the utmost.

However, only a continual growth of fiscal revenues larger than the growth of economic activity would have resulted in an increase in the effective tax collection. Because of tax evasion, the reverse happened. In spite of the fiscal reform, fiscal evasion increased.

A first handicap to the successful recovery of taxes is the lack of statistical data. Sufficient data is necessary to calculate forecasts of fiscal revenues, maintain control over collected taxes and properly evaluate the performance of the tax system. Statistical data would enable the identification of the extent of coverage of the tax system, and also the measurement and analysis of the repercussions that different tax policies may have. Unfortunately, the economic crisis hindered the rigorous elaboration of accounts and reduced the number of available statistics. Under these conditions it is a delicate matter to measure tax evasion, and only with an intuitive approach and the aid of gathered information can we assess the loss of fiscal revenues.

Administrative difficulties and holdups also reduce the system's efficiency and affect the level of revenues effectively collected. However, this phenomenon does not seem to be a major cause, as in the case of the Philippines.[15] The major cause of fiscal evasion for the Côte d'Ivoire comes from the evolution of the base of taxes. First of all, the tax reforms adopted did not have any structural effect; by the end of the 1980s the economic and fiscal structure had hardly changed from that of the 1970s. If the increase in taxes had little impact on the economic structure,[16] it was mainly because of the reduction of the tax base engendered by the adoption of particular tax regimes which favoured certain sectors. An unfavourable environment, nationally and internationally, also contributed. This static economic situation was further induced by the mistaken belief that world prices would eventually regain their 'true level' of the mid-1970s.[17] Thus, no credible effort was undertaken to disentangle the fiscal system from the harmful external shocks.

Given the strength of external trade and the importance of customs duties on fiscal revenues, it is worth noting the following. Imports of manufactured goods have decreased over time, from 80 per cent of imports in 1970 to 54 per cent in 1990. This drop resulted in two joint effects, a drop in activity and the level of taxation during the period of crisis. It was not the result of a dynamic policy having allowed the substitution of imported equipment for local production, but rather of a national reduction in demand. This decrease has corresponded to an increase in the importation of primary goods (especially crude oil). After 1975, there was also an increase in the import of services. Exports experienced a more erratic evolution, with primary exports fluctuating according to world trends. The structural 'changes' arose more from circumstantial change, national and international, than from applied measures and simply explained the impact of the recession on external trade.

The crisis reduced both activity and fiscal revenues collected. The state decided to increase tax rates again to keep this drop in check, but this increase in rates discouraged demand yet again. The removal of this vicious circle will have to be an essential part of future reforms.

Finally, the increased informality of the economy resulted in tax evasion; the high rate of taxation incited businesses to take cover in the informal sector in order to attempt to escape taxes. Statistics relating to this phenomenon confirm that in 1975 less than 10 per cent of the active population belonged to the informal sector, but by 1992 23 per cent of the active population had taken refuge there.[17] The economic crisis and the high tax rates explain the phenomenon of tax evasion.

Within the range of 'traditional' reforms, the choice is very limited (for example budget restrictions), and most of the measures are doomed to fail because of the perverse effects inherent within the particular economic situation of the CI. Moreover, because of membership in the franc zone, devaluation, an instrument which can be used to improve competition and to implement structural changes, is foregone. Measures concerning the different costs of production (reductions in the costs of salaries and energy for example) thus become important. Comparative studies on production costs at the level of manpower, transport, electricity and so forth always indicate that the CI appears to be a 'very expensive' country in relation to other African countries (especially Ghana and Nigeria), but also in relation to Southeast Asian countries. A subsidy policy, theoretically equivalent to a devaluation, is nevertheless difficult because of the heavy budget deficit. The exogeneity of exchange rates remains, however, a real handicap especially since considerable devaluations (up to 30 per cent) have been used by the CI's competitors (Ghana and Malaysia).

What are the options?

The tax reforms of the 1980s were unsuccessful at both altering the taxation structure and at maintaining a stable tax revenue yield. A national economic strategy (comparable to the anti-inflation plans initiated by some South American countries) is indispensable in dealing with the crisis. The previous structural adjustment plans (1981, for the CI) and those following which have been advocated by international institutions have proven to be ineffective because of minimal acceptance by the population. In order for a plan to be effective it must take into account the political considerations, otherwise the plans will be forestalled by affected interest groups. It is important that any further implementation of reforms achieve the desired credibility within the population and the international community for it to be effective. For instance, the day after the devaluation of January 1994, a lot of prices doubled, and such behaviours will change the expected results if not anticipated. Credibility at the international level is equally important to ensure the return of direct foreign investment or to access new mechanisms for relieving the debt–essential factors to rekindle growth.

A modification of the parity of the CFA franc

Within the franc zone, the exchange rate is fixed to the French franc and thus fluctuates in conjunction with it. This is in contrast to most developing countries where currency devaluations are a frequently used economic instrument, especially for the IMF and the World Bank structural policies. The different heads of state of the CFA member countries meet annually and decide the desired parity of the CFA franc in relation to the French franc. Yet parity remained unchanged since 1948[18] until it finally changed on the night of 11 January 1994.[19]

However, national and international circumstances have changed a lot in the 1980s, in particular the difficulties encountered by African countries. Whereas Côte d'Ivoire was regularly compared to other countries in the 1970s, it now has the lowest level of income within this group of intermediate income countries. The different economic upheavals experienced in the past have nevertheless not destabilized the currency value. Under these conditions one can criticize the level of the exchange rate, as a strong consensus was reached with regard to the over-valuation of the CFA franc.[20]

Moreover, the agreements which govern the franc zone stipulate the uniqueness of the exchange rate FF/CFAF and the necessary unanimous agreement to change its level. The different economic situations of the countries, some of which are net importers (for example CI, Senegal, Mali) and others net exporters (for example Congo, Gabon) of oil, and some of which have sea access (for example CI, Gabon) and others are surrounded by land (for example Mali, the Central African Republic) were a great hindrance to achieving modification of the parity. Given that there will be only one optimal exchange rate for each one of these different countries, yet there must be unanimous agreement on one exchange rate 'optimal for all member countries', it is unlikely that all will be satisfied. Nevertheless, political alliances and other considerations (such as compensations to those countries which desire another rate) could aid possible agreement, and the issue of devaluation had to be resolved to counter the negative effects of overvaluation on fiscal revenues and on the economy. There are two possible alternatives available to the CI: a 'national' devaluation, hence a forced exit from the franc zone, or a devaluation in the franc zone as a whole; and this latter solution is preferable since it would enable the CI to keep the advantages of the zone mechanism, in particular the free convertibility of its currency. Given the economic disparities between members, this solution was seen as unlikely[21] but was still the one chosen at the Dakar meeting of January 1994.

The franc zone, as the unique experiment of a monetary zone, has brought with it numerous economic considerations since its inception in the first half of this century. The zone has for a long time portrayed a very strong image of monetary as well as political stability, but the 1980s showed a change in attitude with regard to the zone from both France and the African countries. This was partly because of the costs involved. Although CFA francs had been accumulated in the 'operation account' at the French Treasury during the 1970s and thus sustained the French currency, the reverse (large deficits) had occurred since 1980. Besides, the strong economic crisis strengthened by an unsound management has not changed behaviours but led to an unsustainable situation (easy access to imports, purchase power disconnected from reality, and so on).

The CFA franc parity was also questioned; whereas before 1980 the currency was undervalued, afterwards it became greatly overvalued. In fact, the fixed parity with regards to the FF implied that the CFA franc has been determined by the evolution of the French economy. However, the difference between the two economic situations of France and the CI has varied. The optimal exchange rate for France has little chance of coinciding with that of the CI. As such, the consideration of a devaluation was certainly economically feasible. Given the context in which the CI found itself, in terms of the dilemma between the size of the budget deficit and the stability of the economic structure, a devaluation seemed to be a positive step.

First, devaluation had an immediate effect on export prices; with devaluation the Stabilization Fund could return to its previous situation of a surplus. This then permits an improvement of the budget balance without putting specific fiscal measures into practice. On the contrary, tariffs can be cut down without inducing a great loss of revenue because of the end of fraud. In addition, devaluation facilitates a return to an interior equilibrium. A drop in household buying power following an increase in import prices reduces national demand; and finally, the reduction in production costs (in foreign currency) could encourage foreign investors to re-establish themselves in the CI. The level of salaries, seen as being high by international standards, would automatically be reduced, as would other costs (such as transport and energy) except for costs of imported supplies.[22] But at the same time, automatic perverse effects remain, the increase in the value of the debt, the increase in the prices of investment and so on. Besides, the optimistic predictions on exports[23] should be cautioned because of the nature of the agricultural products involved and the nature of the markets (for example quotas, low elasticity prices, saturated demand). Moreover, the expected gains to be derived from external trade would be further reduced by the increase in the prices of imports, especially since they comprise such an important role in the Ivoirian economy.

All in all, the short-term advantages – the improvement of public finances and the long-term improvement of external trade – may be compromised by the weak industrial development of the country and the extent of its debt. Until 1994 CI has preferred real adjustment (fiscal measures can be equivalent to a devaluation, with export subsidies and import taxes), but now the capacity of the CI to counteract the devaluations of other economies is reduced thus hindering the economy as a whole (with an extremely high level of taxation). Devaluation thus was a reasonable alternative.

Nevertheless, an isolated devaluation without a devaluation of all the countries in the franc zone would have forced the CI to withdraw from this monetary zone. A first handicap would been have the important economic repercussions of causing political offence. The deterioration of relations with France and with other member countries would not have been favourable to the CI. France still remains the CI's most important partner in trade relations[24] and in providing financial flows, loans and development aid.[25] A second inconvenience, relative to the departure from the zone, relates to the credibility of the currency and its convertibility. The free and unlimited conversion of the CFA franc is certainly the most appealing element. Also, since devaluations are often interpreted as a result of economic failure, repeated devaluations could be unavoidable (social and economic troubles). Removal of capital has been a regular occurrence in the history of the Ivoirian economy, and the loss of confidence in the currency[26] and its loss in status could also lead to the suppression of convertibility. Finally, inflation could rocket following a devaluation and all advantages could be cancelled out. It is a question of whether Ivoirians could have monetary discipline by themselves. Numerous examples of hyperinflation can be seen in South America (for example Brazil, Argentina) and in Africa (Zaire), and membership of the franc zone, which implies a certain monetary discipline, has enabled a control of inflation and hence also isolated the countries from price shocks.[27] This relative stability of prices is a real advantage of the franc zone.[28]

Thus, the second choice, a devaluation within the monetary zone as a whole seemed to be the preferable one. But the problem of the optimal level of the exchange rate remains as well as the unanimous consent of all members.[29] In fact, support from international institutions and recently from France[30] played in favour of such a devaluation, especially concerning the reduction in debt.[31] However, some inconveniences remained such as explosive inflation. If the inability to monetize debt and the adoption of restrictive measures, such as a strict control of credit,[32] played an important role in controlling inflation (advantages of the zone), success is not certain. In fact, because of the economic structure (lots of monopolies), imported inflation will be automatically reflected through the maintenance of fixed margins. Facing this phenomenon, workers will ask for wages rises. And in the context of a new democracy and the approach of presidential elections in 1995, a vicious circle was not impossible.

A true fiscal reform

In the longer term the difficulty of implementing a devaluation and the downward rigidity of public expenditures[33] play in favour of fiscal reform. These problems are the essence of such a tax reform.

The study of the existing fiscal structure has shown the preponderance of indirect taxes, in particular customs taxes. A switch of taxes towards VATs and direct taxes would help insulate the tax system from external shocks. In fact, VAT has been at the centre of reforms in several countries (for example the Philippines and in South America), where VAT previously did not exist or its rate was very low. In the CI's case, VAT rates were about 20 per cent in the early 1990s. And because of the strong correlation between VAT and the GDP, an increase in rates will probably have a negative impact on activity. Concerning direct taxes, corporate taxes have been reduced to avoid the closure of firms and the informalization of the economy. The high level of taxation can no longer permit an increase in rates.

The narrowness of the tax base is also a characteristic of the tax system; for instance, 40 per cent of imports belong to special fiscal regimes. Only the formal sector and the formal workers are subject to taxation. Moreover, fraud reduces the base. The enlargement of the tax base appear to be necessary to reduce distortions and also to maintain or increase tax revenues. In 1994, the problem was an institutional one and the fiscal administration did not have sufficient power and means to implement such a reform, that is to tax the informal sector and to reduce fraud. There was need for a much stronger political will.

Moreover, the privatization of businesses can be conceived as a desirable activity since it allows a reduction of public expenditure, an increase in tax revenues and eventually a reduction in production costs through a drop in prices. The elimination of state subsidies theoretically leads to greater efficiency and should induce gains in productivity. Since 1990, the CI has followed a vast privatization programme, which has checked the drop in fiscal revenues but has not modified the prices of products by the same extent. The first reason is the existence of monopolies which still have excessive control of markets; such as the SODECI for water, the CIE for electricity, and so on. There is also the economic and political context in which these privatizations occurred. However, in becoming involved in a process of state disengagement in the long run, the policy may enable a reduction in public expenditure. In addition, no matter what the means used to obtain a reduction in prices (administrative measures or competition) the latter will have two motivating effects. On the one hand a boost in consumption and thus production, and on the other the creation of a favourable environment for investment. The dramatic fall in public investment during the 1980s to, on average, only 4 per cent of public expenditure, has to be compensated through the initiative of the private sector in order to avoid a great deterioration of the industrial base of the Ivoirian economy. The reduction of production costs proves itself to be essential.

Finally, a true tax reform consists in reducing some rates (especially on intermediary goods) without elevating others, and in reducing exemptions and implementing an enlargement of the tax base. However, these methods have been unsuccessfully attempted from 1990 to 1994. Thus success depends on the means (financial and human) involved to recover taxes, which depend on political choices.

Conclusion

The economic evolution of the Côte d'Ivoire, and in particular the fast succession from a period of prosperity (1970–80) to a period of crisis (1981 onwards) is partly explained by the international circumstances. The drop in world prices of raw materials, coffee and cocoa prices considerably reduced export revenues (the engine of growth in 1970–80) as well as stabilization revenues (the basis of vast investment programmes). Also, the increase in world interest rates increased the burden of debt-servicing. Nevertheless, the specific economic structure of the CI, especially its structural inflexibility, were equally the cause of the crisis. In fact, the external orientation of the economy, with exports of primary agricultural products and necessary imports of capital goods, automatically amplifies all exterior shocks. In addition, the CI belongs to the franc zone, through which it restricts its own monetary policy and foregoes control over exchange rates.

Fiscal policy, therefore, must be the instrument by which the government tries to protect the economy from external shocks. By changing the structural composition of the GDP, for example by influencing external trade by means of relative prices, fiscal reforms are capable of stopping or mitigating economic recession as well as the deterioration of public finances. However, the experience of the 1980s, where numerous measures were adopted remains disappointing. The economic structure hardly changed and fiscal revenues were not improved.

In this context, there are few alternatives. Whether choosing devaluation or adopting drastic fiscal measures, it seems that the political domain encroaches upon the economic domain. The announcement of the devaluation of the CFA franc by 50 per cent in 1994 confirmed this political aspect and will open new perspectives to the Côte d'Ivoire.

Appendix 1: chronology

1975–80

Context

The 1975–80 period was characterized by the rapid growth of foreign markets, and, in particular, by a very strong rise in coffee and cocoa prices in 1976–7. In response to the high prices for export-oriented agricultural products, the government initiated a vast public investment programme. In 1978, prices fell to much lower levels. The corresponding decrease in export receipts from coffee and cocoa in the latter part of the 1970s comprised the realization of Côte d'Ivoire's investment plans. The resulting internal macroeconomic disorders at the end of this period provoked a serious financial crisis which necessitated turning to the alternative of foreign borrowing.

Strong GDP growth (averaging 8 per cent) and a balanced state budget ensured the favourable conditions necessary for a continuing increase in fiscal receipts. However, the adverse external shock of the price decline in 1979, with the added effect of the second oil shock, implied the necessary adoption of a series of measures to maintain the level of government receipts. The Stabilization Board played a significant role in this period by providing a high level of receipts. Other taxes also contributed a significant proportion to the high receipt levels. Thus, the existing tax system enabled a strong increase in government expenditure without a deterioration in the government's budgetary balance.

Policy actions

In 1978–9 there was an elevation of the VAT and TPS taxes, and of taxes on fuels and tobacco.

1981–3

Context

This period covers the initiation of the first phase of structural adjustment and stabilization policies. The policies principally outlined a drastic cut in government expenditure, the reduction of available credit in the economy through a restrictive monetary policy, management of the public debt, and growth of fiscal receipts. A strong commitment was undertaken by the Côte d'Ivoire, in accordance with the IMF, for the reduction of the level of government deficit which had recently ballooned to 12.5 per cent of GDP in 1980 from its lower average levels of 2.3 per cent between 1965 and 1975. One of the principal targets of reduction was the public sector, which underwent considerable reorganization. Public corporations were also restructured (four were privatized).

Public investment which had already been reduced in 1979 and 1980 faced a sharp decline in 1981. Its real value was reduced by 30 per cent in 1981 and by 12 per cent in 1982. Over this entire period, total public investment fell by 15 per cent in nominal terms, and by 32 per cent in real terms. For current expenditures, the aggregate salary level of the public sector had been seriously controlled with a freeze on salaries in 1982, and a progressive reduction of wage rate increases of public workers. The economy grew at a rate of 9 per cent for 1981/2, and 5 per cent for 1982/3. Budget deficits grew to worrisome levels at about −10 per cent of GDP, and there was a strong deficit in the current account portion of the balance of payments (averaging CFAF 350 million, or 14 per cent of GDP).

Policy actions

In 1981 there was an elevation of fuel taxes, entailing a 10 per cent increase in the price of gas, and increases in the price of electricity.

1984–7

Context

The second phase of the adjustment and stabilization process consisted in reducing public expenditure and strengthening the tax system to attain an average level of fiscal pressure of 20 per cent.

There was a reduction in subsidies awarded, entailing an increase in the price levels of basic goods such as water (+25 per cent), urban transport (+25 per cent), and so on. Also, the removal of subsidies on fertilizers and crop seeds for local consumption implied higher production prices for coffee and cocoa (+33 per cent), for cotton (+43 per cent), and for palm oil from small farmers (+35 per cent). Public investment was further amputated bringing its level to 8 per cent of GDP in 1984, 5.8 per cent in 1985, 6.2 per cent in 1986 and 6.3 per cent in 1987. Finally, salary levels of both the private and public sectors were frozen. From 1985 onwards, salary levels of parapublic organizations were aligned with those of the public sector.

External events continued to contribute to Côte d'Ivoire's worsening economic situation. Prices of primary products for export decreased (the collapse of world coffee prices in 1987 entailed a decrease in the sale of coffee receipts by 40 per cent). Higher interest rates rendered the servicing of the external debt more difficult, and fluctuations of the US dollar, the currency in which Ivorian exports are paid, also accentuated the difficulties. The budget deficit averaged CFAF 84 billion, or about 3 per cent of GDP. The growth of the economy diminished throughout the period, reaching a negative growth for the first time in 1986/7 (−4 per cent). Despite an improvement in 1985, the current account of the balance of payments remained strongly negative.

Policy actions

Actions for 1984/5 included the promotion of a revised code of investments; an elevation in the value of the price of foodstuffs, serving as a base for export duties on coffee and cocoa; an elevation of DTIs and fuel taxes; reform of customs tariffs; and substitution of quantitative restrictions on imports in favour of a temporary increase in import duties.

Actions for 1987 included the adoption of an export subsidy based on the value added; an elevation of taxes on petroleum products; an increase in coffee and cocoa taxes from CFAF 80.5 to CFAF 100.5 per kilogram; and an increase of the tax on imported rice.

1988–90

Context

At the end of 1987, the government adopted a stabilization policy with the objective of restoring economic growth and reducing internal and external disequilibrium for 1988 onwards. Because of Côte d'Ivoire's strong dependence on export receipts, the terms of trade are very important to the health of the economy. The deterioration of the terms of trade (averaging 10 per cent since 1987), and the aggravation of the debt situation (CFAF 216 billion in 1989 versus 74 billion in 1980), amplified the external disequilibrium of the Ivoirian economy. The trade balance, which had always been at a surplus, became negative starting in 1987 (CFAF −147.6 billion).

The policy of stocking coffee and cocoa products in 1988/9 weighed heavily on the liquidity of the banking system, and indirectly provoked bottlenecks in the economy. This policy did not permit a regeneration of the economy. The Ivoirian economy was seriously weakened with an accumulation of arrears (from CFAF 255 billion in 1987 to 696 billion in 1989).

The consecutive decreases in GDP in 1987 and 1988 (respectively −1.6 per cent and −2 per cent) indicate the persistence of the crisis and the difficulties encountered in trying to meet the objectives of the stabilization plans. This contraction in economic activity entailed a fall in fiscal receipts.

Policy actions

Actions in 1988 included the elevation of import duties to an average of 30 per cent; and the extension of the VAT (at 25 per cent) to the commercial retail and service sectors.

In 1989 they included a reduction in producer prices of cocoa beans from CFAF 400/kg to CFAF 250/kg and then to CFAF 200/kg and of coffee (cerise) from CFAF 200/kg to CFAF 100/kg; and a tentative reduction in salaries (aborted for social reasons).

1990–1

Context

The negotiated programme with the IMF showed the necessity of bypassing the policy of cutting public expenditures in favour of initiating structural reforms to restart economic growth in the short term. The obstacles previously encountered showed the need to focus on modifying the process of institutional decision-making and in the way the administration takes action.

The central objective of the stabilization and recovery programme of 1990 was the realization of a primary surplus of 0.9 per cent of GDP, an ambitious goal given the years of preceding deficits. This implied not only a curbing of expenditures, but also a mobilization of internal resources and a reduction in payment arrears with competition or external pressures which would permit the regulation of debt servicing.

Nevertheless, the results fell below the target objectives. For the fourth consecutive year the volume of economic activity decreased (by 3 per cent) in spite of strong growth in agricultural production (+4 per cent). The trade balance was restored under the impetus of both traditional (coffee, cocoa) and non-traditional (+17 per cent in volume for transformed products) product exports, and with the reduction in imports. Also, efforts at financial stabilization enabled a reduction in the government budget deficit from 7.4 per cent in 1989 to 2 per cent of GDP in 1991.

Policy actions

Actions in 1990 included a strong reduction in the stabilization deficit with a fall in producer prices and a broadening of the tax base and enforcement in tax collection. Various taxes were imposed at the source of purchases by importers, or by public regulations designed to cautiously integrate the informal sector into the tax system.

From 1991 to the present

Context

In the context of policies for restimulating the economy, Ivoirian officials have adopted an interim programme which takes into account the social dimensions of these macroeconomic and structural measures. They have obtained the agreement of financial backers for the short term. The objectives are articulated in a dual framework:

- balancing the government's internal financial operations and attaining a primary surplus (of 2 per cent of GDP in 1992 and 5 per cent in 1995) towards the goal of gradually obtaining an increasing coverage of the sums due for payment of the external debt;

- adopting structural reforms to improve internal and external competitiveness with the goal of achieving a primary surplus in the balance of payments (4 per cent of GDP in 1995) and to ensure a long-term growth of 5 per cent in 1995.

A large number of reforms are envisaged concerning each of the different sectors, most notably the financial sector (with its problems of liquidation and restructuring), government intervention (an increasing disengagement from the economy), and liberalization of certain prices and modifications in the framework of labour.

The only results to date from 1992 do not permit an adequate interpretation of their meaning.

Policy actions

Actions in 1991 included the removal of export duties and licences to export; and the alleviation of the fiscal burden on businesses.

In 1992 they included the reduction of the portion of receipts tied to imports through the lowering of the rate charged to the modern sector (from 8.6 per cent of GDP in 1991 to 7.3 per cent in 1995); the growth of

Appendix 2: employment in Côte d'Ivoire

Table A.1 Distribution of active population

	1975 (%)	1980 (%)	1985 (%)	1990 (%)	1992
Active population	2 555 000	3 812 000	3 812 000	4 593 000	4 950 000
Agricultural sector	1 900 000 (74)	2 284 000 (70)	2 547 000 (67)	2 964 000 (65)	3 150 000
Modern sector	340 000 (13)	440 000 (13)	405 000 (11)	385 000 (8)	380 000
Informal sector	245 000 (10)	430 000 (13)	678 000 (17)	964 000 (21)	1 090 000

Source: Direction de l'emploi et de la réglementation du travail.

Table A.2 Evolution of active population (annual growth rate)

	1975–80	1980–5	1985–90	1990–2
Active population	5.2	3.8	3.8	3.8
Engaged population	4.7	2.1	3.5	3.5
agricultural sector	3.6	2.2	3.1	3.1
modern sector	6.6	−3	−1	−1
informal sector	10.4	11.1	7.3	6.3
Unemployment	9.5	10.6	9	8.6

Source: Government of Côte d'Ivoire (1993).

receipts coming from goods and services (5.9 per cent in 1991 to 7.8 per cent in 1995) through the broadening of the coverage to businesses which evade tax policy measures; the re-establishment of export duties on cocoa beans (2 per cent in 1995); and that receipts to be taken from stabilization will be nullified after removing the vulnerability of receipts to the uncertainty of export receipts.

Table A.3   Structure of employment in the modern sector

	1980 %	1985 %	1990 %
Private sector	326 400 (74)	257 700 (64)	233 300 (61)
Administration	73 847 (17)	107 460 (27)	116 000 (30)
Other	40 000 (9)	40 000 (9)	35 700 (9)

Source: Direction de'emploi et de la réglementation du travail.

Appendix 3

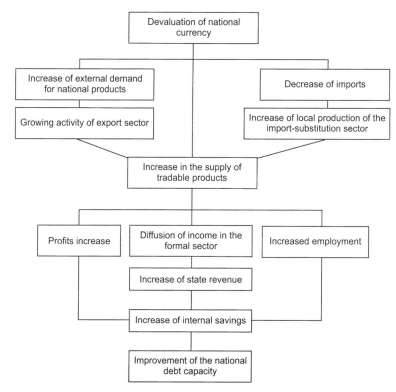

Figure A.1   Virtuous cycle of a devaluation

Appendix 4

Concerning modifications of the zone, different suggestions have been put forward which are orientated more towards European monetary mechanisms. It is important to note that contrary to the EU, where trade cooperation has always been preferred, countries of the franc zone have begun with monetary cooperation. Today the trade cooperation generates great interest and the existence of a monetary cooperation contributes to the promotion of trade relations and trade in the region. However, a form slightly different from that of the actual franc zone has been suggested.

The different African countries would create their own national currency but the CFA franc would continue to exist as a unifying mechanism between the countries (note the analogy to the ecu). Each currency would thus have a defined course in relation to the CFA franc and would be specific to each of them. An African Monetary Fund would secure the administration of this cooperation. In this way the CI would once again find a monetary and economic autonomy without losing certain advantages of the franc zone.

Another proposition is the linking of the CFA franc to the ecu, which would allow a better exchange rate in view of the evolution of trade relations. If

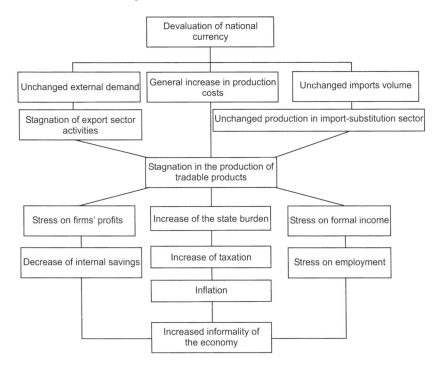

Figure A.2   Vicious cycle of a devaluation

France remained the privileged partner, the diversification of exchange rates would justify this choice. The majority of Ivoirian imports come from France, but the Netherlands has become the most important buyer since 1985 and Italy and Germany are becoming more important trade partners. The change of the franc zone into the ecu zone would also be an opportunity to readjust parities.

All in all, a well-defined monetary status is conducive to external trade but also to the economic stability of the country in terms of monetary speculation and inflation. The intensification of trade relations between countries of the region would make the union necessary in order to simplify transactions and to limit exchange risks.

The maintenance of a credible monetary union would have further implications with the Ivoirian devaluation. It enables the restoration of public finances and, at the same time, an increase in competitiveness without harming the reputation of the currency's stability and convertibility. On top of this, the threat of consecutive devaluations would be eliminated and would enable the creation of a favourable environment for national and foreign investors. Support from France or from other countries would enhance this proposal.

Notes

1 See Kay (1990).
2 Moreover, the national contribution to security is a standard 1 per cent tax.
3 The priority of most developing countries' reforms is first to increase revenues by any means and then acquire a new tax structure (more allocative and distributive).
4 93 per cent of total exports in 1965 and 86 per cent in 1987.
5 See Appendix 1 on the chronology and measures of adjustment.
6 State expenditure is essentially devoted to administration costs. Capital spending represents only 10 per cent of total expenditure.
7 Anticipated retirements and voluntary resignations appear to be preferred by the authorities and are more palatable to the population.
8 With a sum of CFAF 200 billion for only 12 billion inhabitants, the CI heads the list of countries in debt.
9 The parity of the CFA franc depends on all franc zone members.
10 Benin, Burkina Faso, Côte d'Ivoire, Niger, Senegal, Togo, Mali, Cameroon, Central African Republic, Congo, Gabon, Chad and Equatorial Guinea.
11 As well as the territorial collectivity of Mayotte, Monaco and the Comoro Republic.
12 France and the two monetary unions: WAMU for West African countries and 'BEAC' for Central African countries.
13 See Samen (1990).
14 See Appendix 1.
15 See Clarete and Diokno (1994).
16 Strong import taxes in support of import-substitution policies did not allow the development of the secondary sector, which remained constant throughout the period.
17 See Appendix 2 on employment in Côte d'Ivoire.
18 1 CFA F = 0.02 FF.
19 1 CFA F = 0.01 FF.

20   This consensus (in the economic literature) is limited to the actual parity; the measures that can be used in order to end the crisis remain very different.
21   For a long time (and more frequently since 1991) there have been a lot of unsuccessful negotiations to convince those who do not want to devalue.
22   See Appendix 3.
23   The drop of foreign currency prices of Ivoirian exports would allow market shares to grow and export revenues to increase.
24   In 1987, France bought 15 per cent of Ivoirian exports, and Ivoirian imports from France represented a total of 32 per cent.
25   French bilateral public aid in 1988 represented FF 969.5 million, 18 per cent of French bilateral public aid in the countries of the franc zone. Source: 1989 report, *ibid.*
26   With regards to this a practical detail occurs: the circulation of the CFAF as a national currency would no longer be possible and would lead to the creation of a new currency.
27   The evolution of inflation rates during the course of time shows the unity of rates between the different countries and, in particular, France. The budget deficits explain the inflation residuals (the difference between the inflation rates of two countries), Honohan (1990).
28   Budget deficits cannot be financed by issuing money.
29   See Appendix 4 on suggestions about a modification of the zone.
30   After having paid the Bretton Woods CI's debt, the necessity of an agreement between CI and these institutions was stipulated by France.
31   France has suppressed the 'public aid for development' debt for the less-developed countries and has reduced it by half for the intermediary-income countries.
32   After the devaluation, the BCEAO has elevated its rate from 11 to 14.5 per cent in order to restrain credit.
33   Only a reduction in salaries can reduce expenditure, but this measure does not seem possible.

References

Assidon, E. and P. Jacquemot (1988) *Politiques de change et ajustement en Afrique*, Études et Documents, Ministère de la Coopération.

Banque Mondiale (1988) *Côte d'Ivoire: La mobilisation des ressources internes en vue d'une croissance stable*, rapport principal.

Blejer, M. and A. Cheasty (1992) 'How to Measure the Fiscal Debt', *Finance and Development*, vol. 29.

Bliss, C. (1992) 'The Design of Fiscal Reforms in Revenue-Constrained Developing Countries', *Economic Journal*, vol. 102, pp. 940–51.

Brasseul, J. and P. Engelhard (1985) 'Intégration monétaire et développement économique: le cas de la zone franc', *Mondes en développement*, tome 23, no. 52.

Charles, E. and J. R. Lure (1992) 'Incomes Tax Reform in Colombia and Venezuela: A Comparative History', The Hoover Institution, Stanford, *World Development*, vol. 20, no. 3.

Clarete, R. and B. Diokno (1994) 'Relative Marginal Tax Collection Costs of Border and Domestic Taxes: Case of Philippines', preliminary draft, IDRC International Development Research Center, Ottawa, Canada.

Devarajan, S. and C. Sussangkarn (1991) 'Effective Rates of Protection when Domestic and Foreign Goods are Imperfect Substitutes: The case of Thailand', *Review of Economics and Statistics*, vol. 73.

Devarajan, S. and D. Rodrik (1990) 'Pro-competitive Effects of Trade Reform: Results From a CGE Model of Cameroon', *European Economic Review*, vol. 34.

Easterly, W. and K. Schmidt-Hebbel (1992) *Fiscal Deficit and Macroeconomic Performance in Developing Countries*, CECMG, the World Bank.

Frankel, J. and A. Razin (1989) *Fiscal Policies and the World Economy*, Cambridge, Mass.: the MIT Press.

Government of Côte d'Ivoire (1993) *Direction d'emploi et de la réglementation du travail*, Abidjan, Côte d'Ivoire.

Guillaumont, S. (1988) 'Dévaluer en Afrique?' *Observation et diagnostics économiques*, no. 25.

Gupta, S. and K. Nashashibi (1992) 'The Fiscal Dimensions of Adjustment', *Finance and Development*, vol. 29.

Hamilton, B. and J. Whalley (1986) 'Border Tax Adjustments and U.S. Trade', *Journal of International Economics*, vol. 22.

Honohan, P. (1990) *Monetary Cooperation in the CFA Zone*, World Bank working paper no. 389.

Kay, J. A. (1990) 'Tax Policy: A Survey', *The Economic Journal*, vol. 100.

Krumm, K. (1985) *Adjustment Policies in the Ivory Coast in the Framework of UMOA*, World Bank discussion paper no. 19856.

L'Heriteau, M. F. (1987) *La zone franc dans une perspective d'adjustement et de croissance*, Caisse Centrale de Coopération Économique, Pakar, Senegal.

L'Heriteau, M. F. (1990) *Le FCFA: taux de change et adjustement*, Caisse Centrale de Coopération Économique, Pakar, Senegal.

O'Connell, S. (1988) *Fiscal Policy in Low Income Africa*, working paper no. 39.

Özler, S. and D. Rodrik (1992) 'External Shocks, Politics and Private Investment', *Journal of Development Economics*, vol. 53.

Samen, S. (1990) *Protection effective et développement industriel: l'exemple du Cameroun* Paris: Presses Universitaires de France.

Shah, A. and J. Whalley (1991) 'Tax Incidence Analysis of Developing Countries: An Alternative View', *The World Bank Economic Review*, vol. 5.

Schneider, H. (1992) *Adjustement et équité en Côte d'Ivoire*, Paris: Organization for Economic Cooperation and Development.

Thill, J. (1991) *Fiscalité et adjustement structurel en Afrique francophone*, Ministère de la coopération française, Paris.

8

Using a Computable General Equilibrium (CGE) Model to Evaluate the Singapore Tax System

Chia Ngee Choon

Introduction

Singapore is an island city state with a population of 3 million people and a land area of 641 square kilometres. Except for its strategic location and well-trained labour force, Singapore does not have any other natural endowments. Tax policies are often derived from land and labour policies whose main goal is to maintain economic competitiveness and growth. Fiscal policies have also been utilized to allocate resources to certain priority sectors to maximize economic growth. The general consensus is that sound economic policy has played an important role in the economic success of Singapore. A recent World Bank report on the *East Asian Miracle* (1993) also highlighted the importance of the role of government in orchestrating the economic growth of Singapore. In addition to economic priorities, fiscal policies target social objectives. These include reducing road congestion via vehicle ownership and usage taxes; social engineering through personal income tax measures relating to the number of children; and a foreign worker levy to obtain the desired mix of local and foreign workers in various sectors.

A 'paternal approach' is an appropriate description of tax policies in Singapore. Tax policies over the last three decades have been dynamic and flexible, adjusting to the changing needs of the economy. They have varied for each phase of economic development in Singapore. At the initial stage of development in the early 1960s, when an export promotion strategy was adopted to solve the problem of massive unemployment, tax incentives were used liberally to attract multinational manufacturing companies utilizing light to medium labour-intensive technology.[1]

By the late 1970s, Singapore had attained full employment and was faced with a serious labour shortage. The main concern of economic restructuring in 1979 was to maintain international competitiveness *vis-à-vis* the rest of the Asian newly industrialized countries. Tax incentives were used extensively to phase out labour-intensive activities and promote higher value-added, more technology and capital-intensive operations. Incentives were given to promote automation, mechanization, and research and development. In addition, aggressive and active fiscal policies were used to promote the growth of the financial centre, which was identified as another priority sector.

In the late 1980s, with increased globalization of the world economy and having established a well-developed infrastructure and telecommunications system, tax policy was utilized to nourish the growth of yet another priority sector, namely the producer service sector. This sector includes activities such as banking and finance, insurance, telecommunications, research, management, consulting, engineering and design, software and data processing.

The 1990s have witnessed increasing economic liberalization in many Asian countries resulting in their increased integration with the rest of the world. Singapore's growth strategy has been to tap these booming markets. In the recent budget tax incentives were given to develop the 'external' wing of the economy.[2] While tax policies are used to achieve economic and social objectives, it is well-known that they induce inefficiency by distorting production and consumption decisions. Resources move from more to less heavily taxed sectors, and households substitute away from more to less heavily taxed goods. Tax-induced distortions in behaviour can lead to inefficient allocation of resources. As taxes change the economic equilibrium, they alter the prices of goods and relative factor prices, changing the distribution of economic welfare.

This chapter uses a general equilibrium model to evaluate the effects of the Singapore tax system on resource allocation and income distribution. When one considers the intersectoral effects of tax changes, the need for a general equilibrium model to analyse tax policies becomes clear. For example, changes in corporate income tax affect the demand for capital, resulting in a new equilibrium rental price for capital. This in turn affects the income of capital owners, which changes the demand for consumer goods. Therefore, to study the incidence and welfare effects of taxes, it is important to capture effects on users and suppliers. Partial equilibrium tax incidence studies, such as that by Pechman and Okner (1974), cannot capture these general equilibrium effects.

The first numerical general equilibrium model was used by Shoven and Whalley (1972) to evaluate the incidence of corporate income tax for the United States. This methodology has since been applied to many public finance and trade policy issues for other countries. Besides the United States, general equilibrium models have been used to analyse tax and trade policies in, for example, the United Kingdom (Piggott and Whalley, 1985) and Canada (Hamilton and Whalley, 1989). General equilibrium models applied to developing countries include studies on the Philippines (Clarete and Whalley, 1987) and Mexico (Serra-Puche, 1984).[3] The World Bank has also applied computable general equilibrium (CGE) models to developing countries.[4] Recently, general equilibrium modelling techniques have been used to address environmental issues, for example, Jorgenson and Wilcoxen (1991) and Whalley and Wigle (1990).

This chapter is organized as follows: the next section is a summary of the main features of the Singapore tax structure, followed by a description of the model structure and its numerical implementation. An evaluation is then made of the efficiency and distributive impacts of the alternative tax policy options, and finally a summary given of the major findings and a discussion of some of the policy implications.

The tax structure of Singapore

In this section we will provide an overview of the major characteristics of the Singapore fiscal system and compare it with those of the Association of South East Asian (ASEAN) countries, South Korea and some selected industrial countries. One distinctive characteristic of the Singapore fiscal system is a budgetary surplus, which has been achieved since 1968 (including the recession year of 1985). Another characteristic is the low income tax burden, 7.58 per cent, compared to the developed countries (Australia, Canada, Japan, the USA and the UK) where income tax, on average, forms 12.3 per cent of GDP. However it is higher than the Philippines and Thailand (see Table 8.1).

The aggregate fiscal indicators in Table 8.1 reveal another distinctive feature of Singapore's fiscal system: the importance of non-tax revenue. Singapore has the highest ratio of non-tax revenue as a percentage of gross domestic product (GDP) of all the countries in the sample. Non-tax revenue includes investment incomes, revenue from the sale of land leases, sale of goods and services, fines and various fees, and regulatory charges such as collections from motor vehicle quota premiums and foreign worker levies.

Table 8.1   Aggregate fiscal indicators, 1991 (as % of GDP)

	Total revenue	Current revenue	Tax revenue	Non-tax revenue	Income tax
Indonesia	18.16	18.16	16.74	1.42	10.54
Malaysia	28.53	28.50	21.20	7.30	9.57
Philippines	17.48	17.15	14.64	2.50	4.88
Singapore	32.80	28.12	18.70	9.42	7.58
Thailand	24.22	24.21	22.36	1.85	6.24
South Korea	17.63	17.22	15.42	1.80	5.38
Australia	27.11	27.07	24.39	2.67	17.53
Canada	20.12	20.12	17.77	2.34	10.55
Japan	14.38	14.34	13.59	0.75	9.92
UK	37.05	36.98	33.77	3.20	13.45
US	19.84	19.83	18.24	1.59	10.06

Source: Calculated from IMF (1993).

Table 8.2   Tax mix in Singapore and selected Asian and industrial countries, 1991 (as % of total tax revenue)

	Income taxes	Social security and payroll taxes	Property taxes	Domestic taxes on goods and services	Trade taxes	Others
Indonesia	62.97 (86.96)	0.00	2.24	28.52	5.50	0.77
Malaysia	45.14	1.06	0.43	27.20	23.06	3.12
Philippines	33.34	0.00	0.29	30.27	33.32	2.78
Singapore	40.55	0.00	10.28	34.32	3.27	11.59
Thailand	27.90	0.78	2.52	47.24	20.70	0.86
South Korea	34.90	5.59	1.62	37.14	10.23	5.77
Australia	71.86	1.42	0.27	22.81	3.64	0.00
Canada	59.35	15.31	0.00	21.25	3.96	0.13
Japan	72.98	0.00	4.76	17.83	1.41	3.03
UK	39.81	17.73	8.70	33.66	0.09	0.00
US	55.12	38.12	1.08	4.08	1.59	0.01

Table 8.2 compares the tax mix in Singapore with that of Asian and selected OECD countries. Income tax is the main source of tax revenue, constituting almost 41 per cent of total revenue. In the sample of developed countries, personal income tax is more important than the corporate income tax as a revenue source. Singapore, however, relies more on the corporate income tax; on average, corporate income taxes comprised 70 per cent of total income tax revenue between 1975 to 1987. Table 8.2 also shows that unlike Canada, the USA and the UK, who rely heavily on social security and payroll tax, there are no such taxes in Singapore. Singapore has a fully-funded system where there is a one-to-one correspondence between contributions and benefit payments. Being a free port, Singapore has very low trade taxes. The relative importance of consumption-based taxes is comparable to that for other countries in the sample. Appendix 1 describes the main features and issues of the Singapore tax structure.

A numerical general equilibrium model for Singapore

The general equilibrium model used here is for a competitive, small open-price-taking economy. The model consists of 21 sectors producing four non-traded goods, four quasi-traded goods and 13 tradeable goods.[5] The sectors in the detailed *input–output table* were aggregated to give an indication of the impact of alternative tax policies on the main sectors of the Singapore economy, namely primary industry, construction, manufacturing, utilities, commerce, transport and communications, financial and business services, services and the government sector. Since manufacturing is the largest economic activity, accounting for 23 per cent of GNP, it is further disaggregated into 10 industries.

Each sector uses two primary factors and sector-specific capital. All variable factors are assumed to be perfectly mobile across sectors; capital is internationally mobile but not labour. All factors are fully employed with payments to factor owners being income for the households. There are eight household types consuming 15 types of consumer goods. Each household is endowed with exogenous fixed amounts of the variable and sector-specific capital. All taxes levied in Singapore are incorporated in the model.

As all agents in the economy are assumed to be neo-classical utility maximizers, by solving the maximization problem a system of excess demand equations for the commodities and factor demands can be derived. The model then solves for equilibrium product and factor prices, activity levels and tax revenue that would satisfy all the equilibrium conditions; that is, market clearing for all goods and factors, the zero profit condition holding for every sector, trade balance and budget balance for all households and the government. The model is solved using MPS/GE (Rutherford, 1989).

Model structure

Appendix 2 contains a glossary of terms used to describe the model.

Production sector

There are two levels of nesting. At the top level, producers in sector j use composite intermediate input (A_j) and value-added (VA_j) to produce output (Q_j). It is a Leontief production function, which combines A_j and VA_j in fixed proportions. A Leontief function is used because we assume there is no substitution between A_j and VA_j.

$$Q_j = \min (A_j, VA_j) \quad j = 1 \dots 21$$

For intermediate inputs a Leontief input–output technology is assumed for intermediate demands. Let A_{ij} be the amount of intermediate inputs i used in sector j and let a_{ij} be the fixed intermediate input–output coefficient. The demand for intermediate inputs by sector j is:

$$A_{ij} = a_{ij}Q_j \quad i = 1 \dots 21$$

A Leontief specification for intermediate inputs implies that demand for intermediate inputs depends only on the technical requirements (a_{ij}) and is independent of prices.[6]

For industry value-added functions, value-added (VA_j) has two sub-levels of nesting. The first sub-level is a Cobb–Douglas function of a composite of variable factors (M_j) and a sector-specific capital (F_j). It is necessary to introduce F_j to avoid the problem of extreme specialization typical in a small open economy under homogeneous product assumption. F_j are immobile across sectors.

Sub-level 1: Cobb–Douglas function of M and F[7].   At the first sub-level, *VA* is a Cobb-Douglas function of *M* and *F*:

$$VA = M^{\beta} F^{1-\beta}$$

Let p_m be the composite of the composite variable factors. Let π_F and π_F^* represent the net-of-tax and gross-of-tax price of the sector-specific capital such that $\pi_F^* = \pi_F(1 + t_F)$, where t_F is the tax rate levied on the sector-specific capital. If the sector-specific capital is constrained at the level F, then the restricted profit maximization problem is :

$$\text{Max } \pi_{va} VA - (\pi_m M + \pi_f \bar{F})$$

subject to:

$$VA = M^{\beta} \bar{F}^{1-\beta}$$

Solving, we obtain the demand for *M*:

$$M = \left\{ \frac{\pi_m}{\beta \, \pi_{va}} \right\}^{1/(\beta-1)} \bar{F}$$

Sub-level 2: M is a CES function of K and L:.   *M* is a CES function of labour (*L*) and variable capital (*K*). *L* and *K* are perfectly mobile across sectors. Let ϕ be the efficiency parameter; δ_k be the distribution of factor *k* and σ_v be the elasticity of substitution between the factors. The CES composite *M* is given by:

$$M = \phi[\delta L^{(\sigma_v-1)/\sigma_v} + (1-\delta)K^{(\sigma_v-1)/\sigma_v}]^{\sigma_v/(\sigma_v-1)}$$

Demand for variable factors.   Factor demands are derived from cost-minimizing behaviour. Let π_L^* and π_K^* represent the gross of tax price of the factors *L* and *K* respectively. Let π_L and π_K represent the net-of-tax price received by *L* and *K* respectively. If t_L and t_K are the tax rates levied on *L* and *K* respectively, then,

$$\pi_L^* = \pi_L(1 + t_L) \tag{8.1}$$

$$\pi_K^* = \pi_K(1 + t_K) \tag{8.2}$$

Producers in sector *j* solve the following problem: minimizing the after-tax factor cost subject to *M* is 1. The Lagrangean is:

$$\psi = \pi_L^* L + \pi_K^* K + \lambda \left\{ 1 - \phi[\delta L^{(\sigma_v-1)/\sigma_v} + (1-\delta)K^{(\sigma_v-1)/\sigma_v}]^{\sigma_v/(\sigma_v-1)} \right\}$$

Solving the Lagrangean yields the derived demand for L and K per unit of M, represented by f_1 and f_2 respectively:

$$f_1 = \frac{1}{\phi}\left\{(1-\delta)\left(\frac{\delta\pi_K^*}{(1-\delta)\pi_L^*}\right)^{1-\sigma_v} + \delta\right\}^{\sigma_v/(1-\sigma_v)}$$

$$f_2 = \frac{1}{\phi}\left\{\delta\left(\frac{(1-\delta)\pi_L^*}{\delta\pi_K^*}\right)^{1-\sigma_v} + (1-\delta)\right\}^{\sigma_v/(1-\sigma_v)}$$

Demand sector

The demand side of the economy is represented by the government and eight household groups differentiated according to income. Each household is different in terms of their initial endowments and preferences over consumer goods (G_i) and leisure (l). The consumer good G_i is fixed coefficient combination of the 21 products $X_j (j = 1 \ldots 21)$ via a transformation matrix (Z_{ji}).

In the central variant of the model, preferences are represented as a two-level nested CES function (U_2 and U_3).[8] Household saving (S^h) is exogenously determined as a fixed proportion of income. S is transferred to a fictitious investment agent who invests savings in new vintage capital, which corresponds to the fixed capital formation as given in the Input–Output table. Investment in the static model is therefore 'savings-driven'.

Each household has a fixed exogenous endowment of labour, capital and sector-specific factors. Income of household $h(Y^h)$ consists of factor payments from labour and capital; rents from the endowed sector-specific factor and transfers from government, given as:

$$Y^h = \sum_{k=1}^{3} \pi_K \omega_k^h + \alpha_h \lceil$$

where $\lceil$ is the total government transfer; α_h is the proportion of government transfer to household h; ω_k^h represents household h's share of economy endowment of factor k, and π_k is the rental price received by households as factor owners, and is net of all factor taxes, and π_k is equal to one in the benchmarking.

At the second level, the household solves the following problem:[9]

$$\max U_2 = \left\{\beta_l G^{(\sigma_l-1)/\sigma_l} + (1+\beta_l)/^{(\sigma_l-1)/\sigma_l}\right\}^{\sigma_l/(\sigma-1)}$$

subject to:

$$p_g G + p_l I = Y_d - p_s S$$

Solving, yields the optimum G and l:

$$G = \frac{\beta_l(Y_d - p_s S)}{p_g^{\sigma_l}[\beta_l^{\sigma_l} p_g^{1-\sigma_l} + (1 - \beta_l)^{\sigma_l} p_l^{\sigma_l}]}$$

At the third-level nesting, the maximization problem is:

$$\max U_3 = \sum_{i=1}^{14} Y_i \log G_i$$

subject to:

$$\sum_{i=1}^{14} p_i(1 + T_i)G_i = Y_d - p_s S - p_l I$$

Taking the first-order condition gives the demand for each consumer good $i(= 1 \ldots 14)$.

$$G_i = \frac{Y_i(Y_d - p_s S - p_l I)}{p_i(1 + T_i)}$$

The above equation implies that any change in the tax rates (T_i) will affect the demands for G_i, which will, in turn, influence the production of Q_j. These would then affect factor demands and the equilibrium factor prices, hence affecting a household's income.

Since utility functions are well-defined, individual demand functions and hence market demand functions are continuous for all strictly positive price vectors and satisfy Walras' Law. Aggregating across all the households' demands yields the market demand for consumer good i, given by:

$$\overline{G}_i = \sum_h G_i^h$$

The aggregate excess demand for sectoral good j is given by:

$$XD_j = Z_{ji}\overline{G}_i - Q_j$$

where Z_{ji} is a transformation matrix linking the sectoral goods j to the consumer goods i.

Government sector

The government sector refers to the producers of government services – such as public administration, economic and social planning, defence and security services – which are normally provided at nominal cost to the public. Other profit-earning enterprises and statutory boards are treated like other producer sectors in the economy.

The government collects all the tax revenue (R) and spends part of the revenue (βR) on goods and services. The remainder is either redistributed back to households as transfers (f) or saved as government savings (S^g). The government has a utility function defined over the producer goods and savings. From the government utility function, is calculated the corresponding expenditure function. From the counterfactual tax regimes is calculated the revenue that is required to restore the government to the benchmark utility level at any set of prices. This is because with different tax regimes there are different equilibrium prices, so that the same dollars of revenue collected will not yield the same utility.

External sector

External sector closure refers to the assumptions made on export demand and import supply.[10] The small open price-taking economy (SOPTE) model used here assumes domestic and foreign goods to be perfect substitutes (the non-Armington assumption). The use of this assumption avoids the major problems associated with the use of the Armington assumptions, namely (1) the need to specify the degree of substitutability between domestic and imported products, and (2) the large terms-of-trade effects which tend to dominate the welfare effects. However, the major drawback of using the non-Armington assumption is that we need to specify some sector-specific factors to avoid problems of extreme specialization in the numerical simulations. Data on these factors are often not available.

For a SOPTE model, prices of traded goods are determined by the world markets, whereas prices of non-traded goods are endogenously determined. For a SOPTE model, in the absence of non-traded goods, the given world prices will fully characterize the equilibrium. With non-traded goods, the relative price between traded and non-traded goods becomes endogenous. Relative prices will adjust until excess demands of non-traded goods are negative. So long as there is market clearance for non-traded goods, trade balance will hold by Walras' Law.

Investment and savings

Although the basic variant model is static, for internal consistency we have to specify the savings and investment behaviour. Savings are assumed to be transformed into new vintage capital (V) without any time lag. An investment activity produces V, which is different from capital today K in the production function. For an open economy, two sources of savings are available – foreign and domestic. Capital inflow is modelled as foreign savings. Domestic savings include S^h and S^g. In equilibrium, total investment is equal to total savings:

$$p_s V = \sum_h p_s S^h + p_s S^g$$

Equilibrium conditions

The behaviours of profit maximization for producers and utility maximization for consumers yield the producers' demands for intermediate inputs and factors and consumers' demands for consumer goods, respectively. The competitive market equilibrium in the presence of taxes is defined by a vector of factor and product prices, activity levels, income and tax revenue such that the following equilibrium conditions hold:

(i)   *Market clearing for all goods and factors*:

$$\sum_{j=1}^{21} f_{1j} Q_j \leq \overline{N}_1 = \sum_{h=1}^{8} (L_s^h - I^h)$$

$$\sum_{j=1}^{21} f_{kj} Q_j \leq \overline{N}_k$$

$$\sum_{i=1}^{15} \sum_{h=1}^{8} Z_{ji} G_i^h + \sum_{i=1}^{21} a_{ij} Q_j \leq Q_j$$

(ii)   *All sectors ($j = 1 \ldots 21$) earn economic zero profit*:

$$(1 - t_{pj}) \pi_j = \sum_{k=1}^{3} \pi_k (1 + t_k) f_{kj} + \sum_{i=1}^{21} \pi_i a_{ij}$$

Other properties of equilibrium are:

$$\sum_{i=1}^{14} p_i (1 + T_i) G_i^h + p_s S^h + p_l I^h = (1 - T_h) \sum_{k=1}^{3} \pi_k \omega_k^h + \alpha_h] = Y_d$$

(i)   *Budget balance for all households ($h = 1 \ldots 8$)*
(ii)   *Budget balance for the government*:

$$\sum_{i=1}^{14} p_i (1 + T_i) G_i^g + p_s S_g + p_\lceil \lceil = R^T + \sum_{k=1}^{3} \pi_k \omega_k^g$$

Numerical implementation

To implement the model numerically, I follow the procedure of counterfactual equilibrium analysis developed by Mansur and Whalley (1984). This approach involves calibrating the model to an equilibrium data-set, assumed to be a representative equilibrium of the economy for the year 1983.[11]

Following the Harberger (1962) tradition, in the benchmark equilibrium all quantities and net-of-tax prices are scaled to one. This unit convention is used because it allows the translation of data, which are in value terms, into observations of physical quantities. For example, assuming the net-of-tax price of labour to be one, the quantity of labour demanded by sector *i* is determined simply from the value-added data on labour in sector *i*. With this separation complete, model calibration is straightforward for Cobb–Douglas functions and is implemented for the CES functions in the ways described in Mansur and Whalley (1984) using elasticity parameters from related literature.

Simulation experiments and results

The model described in the preceding section is used to analyse the allocative and distributive impacts of Singapore's tax system. A number of simulations were run under alternative equal-yield tax policy options. In the counter-factual equal-yield tax experiments, the revenue that is required to restore the government to the benchmark utility level at the new equilibrium set of prices is computed by setting the tax rate for the lump-sum tax endogenously.

To evaluate the efficiency and distributive effects of the existing tax in Singapore, all existing taxes are replaced with a yield-preserving and broad-based lump-sum tax. Then the welfare gain from such a non-distortionary lump-sum tax is computed. To compare the efficiency and distributive impacts of each tax, counterfactual equilibria are computed by piecewise abolition of each tax and replacing it by an equal yield lump-sum tax. Policy evaluation is done by comparing the counterfactual equilibrium with the benchmark equilibrium, using the Hicksian compensating variations (*CV*) and equivalent variations (*EV*).

Efficiency and distributive impacts of the overall tax system

Efficiency cost of the entire tax system

Table 8.3 shows the deadweight loss induced by the tax system. Efficiency cost is reported in terms of different welfare measures. The arithmetic sums of welfare gains/losses over all households in terms of *CV* and *EV* are S$553.8 million and S$570.3 million, respectively. The annual welfare cost of the tax system is around 1.8 per cent of GNP. The amount of distortion created by the tax system represents 14.5 per cent of the total tax revenue collected. However, the amount of cost inflicted on society by the tax system is relatively small compared to other studies. For example, the tax/subsidy system in the United Kingdom introduces a welfare cost amounting to 7.6 per cent of GNP (Piggot and Whalley 1985).

Table 8.3   Aggregate welfare impacts of the 1983 Singapore tax system using different welfare measures (central case replacement: all tax distortions are abolished and replaced by an equal yield non-distorting tax)

Aggregate welfare measures:	
1. Arithmetic sum of CV across all households (S$m)	553.8
2. Arithmetic sum of EV across all households (S$m)	570.3
3. $\sum CV$ as per cent of counterfactual GDP	1.8
4. $\sum EV$ as per cent of benchmark GDP	1.76
5. $\sum CV$ as per cent of benchmark of tax revenue	14.5

One possible explanation for the smaller efficiency cost of the Singapore tax system could be due to the smaller effort ratio in Singapore. Effort ratio, which measures the proportion of GNP that has been withdrawn by taxes, is 20 per cent for Singapore compared to 56 per cent for the UK. Another possible reason for the small tax subsidy distortions is that in Singapore, while the government adopts a paternalistic attitude to most social issues, old age savings and health care have been largely left to the individual.

Distributive impacts of the overall tax system

Table 8.4 reports on the income distribution impacts of the tax system in terms of welfare loss as a percentage of their benchmark income and summary statistics such as the Gini coefficient, the coefficient of variation and the Atkinson index. With the replacement of all taxes by a lump-sum tax, the top 5 per cent of households realize huge welfare gains at $625.67m (7.52% of benchmark net of tax income), and the bottom 10 per cent of households suffer a welfare loss of $39.97m (3.05% of benchmark net-of-tax income). The welfare gains and losses for the middle-income households are smaller. The larger Gini coefficient (which increases by 10.23%) indicates that income inequality increases with the replacement of existing taxes. The coefficient of variation, which emphasizes movement in the upper tail of the income distribution, changes substantially, indicating the relatively high income tax liability faced by this group of households. The Atkinson index also confirms that the replacement of the existing tax system worsens the income distribution.

There is significant redistribution in the overall tax system. This is contrary to partial equilibrium studies by Pechman and Okner (1974) who indicate that there is negligible redistribution in the tax system since the progressivity of the personal income tax system offsets the regressivity of the sales tax.[12] Piggot and Whalley's result also indicates significant redistribution in the tax system, with most of the redistribution coming from housing subsidies. The redistributive feature of the Singapore tax system comes mainly from the personal income tax (PIT). To isolate the impact of PIT on redistribution, the counterfactual is re-run with the PIT left in place. As expected, the distributional impact becomes less extreme. Instead of gaining 7.5 per cent of benchmark income, the top income decile gains around 4 per cent. The bottom income group loses 0.25 per cent of the benchmark gross income instead of 3 per cent when PIT is abolished together with all other taxes. The smaller increase in the Gini coefficient in the new equilibrium (2.7 % increase from benchmark) indicates that income inequality is less pronounced when the broadly-based PIT is left in place.

Effects on outputs, prices and factor demands

Table 8.5 shows that there is a substantial increase in the output of the banking and finance sector in the simulation, indicating that this sector is heavily taxed under the existing tax system. Output from the construction, real estate and retail trade sector also increases. Except for the food and beverage sector, there is a fall in production in the various manufacturing sectors, confirming the preferential tax treatment received by this sector. The increase in output of the food and beverage sector largely reflects the abolition of excises. This result implies that the recent tax changes to extend preferential tax treatment to the service sector might increase production in the service sector.

Since this is a small open price-taking economy, prices of tradeables are given by the world market and depend on the movement of the exchange rate. The exchange rate depreciates in the simulation. There is significant price movement in the non-traded sector and a substantial increase in the demand for labour services in the banking and finance, real estate, construction and retail trade sectors. This seems to be a direct impact from the increase in production in these sectors.

Marginal welfare cost

In this sub-section we simulate the marginal welfare cost of individual components of the tax system when the tax rate is increased by 0.1 per cent. The marginal welfare cost (MWC) is shown Table 8.6. The MWC of raising a dollar of revenue from indirect taxes, such as the excises on consumption and the indirect production taxes, is significantly higher than a dollar raised from direct taxes. This is because, at the time of the study, excises on consumption are levied at very high rates and on narrowly-based commodities such as liquor, tobacco, sugar and petroleum. This result implies that a cut in direct taxes results in lower welfare gains than a cut in indirect taxes. This has implications for the tax reform of introducing a consumption tax and reducing personal and corporate income tax and changing the composition of direct and indirect taxes in the tax system.

Table 8.4 Distribution and efficiency impacts of replacing the 1983 Singapore tax system with a lum-sum tax and when personal income tax (PIT) is left in place

Household types (monthly gross-of-tax income)	% of households	All taxes abolished				All taxes except PIT abolished	
		Hicksian EV ($m)	EV as % of benchmark income	Share of net-of-tax income		Hicksian EV ($m)	EV as % of benchmark income
				Benchmark	New equilibrium		
HH1 (less than $500)	16.03	−39.97	−3.05	4.04	3.63	−3.32	−0.25
HH2 ($500–999)	28.01	−73.51	−1.93	11.78	10.87	60.52	1.59
HH3 ($1000–1499)	18.60	−36.24	−0.90	12.45	11.75	45.31	1.12
HH4 ($1500–1999)	11.22	−23.41	−0.68	10.67	10.14	28.72	0.83
HH5 ($2000–2999)	12.14	−0.66	−0.01	16.16	15.85	57.68	1.10
HH6 ($3000–3999)	5.96	55.12	1.49	11.43	11.53	63.45	1.71
HH7 ($4000–4999)	3.13	63.25	2.51	7.77	8.00	51.04	2.03
HH8 ($5000 and above)	4.92	625.67	7.52	25.68	28.21	328.63	3.95

Summary statistics:
$\sum EV$ over all households $570.25m $632.05m
$\sum EV$ as % of benchmark GDP   1.76%   1.95%

Gini coefficient (benchmark=0.3369) :   0.3753
Coefficient of variations (benchmark=0.4703) :   0.5308
Atkinson Index ($e = 0$):   0.1017
Atkinson Index ($e = 1.0$):   0.1957

Table 8.5 Effects of abolition of all taxes on factor demands, output and prices, and sensitivity of these impacts to elasticity of substitution between factors

Aggregated sectoral groups	Central case elasticity			$skl = 2.0$			Central case		$skl = 2.0$	
	Labour	Capital	Specific factor	Labour	Capital	Specific factor	Output $b^2 = 1$	Price $b = 1$	Output $b = 1$	Price $b = 1$
1. Tradables										
Primary production	−7.83	−10.40	12.73	−25.02	−31.19	38.36	0.8909	0.7567	0.7272	0.7442
Manufacturing	−0.84	−5.55	10.86	−7.33	−19.44	50.21	0.9318	0.7567	0.7248	0.7427
Petroleum refining	−1.25	−2.63	14.87	−15.29	−24.83	133.25	0.8705	0.7567	0.4287	0.7442
2. Quasi-tradables										
Retail trade	2.68	−2.48	−4.86	3.39	−5.54	−4.05	1.0510	0.7567	1.0421	0.7442
Transport & communication	−6.36	−15.64	13.55	−15.63	−30.65	29.95	0.8806	0.7567	0.7695	0.7442
Finance	14.13	2.56	−33.68	26.83	3.73	−61.41	1.5077	0.7567	2.5915	0.7442
Services	−7.84	12.78	2.70	−15.76	27.80	1.01	0.9736	0.7740	0.9899	0.7658
3. Non-tradables										
Government services	0.05	−4.19	6.61	−2.73	−9.65	17.06	0.9996	0.7941	0.9983	0.7910
Utilities	1.23	−3.08	−1.19	1.74	−5.53	−1.47	0.9380	0.7872	0.8542	0.7776
Construction							1.0120	0.7850	1.0149	0.7790
Real estate	6.97	5.18	−2.36	23.67	14.77	−7.47	1.0241	0.8559	1.0806	0.7453

Notes: [1] skl = Elasticity of substitution between capital and labour;
 [2] b = Benchmark value.

Table 8.6 Marginal welfare cost of increasing different components of the taxes by 0.1 per cent

	Cents per dollar of revenue collected
1. Personal income tax	15
2. Corporate income tax	4
3. Payroll tax	14
4. Selective excises	82
5. Indirect production tax	25

Efficiency and distributive impacts of other components of the tax system

To analyse the structural features of the tax system, counterfactual equilibria are computed with piecewise abolition of the components of the tax system. These counterfactuals provide possible direction for future tax changes. Figure 8.1 shows the distributive impact of each tax. Table 8.7 shows the efficiency and distributive effects from these counterfactuals using the central

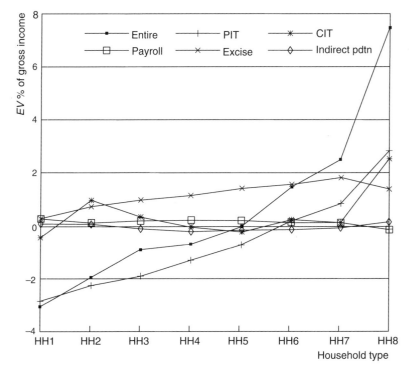

Figure 8.1   Distribution of welfare gain/loss of households, in terms of Hicksian *EV* as percentage of benchmark income

variant of the model and in the extended model where savings are endogenous. Results on efficiency cost using different welfare criteria are presented in Table 8.7. All income groups gain from elimination of excises. The lower income group loses from abolition of PIT, while the higher income group loses from abolition of the corporate income tax (CIT). The main results emerging from each simulation are discussed in turn.

Personal income tax (PIT)

It is interesting to note that abolishing the PIT results in a welfare loss (measured in terms of $\sum EV$). This is because in this model with labour-leisure choice, leisure is subsidized at the effective marginal tax rate. Abolition of the PIT indicates a loss in subsidy and could be welfare-worsening. However, if hypothetical lump-sum transfers are allowed across households so that all households' welfare have the same proportionate change, this same experiment results in a potential welfare improvement of 1.95 per cent from the benchmark.[13]

Corporate income tax (CIT)

The efficiency cost of the corporate income tax (CIT) is the highest after excises, at 0.78 per cent of benchmark GNP, and is generally progressive. This figure is also higher than the estimate obtained by Harberger (1962) using US data. It is interesting to note that the banking sector gains most from the abolition of CIT, not the manufacturing sector, as the former has a higher effective tax rate. The output from the banking sector increases by 48 per cent, while that of the manufacturing sector falls by 9.5 per cent with capital costs increasing by 24 per cent.

Payroll tax

The overall efficiency gains from replacing the payroll tax is small compared to the replacement of the other taxes. Households in the lowest income decile, who receive most of their income from labour, are better off. However, in terms of deadweight loss as a per cent of the replaced tax revenue, payroll tax is the most distortionary. This is because although the rate is low, the variance of the effective tax rates across sectors is relatively high causing intersectoral distortion and penalizing sectors that are more intensive in low-skill labour.[14]

Excises

There is a large welfare gain from abolishing excises compared to abolition of the PIT, CIT, payroll taxes or the indirect production tax. The normative proportionate increase in households' welfare is 1.45 per cent, while the total monetary gain is 1.23 per cent of benchmark GNP. The effective excise varies widely across consumer goods, with very high rates imposed on a few commodities.

Table 8.7 Sensitivity of efficiency, cost and distributive impacts of taxes to alternative treatment of savings

A. Efficiency impacts

	Pareto equalizing welfare level[1]		$\sum EV$ as % of benchmark income	
	Exogenous savings	Endogenous savings	Exogenous savings	Endogenous savings
Entire tax system	6.78	2.36	1.76	0.65
Personal income tax	2.43	1.11	-0.05	0.08
Corporate income tax	2.12	1.86	0.78	-0.25
Payroll tax	0.29	0.27	0.10	0.34
Selective excises	1.47	0.71	1.23	0.97
Indirect production taxes	0.21	0.80	-0.01	-0.08

B. Distributive impacts

	Gini coefficient		Coefficient of variation		Atkinson index	
	Exo. savings	Endo. savings	Exo. savings	Endo. savings	Exo. savings	Endo. savings
Entire tax system	0.3753	0.4414	0.5308	0.5208	0.1957	0.1889
Personal income tax	0.3641	0.4458	0.5117	0.5146	0.1884	0.1766
Corporate income tax	0.3434	0.3438	0.4899	0.4904	0.1596	0.1599
Payroll tax	0.3362	0.3380	0.4772	0.4797	0.1554	0.1574
Selective excises	0.3353	0.3353	0.4763	0.4763	0.1542	0.1542
Indirect production taxes	0.3379	0.3380	0.4799	0.4800	0.1567	0.1568

Notes: [1] Welfare impact is also evaluated using the concept of potential welfare gain/loss, based on Kaldor's (1939) weak compensation principle. A positive arithmetic sum of EV indicates that Kaldor's compensation principle is passed. This implies that gainers can compensate the losers while at the same time have an improvement in welfare, so that a *potentially Pareto-improved allocation* exists. It is, therefore, hypothetically possible to undertake costless lump sum redistribution to achieve an allocation such that every household has the same equilibrium welfare level.

Not unexpectedly, the removal of excises causes consumer prices of these items to fall significantly – 25 per cent for motor vehicles, 41 per cent for gasoline and 45 per cent for alcohol and tobacco. Although excises contain items consumed by both the rich and poor, the rich gain significantly (1.34% of benchmark income) from abolition of excises on petroleum, gas and motor vehicles, while the poor gain less (0.2% of benchmark income) mainly from abolition of excises on tobacco.

Replacing both corporate and personal income taxes by an equal-yield consumption value-added tax

One of the proposals for tax reform is to reduce the reliance on direct taxes and increase reliance on indirect taxes. The extreme case is considered in which all direct taxes (both corporate and personal income taxes) are abolished and replaced with an equal-yield consumption tax on all goods and services. This reform tends to be regressive, since the abolition of direct taxes will benefit households at the upper end of the income distribution, but the equal-yield uniform rate consumption tax hits all households equally. On the other hand, removing CIT and PIT is likely to remove inefficiency caused by the differential rates of CIT across sectors and the labour–income distortions caused by PIT, hence leading to welfare gain.

Table 8.8 shows the effects of replacing both corporate and personal income taxes by an equal-yield consumption VAT. A 14.32 per cent comprehensive goods and services tax is needed to maintain the government at the benchmark utility level. As expected, welfare gains and losses vary across households. Households at the upper end of the income distribution (HH4, HH5, HH6, HH7 and HH8) are better off, whereas those at the lower end (HH1, HH2 and HH3) are worse off. As a group, HH8 has a large welfare gain of $108m (or 1.31% of benchmark income). HH1 has a smaller loss in absolute terms ($30.98m) but a larger loss in term of percentage of benchmark income (2.37%). Compared to the benchmark equilibrium, the Gini coefficient has increased by 4.28 per cent.

The welfare gain from this experiment is small at $211.7m or 0.65 per cent of benchmark GNP. However, if we allow hypothetical lump-sum transfers from the gainers to the losers such that all households have the same percentage change in welfare, the potential welfare gain is larger at 1.43 per cent.

Some very interesting results emerge from the demand and price effects from this tax change. Part D of Table 8.8 shows that the demand for luxury goods increases. These goods include motor vehicles, gasoline, alcohol and tobacco. Abolishing both PIT and CIT generated positive income effects and increased demand for luxury goods.

Table 8.8 Efficiency and distributive impacts of replacing corporate and personal income taxes by an equal yield consumption value added tax

A. Distribution of welfare gain/loss:

Household types	Hicksian *EV* ($m)	Hicksian *EV* as % of income
HH1	−30.98	−2.37
HH2	−45.61	−1.20
HH3	−12.69	−0.31
HH4	1.80	0.05
HH5	71.03	1.36
HH6	63.08	1.70
HH7	56.33	2.24
HH8	108.78	1.31

B. Per cent change in Gini coefficient from benchmark: 4.28

C. Potential Pareto welfare gain 1.43

D. Effects on demand and prices of consumer goods (benchmark price and quantity index =1)

Consumer goods	New demand index	%change in demand index	New price index	% change in price index
Food	0.9745	−2.55	0.9980	−0.20
Clothing	0.9838	−1.62	0.9940	−0.60
Accommodation	0.9587	−4.13	1.0201	2.01
Utilities	0.9922	−0.78	0.9791	−2.09
Durables	0.9823	−1.78	0.9914	−0.86
Motor vehicles	1.1614	16.14	0.8534	−14.66
Gasoline	1.4532	45.32	0.6733	−32.67
Tpt & comm.	0.9871	−1.29	0.9844	−1.56
Education	0.9697	−3.03	1.0069	0.69
Health	0.9606	−3.94	1.0167	1.67
Recreation	0.9989	−0.11	0.9815	−1.85
Alc. & tobacco	1.5803	58.03	0.6139	−38.61
Non-durables	0.9714	−2.86	1.0006	0.06
Services	1.0198	1.98	0.9590	−4.10
Savings	0.9784	−2.16	1.0012	0.12
average		6.48		−6.18

Summary and conclusion

The main findings from the simulation experiments and their policy implications are summarized below:

1. The marginal welfare cost of the overall tax system is approximately 20 cents for every dollar of revenue raised. The deadweight loss of raising a dollar from specific excises is greater than direct taxes.

2. The efficiency cost of the existing Singapore tax system, measured in terms of the arithmetic sum of *EV* as a percentage of GNP, is small.
3. There is a significant redistribution in the tax system.
4. The current tax system gives preferential treatment to the manufacturing sector. Abolishing the current tax system and replacing it with an equal yield, non-distorting tax leads to substantial increase in outputs from the banking and finance, construction, real estate and retail trade sectors.
5. Most of the inefficiency in the tax system comes from selective excises. Efficiency costs from the corporate income tax, personal income tax and indirect production taxes are quite small.
6. Most of the redistribution of the tax system comes from personal income taxes.
7. Replacing both personal and corporate income taxes by an equal yield consumption value added tax, without any exemptions, is highly regressive and leads to very small efficiency gains (0.65%), but it enhances international competitiveness (measured by the percentage change in net exports).
8. The efficiency cost of the various tax sources is robust to different elasticity specifications for the production and consumption functions, and to alternative specifications of savings behaviour.
9. The efficiency cost of the tax system, however, is sensitive to the criteria used to measure welfare. When *potential* welfare measure is used, the welfare cost is around 5.4 per cent of GNP.

The tax system before the introduction of the goods and services tax is relatively efficient with a considerable amount of redistribution. Most of the inefficiency in the tax system is due mainly to the presence of specific excises, which are levied at very high rates on a small base. Over the years specific excises for most of the commodities have remained constant, except for motor vehicles. Indeed, motor vehicle-related taxes have proven to be highly revenue-productive, accounting for 23 per cent of the total tax revenue collected in 1992 compared to 15 per cent in 1983. It is therefore expected that distortions from specific excise taxes will have increased. With the introduction of the goods and services tax and in the absence of rebates and offsets, the tax system becomes less progressive though there are some efficiency gains.

Appendix 1: description of the Singapore tax system, 1993

Personal income tax (PIT)

Main Features

1 Levied at progressive rates, ranging from 2.5 to 30 per cent with 14 brackets.

2 Absence of capital income tax.
3 Used to achieve social objectives:
a Encourage procreation for specially qualified women via enhanced child relief and special tax rebates.
b Encourage old-age savings by exempting contributions to the Central Provident Fund from tax base.
4 Reliance on PIT as revenue source has declined over 1980 to 1992.

Differences from other countries

1 No withholding system, income tax payments lag behind a year. PIT collected once a year, not pay as you earn.
2 Extensive use of one-off tax rebates to encourage and reward work effort. Compared to rates reduction, one-off rebates are more flexible and administratively simpler.
3 Compared to the other ASEAN countries, the tax base is large. About 70 per cent of the labour force pays income tax. However, with the introduction of the goods and services tax (GST), coupled with the increase in personal tax reliefs and income tax rebates, about 50% of the labour force will be in the income tax net.
4 Following the US tax reform, many countries adopted a flatter income tax system with fewer brackets. Singapore, however, continues to have 14 brackets to maintain progressivity.

Major issues

1 Distributive and efficiency impacts of PIT.
2 Effects on savings and labour supply.
3 Different gains from tax shelters in different income groups
4 Tax treatment of housing (tax free imputed earnings).
5 Tax evasion by the self-employed.

Corporate income tax (CIT)

Main features

1 Partial integration of PIT and CIT with full imputation. Corporate profits, whether retained or distributed, are taxed at corporate level. However, credit for corporate tax paid will be given when profits are distributed to shareholders.
2 Statutory rate is 27 per cent; long-term target rate is 25 per cent.
3 Effective tax rate is much lower due to the presence of extensive investment incentives, which are biased towards some targeted sectors.

Differences from other countries

1 Provision of incentives to attract foreign investment and to direct resources to priority sectors remains important. This is contrary to other countries (e.g. United States) who have removed or reduced incentives (e.g. Mexico).
2 Unlike most developed countries, PIT is more important than the CIT as a revenue source. On average, from 1975 to 1987 CIT comprised 70 per cent of total income tax revenue. CIT also includes contributions made by the 13 statutory boards under the Statutory Corporations (Contributions to Consolidated Fund) Act 1989.

Major issues

1 Incidence and efficiency cost of CIT.
2 Tax competition among ASEAN countries for foreign investments.

Taxes on consumption

Main features

1 Introduction of goods and services tax (GST) on 1 April 1994. GST is at 3 per cent, levied on all goods and services including necessities. Exports are zero-rated.
2 Customs and excise duties are levied on five main products – liquor, petroleum products, sugar, tobacco and motor vehicles.
3 Selective sales tax on services include taxes on public utilities, entertainment, telecommunications, and so on.

Differences from other countries

1 Taxes on motor vehicles account for about one-quarter of tax revenue collected. The importance of motor vehicle taxes is an outcome of Singapore's land-use policy to reduce vehicle ownership and usage. Revenue from this source has been on an upward trend, while other urban taxes (e.g. property tax) have remained constant.
2 Consumption-based taxes becoming more important revenue sources.

Major issues

1 The efficiency and distributive impacts of introducing the GST.
2 Welfare implications of the motor vehicle taxes and the efficacy of motor vehicle taxes.
3 With an increase in reliance on indirect taxes and a fall in reliance on direct taxes, what are the efficiency and distributive impacts of the tax system?

Taxes on international trade

Main features

1 No export taxes.
2 Import duties levied on a few traditional products.

Differences from other countries

1 Being a free port, taxes on international trade have never been an important source of revenue, even at the initial stage of economic development. This is in sharp contrast to the other ASEAN countries whose trade taxes constitute important sources of tax revenue. For Malaysia, the Philippines and Thailand, they constitute 23 per cent, 33 per cent and 21 per cent, respectively.

Taxes on labour

Main features

1 To regulate the inflow of foreign workers, the use of foreign workers is subject to levies. The levies differ across different sectors and for different types of workers.
2 Employers contribute to the Central Provident Fund.

Differences from other countries

1 No social security tax and payroll tax as in most developed economies. The social security system is fully funded with one-to-one correspondence between contributions and benefit payments.
2 A higher labour cost due to the employer's contribution to the Central Provident Fund. The long-term target rate is set at 20 per cent.

Major issues

1 Labour market distortions created because of differential pricing of labour.
2 The efficiency implications of the compulsory contributions to the Central Provident Fund imposed on employers.

Appendix 2: glossary of notation

Production

Q_j output from sector j
A_j aggregate intermediate inputs to sector j
a_{ij} fixed intermediate input–output coefficient
Q_{ij} amount of output from sector i used in sector j
VA_j value added in sector j

φ_j efficiency parameter in *VA* function
δ_{kj} input intensity of factor k in sector j in *VA* function
σ_{vj} elasticity of substitution between factors k in jth sector
f_{kj} use of the factor k in sector j
t_k ad valorem tax rate on factor k
π_k net-of-tax price received by owners of factor k
L_j labour use, in service units, in sector j
K_j capital use, in service units, in sector j
$\underline{F_j}$ sector-specific capital use, in service units, in sector j
$\overline{N_k}$ total endowment of factor k

Demand sector

Z_{ij} matrix linking consumer good j with sectoral good Q_i
U^h utility function of household h
C_f composite future consumption
C_p composite present consumption
P_f price of C_f
I leisure consumption
G composite consumer good
$\lceil$ total government transfer
α_h proportion of government transfer to household h
ω_w^h share of household h in the endowment of factor k
Y^h gross income of household h
Y_d^h disposable income of household h
T_h marginal income tax rate on Y^h
S^h savings of household h
C_p^h composite current consumption by h
p_c composite price of the present consumption;
p_s price of S (new vintage capital)
U_1^h CES function of C_p^h and C_f^h
σ_c^h elasticity of substitution between C_p and C_f^h for household h
β_c share parameter of C_p and S in U_1^h
G composite consumption good
p_g price of G
l leisure consumption
p_l price of leisure $= p_L(1 - T_h)$
U_2^h CES function of G and l
σ_1 elasticity of substitution between G and l
β_l share parameter of G and l in U_2^h
G_i^h consumption of consumer good i by h
$!_i$ total household consumption of consumer good i ($! \ G_i^h$)
U_3^h Cobb–Douglas function of G_i
Y_i^h share of G_i in U_3^h
T_i ad valorem tax rate on G_i

Appendix 3: numerical implementation of the model

Step 1: derivation of benchmark equilibrium data (BED) set

The database, to which the equilibrium model is calibrated, represents the Singapore economy in 1983. It is a micro-consistent set which satisfies all the equilibrium conditions, namely, market clearing for all goods and factors, a zero profit condition for every sector, budget balance for households and government and external sector balance. The main sources of data used in assembling the BED are: *Singapore Input-Output Tables, Household Expenditure Survey, Census of Industrial Production, Census of Wholesale and Retail Trade, Restaurants and Hotels* and *Survey of Services*. RAS procedure as described in Bacharach (1971) is used to adjust these data from various sources, which often use different definitions, so that they are micro-consistent with one another.

Step 2: calibration

Calibration involve specification of parameters in the model functions so that the model produces the BED set as the equilibrium solution. Calibration of a Cobb–Douglas function is relatively straightforward. For example, scale parameters in the utility for consumer goods are obtained simply from the consumption shares of these goods obtained from the household expenditure survey. Calibration for the utility function between leisure and goods, and between present and future consumption, involves using elasticity of labour supply and saving elasticity estimates from the literature (e.g. Killingsworth, 1983, and Boskin, 1978). Elasticity estimates for the value-added functions are obtained from Toh (1985).

Step 3: counterfactual equilibrium analysis

Alternative tax policies are introduced and the corresponding equilibrium computed (counterfactual equilibrium) and compared to the benchmark equilibrium. Counterfactual equal yield equilibria are computed by endogenously determining the tax rate such that the tax revenue in the new equilibrium will leave the government at the same benchmark utility. This means that the total resources available for private sector use are the same in both equilibria. Others, like Rutherford and Winer (1990), allow the size of the government sector to vary with tax revenue.

Notes

1 In 1995, Singapore introduced the Pioneer Industries Ordinance which allowed for a tax holiday of 5 years, depreciation and net operating loss carryover for investment in pioneer industries. In 1967, tax concessions on profits from export activities and double tax deduction schemes for expenses incurred in the promo-

tion of exports became available under the Economic Expansion Incentives Act. See Chia and Whalley (1994), tables 8.2 and 8.5.

2   These incentives include a unilateral tax credit for dividend income remitted from countries without a double tax avoidance treaty; double tax deduction for expenses incurred in the promotion of exports, exploring and developing overseas investment opportunities. For more details, see Ministry of Trade and Industry (1993), p. 44.

3   See Shoven and Whalley (1984) for a summary of the application of the general equilibrium models to many other studies. Devarajan, Lewis and Robinson (1986) contains a bibliography of computable general equilibrium models applied to developing countries.

4   The work by Adelman and Robinson (1978) on Korea was probably the first and most comprehensive of CGE models. Other CGE country studies include: Turkey by Dervis and Robinson (1978) and Cameroon by Benjamin and Devarajan (1985). The models used by Shoven, Whalley and their collaborators are strictly in the tradition of Walrasian economies with market clearing in all sectors. Due to the presence of institutional rigidities in most developing countries, World Bank researchers considered full market clearing unreasonable for developing countries. They, therefore, depart from the co-classical Walrasian tradition and relax the assumptions to capture 'structuralist features' of developing countries.

5   The classification of sectors is based on the degree of 'tradeability', using the ratio of exports in total production, the share of imports in total domestic demand, and the ratio of imports to intermediate inputs. Because of the extreme openness of the economy, sectors such as retail trade, transport and communications, which traditionally are non-traded, are traded in Singapore and hence are classified as 'quasi-tradeable'.

6   The main weakness of using the Leontief functional form is that it is unable to capture relative price effects. The demands for intermediate inputs are driven entirely by output levels. This may be a very restrictive and unrealistic assumption.

7   All subscripts j have been suppressed to avoid cluttering in the equations.

8   In the extended model, households make savings decisions based on expectations about the future consumption stream. Saving behaviour is based on utility maximization behaviour represented by another level of nesting, U_1, which is a CES function of present and future consumption. The latter is the expected future annuity stream generated by savings today. The price of the future consumption good is not fixed and is dependent on the cost of capital and the real rate of return of new capital (see Chia, 1991, pp. 27–9).

9   Again, to avoid cluttering, all superscripts h representing the households have been suppressed.

10   The importance of the treatment of foreign trade for external sector closure in the general equilibrium model is discussed in Whalley and Yeung (1984).

11   See chapter 2 of Chia (1991) for the details on numerical implementation and the micro-consistent benchmark equilibrium data-set.

12   It should be noted that this general equilibrium analysis of the Singapore tax study was done before the implementation of the general goods and services tax (GST) on 1 April 1994. Preliminary simulations of the impacts of GST suggest that the degree of progressivity of the tax system is affected by the broad-based consumption tax. However, if offsets/rebates from the government were modelled, then there is considerable redistribution.

13 The concept of a potential welfare improvement is explained in the note to Table
8.7. For further discussion of the issue, see Chia (1991), pp. 106–9.
14 The standard deviation of the effective payroll taxes across the sectors is 9.71.

References

Adelman, I. and S. Robinson (1978) *Income Distribution Policy in Developing Countries: A Case Study of Korea*, Stanford: Stanford University Press.

Atkinson, A. B. (1974) *The Economics of Inequality*, 2nd edn, Oxford: Clarendon Press.

Bacharach, M. (1971) *Bi-proportional Matrices and Input–Output Change*. Cambridge: Cambridge University Press.

Ballard, C., L. Fullerton, D. Shoven, B. John and J. Whalley (1985) *A General Equilibrium Model for Tax Policy Evaluation*, Chicago: University of Chicago Press.

Benjamin, N. C. and S. Devarajan (1985) 'Oil Revenues and Economic Policy in Cameroon: Results from a Computable General Equilibrium Model', *World Bank Staff Working Paper no. 745*, Washington, DC: The World Bank.

Boskin, M. (1978) 'Taxation, Saving and the Rate of Interest', *Journal of Political Economy*, vol. 86, pt. 2, April, pp. S3–S27.

Chia, N. C. (1991) 'Analysis of Tax Policy Options for Singapore: A General Equilibrium Approach', PhD dissertation submitted to the University of Western Ontario.

Chia, N. C. and J. Whalley (1995) 'Patterns in Investment Tax Incentives Among Developing Countries', in A. Shah (ed.) *Fiscal Incentives for Investment and Innovation*, Washington, DC: World Bank.

Clarete, R. and J. Whalley (1987) 'Marginal Welfare Costs of Taxes', *Journal of Public Economics*, August, pp. 357–62.

Dervis, K. and S. Robinson (1978) 'The Foreign Exchange Gap, Growth and Industrial Strategy in Turkey: 1973–1983', *World Bank Staff Working Paper no. 306*, Washington, DC: The World Bank.

Devarajan, S., J. D. Lewis and S. Robinson (1986) *A Bibliography of Computable General Equilibrium (CGE) Models Applied to Developing Countries*, Harvard Institute for International Development no. 224, pp. 1–19.

Hamilton, B. and J. Whalley (1989) 'Efficiency and Distributional Effects of the Tax Reform Package', in J. Mintz and J. Whalley (eds), *The Economic Impacts of Tax Reform*, Canadian Tax Paper no. 84, pp. 373–98, Toronto: Canadian Tax Foundation.

Harberger, A. C. (1962) 'The Incidence of Corporation Income Tax', *Journal of Political Economy*, vol. 70(3) pp. 215–40.

International Monetary Fund (1993) *Government Finance Statistics Yearbook 1993*, Washington DC: IMF.

Jorgenson, D. W. and P. J. Wilcoxen (1991) 'Intertemporal General Equilibrium Modelling of Environmental Regulation', *Journal of Policy Modelling*, vol. 12, no. 4, Winter, 715–44.

Kaldor, N. (1939) 'Welfare Propositions and Interpersonal Comparisons of Utility', *Economic Journal*, vol. xlix, pp. 549–52.

Killingsworth, M. R. (1985) *Labour Supply*, Cambridge: Cambridge University Press.

Mansur, A. and J. Whalley (1984) 'Numerical Specification of Applied General Equilibrium Models: Estimation, Calibration and Data', in H. E. Scarf and J. B. Shoven (eds), in *Applied General Equilibrium Analysis*, New York: Cambridge University Press.

Ministry of Trade and Industry (1993) *Economic Survey of Singapore*, 1993, Singapore: Singapore National Printers.

Pechman, J. A. and B. A. Okner (1974) *Who Bears the Tax Burden?*, Washington, DC: The Brookings Institution.

Piggott, J. R. and J. Whalley (1985) *Applied General Equilibrium Analysis: An Application to U.K. Tax Policy*, New York: Cambridge University Press.

Rutherford, T. F. (1989) 'General Equilibrium Modelling with MPS/GE', University of Western Ontario.

Rutherford, T. F. and S. L. Winer (1990) 'Endogenous Policy in a Computational General Equilibrium Framework', University of Western Ontario, Department of Economics, Research Report 9007, June.

Serra-Puche, J. (1983) 'A General Equilibrium Model for the Mexican Economy', in H. E. Scarf and J. B. Shoven (eds), *Applied General Equilibrium Analysis*, New York: Cambridge University Press.

Shoven, J. and J. Whalley (1972) 'A General Equilibrium Calculation of the Effects of Differential Taxation of Income from Capital in the U.S.', *Journal of Public Economics*, vol. 1, pp. 281–322.

—— (1984) 'Applied General Equilibrium Models of Taxation and International Trade: An Introduction and Survey', *Journal of Economic Literature*, vol. 22, pp. 1007–51.

Singapore, Accountant-General's Department, *Financial Statement, 1982–83*.

Singapore, Department of Statistics, *Report on the Household Expenditure Survey 1972–73 and 1982–83*, September 1973 and 1983.

Singapore, Department of Statistics, *Singapore Input–Output Tables*, June 1983.

Singapore, Department of Statistics, *Yearbook of Statistics*, 1982, 1983, 1984.

Singapore, Inland Revenue Department, *Annual Report*, various years.

Toh, M. H. (1985) 'Technical Change, Factor Elasticity of Substitution and Return to Scale in Singapore Manufacturing Industries', *Singapore Economic Review*, pp. 36–56.

Whalley, J. and R. Wigle (1990) 'The International Incidence of Carbon Taxes', University of Western Ontario, September, mimeo.

Whalley, J. and B. Yeung (1984) 'External Sector Closing Rules in Applied General Equilibrium Models', *Journal of International Economics*, vol. 16, February, pp. 123–38.

World Bank (1993) *The East Asia Miracle: Economic Growth and Public Policy*, New York: Oxford University Press.

9

Fiscal Federalism Dimensions of Tax Reform in Developing Countries

Robin Boadway, Sandra Roberts and Anwar Shah

Introduction

Many countries, especially in the industrialized world, can be classified as federalist because significant fiscal functions are undertaken by lower levels of government, both on the expenditure and on the tax side. Federal economies have developed elaborate forms of fiscal arrangements between the central (federal) and lower (state and municipal) levels of government which jointly determine the way in which tax bases are allocated and shared among the various levels of government, as well as how funds are transferred from one level to another. The existence of multiple levels of the taxing authority gives rise to issues of tax design not found in unitary states.

As the public sectors of developing countries evolve to provide more of the sorts of public services found in industrialized countries, the benefits of decentralized decision making are likely to become more apparent. The reform of tax systems required to streamline revenue-raising will have to take account of the revenue needs of lower levels of government. This will naturally put constraints on the types of tax reforms that are both feasible and desirable. It is the purpose of this chapter to review the special issues that arise in reforming taxes in federal states. The conceptual guidance presented here, however, should be more generally applicable in a multi-jurisdictional setting regardless of the constitutional structure of the country.

In doing so, we draw heavily on the experiences in industrialized countries where federal fiscal arrangements have evolved over a long period of time. Practices in these countries, though highly developed, are far from uniform; they differ because of different institutional, political and geographical circumstances of the countries. Nonetheless, there are a number of economic principles of taxation in a federal setting that have been developed in the literature and that can be applied to any federal economy. Their implications for any country will depend upon features of the economy, such as the extent of decentralization of functions, the degree of heterogeneity of the population, and the extent of government intervention in the economy. Our review will concentrate on these principles.

We begin with a brief review of the economics of fiscal federalism as it relates to fiscal arrangements, that is, the combination of the system of transfers and the system of tax-sharing and harmonization in a federation. Next, we discuss the issue of tax assignment: which taxes ought to be made available to which levels of government? The decentralization of revenue-raising inevitably gives rise to problems of inefficiencies and inequities in the internal economic union. Ways of avoiding these through tax harmonization and coordination are discussed next. Finally, we outline some of the implications for tax reform, especially in developing countries.

Review of the principles of fiscal federalism

Principles of expenditure decentralization

There is a large literature on fiscal federalism. Our purpose here is simply to summarize the basic lessons to be derived from that literature.[1] Federal structures of government allow for decentralization of the provision of public services to lower levels of government. It is argued that, as in the private sector, decentralized decision-making makes allocation of resources more efficient. It does so by enabling governments to provide the mix of services most suited to the needs and tastes of local consumers, by making governments more accountable to their citizens, by devolving decisions to governments which are closer to them, and by instilling greater responsiveness by competition among governments.

A reasonable working principle is to decentralize all functions except those for which it can be demonstrated that centralization is needed because of economies of scale, because the benefits of a particular type of service are highly public in nature, or because uniformity of provision is an important objective (for example to maintain the efficiency of the internal economic union or to achieve national equity objectives).[2] This principle leads to the following suggested division of powers among levels of government.

Public goods and services

Public goods and services which are national in nature should be assigned to the federal government. These include national defence, control of the money supply, international trade and relations, criminal law and national environmental issues. Public goods whose benefits accrue mainly regionally or locally should be assigned to lower levels of government. Examples include roads and waterways, water supplies, regional environmental issues, land and resource use, garbage and recreation. Goods and services that are public make up only a small proportion of government spending. 'Private' goods and services and transfers are much more important.

Quasi-private goods and services

Most goods and services expenditures by government are on quasi-private goods and services which are private services provided through the public sector, usually free of charge. They include large items such as education, health services and welfare. They are delivered most efficiently by lower levels of government since they benefit individuals closest to where the expenditures are performed. Nonetheless, the federal government may have an interest in the way in which these types of services are being provided. They are usually instituted for redistributive purposes and the federal government may have a legitimate interest in ensuring that national equity objectives are being satisfied. As well, differential provision of quasi-private goods and services may distort the allocation of labour across states. We return below to the means by which the federal government may exercise its responsibilities for national efficiency and equity while allowing these services to be decentralized to the states.

Transfers

Transfers to individuals and businesses also comprise a large budget item. Those to individuals serve essentially redistributive purposes, either as a part of the income-based tax-transfer system or as part of the system of social insurance (including unemployment insurance, welfare and pensions). To the extent that the federal government has responsibility for redistributive equity, these are necessary policy instruments. States may nonetheless have some interest in redistribution based on local preferences and may wish to supplement federal transfer schemes with those of their own. Transfers to businesses are more clearly a federal responsibility. At the state level, they are likely to give rise to distortions in the allocation of capital and to beggar-thy-neighbour policies.

Regulation

As well as spending money, governments regulate activities of the private sector (even though economists might prefer that they limit themselves in this area). Regulation of capital markets should clearly be a federal responsibility because of the mobility of capital and the possibility of interfering with the efficiency of the internal economic union. Regulation of goods which are freely traded across internal borders (such as transportation, communications and agriculture) should also be central. Labour market regulation is less clear-cut. Some forms should be clearly federal, such as immigration policies. Others (such as professional licensing), though they may fulfil local needs, can clearly interfere with national labour market efficiency. On the other hand, some forms of labour market regulation (such as standards in the workplace or labour training) need to be decentralized to conform with local customs or be coordinated with education or other policies.

The exact application of these principles depends on the features of the particular country. The benefits of decentralization will be greater if the population is widely dispersed and not homogeneous. There is obviously a great deal of judgement involved in their application. One important factor in determining the limits of decentralization is the extent to which government in general, and the federal government in particular, is relied upon for redistributive objectives. In industrialized countries, much of what governments do is redistributive. Generally speaking, those who place greater weight on the redistributive role of government tend to support a larger role for the federal government and more responsibility for redistribution being assigned to the federal government. Those who would prefer less government interference in the economy and less redistribution, tend to favour greater decentralization (since competition by lower levels of government is thought to reduce both the size of the public sector and its ability to redistribute).

Principles of revenue decentralization

The decentralization of expenditure responsibilities brings with it the need to decentralize revenue-raising responsibilities. Otherwise, the lower levels of government would be dependent upon funding from the central government and the full benefits of decentralized decision-making and political accountability would not be achieved. It is the purpose of the following sections of this chapter to discuss the best ways to decentralize taxing responsibilities. However, the extent of decentralization of revenue-raising need not correspond exactly with that of expenditure responsibilities. Indeed, in virtually all multi-government economies, lower levels of government finance some of their expenditure responsibilities by transfers from the higher level. There are two reasons for this. The first is simply that the case for decentralizing expenditure responsibilities is stronger than that for decentralizing revenue-raising. While decentralizing expenditures leads to more efficient service delivery, it is not clear that there are equivalent efficiency advantages (apart from fiscal accountability) of decentralizing revenue-raising. On the contrary, decentralization of taxation can lead to significant inequities and inefficiencies in the federal economy. Thus, there are economic advantages to having more taxes collected at the higher level of government than are necessary for its own expenditures and transferring some of them to the states.

The second is that the transfer of funds from the higher to the lower level of government can itself achieve important objectives in a federal state. In particular, appropriately designed transfers can be used to ameliorate the inefficiencies and inequities that accompany fiscal decentralization while still preserving its benefits. The form that these inefficiencies and inequities take has a bearing on the form of the transfers. We can identify four main objectives for federal-state grants.[3]

Fiscal efficiency

The decentralization of expenditure and tax responsibilities inevitably leaves different jurisdictions with different fiscal capacities as they can only provide given public services at very different tax rates to their citizens. In other words, depending on the state of residence, the net fiscal benefits (NFBs) for a given type of citizen will differ. In general, the existence of differential NFBs provides an incentive for resources (especially labour) to be allocated inefficiently.[4] The quantitative importance of fiscal inefficiency depends upon the degree of mobility of labour across states, as well as the difference in state tax capacities. Fiscal inefficiency can be largely alleviated by transfers to states to equalize their tax capacities; the grants should be unconditional and unrelated to actual tax rates or tax efforts within a state.[5]

Fiscal equity

NFB differences also give rise to horizontal inequities in the federation, as originally pointed out by Buchanan (1950), since otherwise identical persons would be treated differently by the public sector depending on the state in which they reside. The same sort of equalizing unconditional transfers that can deal with fiscal inefficiency are also appropriate for addressing these fiscal inequities. This is one of the rare cases in economics in which efficiency and equity concerns coincide.

Efficiency of the internal economic union

The exercise of fiscal responsibilities by states is also likely to give rise to distortions in the free flow of goods, services, labour and capital across the states. This can occur in both taxes and expenditures. In the case of the former, the appropriate action is to institute some form of tax harmonization among or between the states and the federal government; we deal with that in a later section. However, expenditure policies can also interfere with the efficiency of the internal economic union. Differences in programme design across states can induce labour misallocation (for example, states may impose residency requirements or restrict portability). Also, the terms of the programmes may be designed to attract desirable residents (skilled or wealthy persons) and to drive away less desirable ones (low-income and low-skilled persons). The federal government may also wish to impose guidelines on states to prevent their programmes from distorting the internal common market. One way to do so is through conditional grants that provide financial incentives for provinces to design their programmes according to criteria set out by the federal government. This is referred to as the use of spending power. Ideally, the criteria should be general ones, no more restrictive than necessary to induce provinces to cooperate. In particular, the provinces should maintain legislative control over programmes in their areas of responsibility and should not be deterred from exercising that authority in innovative and effective ways. Generally speaking, the conditional grants needed to foster the internal economic union need not be matching ones. They could be block grants disbursed according to simple aggregate formulas (for example, equal per capita or needs-based), but with penalty provisions attached for non-conformity with national standards.

National equity objectives

Federal interest in fostering national standards of redistributive (vertical) equity may also lead to a role for the spending power. Much actual redistribution takes place on the expenditure side of government budgets and is delivered through quasi-private goods. To the extent that these are the responsibility of the states, the only way for the federal government to achieve its national equity objectives is through the spending power. As with efficiency, the federal government can provide block grants to the states with conditions attached stipulating general standards to which programmes should conform. These could include such things as accessibility, coverage of the programme and portability.

The system of intergovernmental transfers makes up part of the fiscal relations between different levels of government made necessary by the decentralization of responsibilities to the states. The other main part consists of harmonization and sharing tax arrangements. These are also important to ensure the efficiency of the internal economic union, to foster national equity objectives and to maintain the administrative efficiency of the tax collection system, while at the same time giving the states the responsibility required for financing their own expenditures (at least at and near the margin). The combination of the system of transfers and the system of tax-sharing and harmonization comprise what is referred to as the fiscal arrangements of the federation. The fiscal arrangements taken as a whole enable the federation to achieve the fullest benefits of decentralized fiscal responsibility while preserving the efficiency and equity of the national economy. Decentralization and the fiscal arrangements go hand in hand: the more decentralized the federation, the more important the system of fiscal arrangements and the more effective the fiscal arrangements, the more confidence one can have in advocating the decentralization of decision-making. Though we concentrate on the tax side of the fiscal arrangements in this chapter, the design and effect of various tax harmonization measures are not independent of the transfer system.

Finally, though we are ultimately concerned with tax reform in developing countries, much of the experience we draw on is in industrialized economies with longer histories of federal decision-making. There are some very fundamental differences in the roles assumed by governments in the two sorts of economies which will set limits on how far tax reforms in a federal system can be taken. By and large, governments in industrialized countries have more advanced social programmes and redistributive schemes, have tax mixes that rely more on direct taxes and general taxes and are more decentralized than those in developing countries. This will have an influence on how far the principles of this chapter can be applied.

Tax assignment

Governments rely on a wide variety of tax instruments for their revenue needs, including direct and indirect taxes, general and specific taxes, business and individual taxes. The question we address here is which types of taxes are most suitable for use by lower levels of government. We begin with a statement of general principles and then consider how these principles might apply to each of the common types of taxes levied.

Principles of tax assignment

The assignment of taxes by jurisdiction depends partly on the mix of various taxes used in the country. In public finance theory, the issue of the ideal tax mix even in a unitary state has not been widely developed. Governments almost universally employ balanced tax systems in which different taxes apply to basically the same bases. For example, general sales taxes, payroll taxes and income taxes have bases which overlap considerably. From the point of view of standard efficiency and equity, one should be able to make do with a single general tax base, yet no governments behave that way. The usual reason given for this is administrative. A mix of taxes keeps the rate on any one tax low, thereby reducing the incentive to evade or avoid the tax. Furthermore, by using a mix of taxes, taxpayers who would otherwise be able to avoid taxation of one type are caught by another, making the tax system fairer. The importance of various taxes in the overall mix remains, however, a matter of judgment rather than something that can be deduced from principles.

These same general considerations apply in the case of assigning taxes in a federal government system. Efficiency and equity arguments have to be tempered by administrative considerations and the exact assignment depends upon informed judgement. We can, however, outline the economic principles that come into play when deciding which taxes to assign to lower levels of government. They are as follows:

Efficiency of the internal common market

The internal common market will function efficiently if all resources (labour, capital, goods and services) are free to move from one region to another without impediments or distortions imposed by policy. Decentralized tax systems can interfere with the efficiency of the economic union in two ways. First, uncoordinated taxation is likely to lead to distortions in markets for resources which are mobile across states, especially capital and tradeable goods. This problem will be lessened considerably if state governments recognize that resources are mobile. However, if they do recognize that, they may engage in socially wasteful beggar-thy-neighbour policies to attract resources to their own states. If all jurisdictions engage in such policies, the end result will simply be inefficiently low taxes (or high subsidies) on mobile factors.

National equity

The tax-transfer system is one of the main instruments for achieving redistributive equity. The argument for making equity a federal objective is simply that all persons ought to enter into society's 'social welfare function' on an equal basis, and the federal government is the only level that can ensure that residents in different regions are treated equitably. This may be tempered if states have different tastes for redistribution or if centralized decision-making is not guided by normative criteria. To the extent that equity is viewed as a federal policy objective, decentralized taxes can interfere with achieving that objective. As with efficiency, uncoordinated state tax policies may unwittingly induce arbitrary differences in redistributive consequences for residents of different states. Also, given the mobility of labour and capital across states, states may engage in perverse redistributive policies using both taxes and transfers to attract high-income persons and repel low-income ones. Beggar-thy-neighbour redistributive policies are likely to offset resource allocation but will result in less redistribution than in their absence. (Of course, those who abhor redistribution through government will prefer decentralized redistributive policies for precisely the same reason.) This is obviously likely to be a greater problem for those taxes that are redistributive in nature, as well as for transfers.

Administrative costs

The decentralization of revenue raising can also serve to increase the costs of collection and compliance, both for the public and the private sector. There are fixed costs associated with collecting any tax which will have to be borne for each tax type used by the states. Taxpayers will also have to incur costs of compliance for all taxes levied. The possibilities for evasion and avoidance increase with decentralization for some types of taxes, and this will be true where the tax base is mobile or straddles more than one jurisdiction. In the latter case, there will have to be rules for allocating tax revenues among jurisdictions; in their absence, some tax bases may face either double taxation or no taxation at all. Auditing procedures may also be distorted for those tax bases which involve transactions across state boundaries.

Fiscal need

To ensure accountability, revenue means should be matched as closely as possible to revenue needs. Thus tax instruments intended to further specific policy objectives should be assigned to the level of government that has the responsibility for such a service. Thus progressive redistributive taxes, stabilization instruments and resource-rent taxes would be suitably assigned to the national government, while tolls on intermunicipal roads are suitably assigned to state governments. In countries with a federal-level VAT (value added tax), it may be too cumbersome to have sub-national sales taxes. In such circumstances, the fiscal-need criterion would suggest allowing sub-national governments access to taxes (such as personal income taxes) which are traditionally regarded as more suitable for national administration.

Assignment by type of tax

The relevance of each of the above principles varies from tax base to tax base. It also depends on how much responsibility for revenue-raising has been devolved to the states. In this section, we consider how the principles apply to each of the main types of taxes. Where relevant, we note particular issues and practices in developing countries. Of course, there may be institutional impediments to the ability to assign taxes according to economic principles. In particular, national constitutions may restrict the ability of either the federal government or the states from assuming responsibility for certain types of taxes. In some countries the federal government may be able to override state policies where it is justified by national objectives, such as maintaining efficient internal economic union. Thus, for example, the interstate commerce clause in the US constitution allows the federal government to strike down state laws that interfere with interstate trading.

Personal income taxes

Income taxes applied to individuals (or households) represent an important instrument for redistribution. For redistributive purposes, they should be available to the federal government; assignment of personal income taxes to the states runs the risk of national equity objectives being violated through different degrees of progressivity across states and of state policies competing away redistribution.

Moreover, since capital income is typically a component of these taxes, there is a possibility of capital markets being distorted. For example, state income tax regimes could give preferential treatment to capital income generated within the state. As well, because capital income can be earned both within the state and outside, compliance and collection costs and the possibilities for evasion are likely to increase substantially as responsibility for personal income taxes is decentralized. For these reasons, it is preferable that responsibility for the personal income tax rest with the federal government.

The same might be said for other direct taxes on persons, such as taxes on personal wealth and on wealth transfers (for example, estate taxes). Indeed, the case for centralization of these is perhaps stronger as their bases are highly mobile and they are very effective instruments for pursuing equity. By the same token, subsidies to persons (which are essentially negative direct taxes) might also be levied federally and integrated with the income tax system.

It should be noted that in low-income agrarian societies and lower-middle income countries, the coverage of the personal income tax is quite limited and its role as a redistributive element of the fiscal system is further clouded by widespread tax evasion. Shah and Whalley (1991) have argued that when one considers the rural–urban migration effects associated with a tax on urban incomes, as well as the reverse redistribution effects of the income tax through the bribe system, personal income tax may not be viewed as a progressive element of the tax structure in lower-middle income countries. Under such circumstances, an exclusive federal role for personal income tax is difficult to justify. Furthermore, many of the services provided by sub-national governments in developing countries could not be directly related to property and are redistributive in nature. This suggests that while the federal government may impose a progressive income tax structure, sub-national governments should be given access to flat charges on the federal base.

To the extent that states are allowed access to personal income tax revenues, the allocation of the tax base across states becomes important to ensure that each person is taxed only once. In principle, allocation by place of residence rather than place of employment is preferred. However, establishing place of residence may be difficult if people move during the tax year, and assigning proportions of a tax base to each state according to the share of a tax year spent in the state would be complicated. Countries with decentralized income tax systems usually assign residency to a given state for the entire tax year according to residency on a given date (for example, the last day in the year).

China has assigned personal income taxation to the provincial-local governments, while retaining for the central government a joint role with the provinces in determining its base. In most other developing countries, the determination of the personal income tax base and rate is a central responsibility, whereas tax administration is occasionally shared with sub-national governments. Exceptions are India where this tax field is shared by the federal and state governments, and Brazil where states are allowed a supplementary rate on the federal base. Nigeria is unusual insofar as the federal government collects only a limited share of income taxes. It has access only to taxes paid by the armed forces, external affairs employees, and residents of the Federal Capital Territory. The predominance of state-level income tax collection hinders redistribution. In some cases, state governments control instruments other than income tax which may affect income redistribution. In Brazil, for example, the taxes on inheritances, gifts and supplemental capital gains are state levies.

Corporation taxes

As with personal income tax, there is a strong case for making corporation income tax a federal responsibility. For one thing, the corporate tax can be viewed partly as an adjunct to the personal tax or, more precisely, as a with-holding device for the personal tax (to tax at source shareholder income which could otherwise be reinvested in the corporation and escape immediate taxation). To this extent, it is better levied at the same level as the personal tax so that it can be integrated easily. In an open economy, the corporate tax also serves as a useful device for obtaining revenues from foreign corporations, especially those that are able to obtain tax credits from their home govern-ments. Again, the federal level seems the most appropriate one for this pur-pose. More to the point, since the corporate tax base is capital income within a jurisdiction, decentralizing it to the states would jeopardize the efficient functioning of capital markets and give rise to the possibility of wasteful tax competition to attract capital at the expense of other jurisdictions.

Administrative simplicity also favours centralizing the corporate tax. Many corporations operate in more than one jurisdiction at the same time, and tax administration in a multi-jurisdiction setting can be a complicated matter. For any jurisdiction, the appropriate share of the tax base must be allocated to that jurisdiction and the taxing authority must have some way of monitoring a firm to ensure compliance. With complete independence of taxing author-ities, this would be difficult. A firm may well have an incentive to engage in transfer pricing or financial and book transactions to shift its profits around to reduce its tax burden. The firm itself will have an increased cost of com-pliance if it faces different tax regimes in different jurisdictions. In practice, tax bases are typically allocated among sub-national jurisdictions according to methods of formula apportionment which attempt to minimize the administrative and incentive problems associated with determining tax shares. Common methods include allocating tax revenues of a given corpora-tion among jurisdictions according to a mix of shares of a firm's payroll, revenues and possibly capital stocks.

Thus, the case for centralizing corporate tax is very strong. The same might be said for other taxes that effectively fall on corporate capital, such as capital taxes. By symmetric arguments, subsidies to corporations should be central-ized, given the obvious tendency for lower levels of government to use them to attract capital in competition with other jurisdictions in ways which might be distorting.

Of course, not all tax competition need be wasteful; it could also serve to improve the efficiency of lower-level governments. Some of the distorting effect of tax competition could be avoided if the taxes involved were designed to be non-discriminatory so that they treated all capital within their jurisdic-tions alike. This is equivalent to the principle of national treatment in inter-national trade policy.

In most developing countries, the determination of the corporate tax base and rate structure is a central government responsibility. The exception is China, where it is a joint responsibility of the centre and the provinces. Administration of the corporate tax is a joint responsibility of national and sub-national governments in Pakistan and the Russian Federation; it is the sole responsibility of sub-national governments in China. There are cases in which sub-national governments control instruments that may affect capital mobility; in India, for example, the capital transactions tax is a state instrument.

Sales taxes

Sales taxes are much better candidates for decentralization to the states, especially if significant revenue sources are required. Typically, general sales taxes are levied on consumption goods defined with varying degrees of inclusiveness and on a destination basis. As such, they are essentially general taxes on residents of the taxing jurisdiction. Given the relatively low degree of mobility of households, they are likely to be much less distorting than taxes on mobile bases like capital (at least as long as investment goods are not included in the base). Also, since sales taxes are not significant instruments for redistribution, little equity is lost from decentralizing them to the states.

However, some distortions and administrative problems are likely to arise from state sales taxes. The main source of inefficiency has to do with cross-border shopping. Residents of high-tax jurisdictions would have an incentive to shop in neighbouring low-tax jurisdictions to reduce their tax burdens. Given the absence of border controls, this would be difficult to avoid. As a consequence, tax competition is likely to result in rate levels and structures that do not vary greatly across jurisdictions. On the surface of it, this might pose a problem for poorer jurisdictions that might otherwise need higher tax rates to finance their basic services. However, this disadvantage would be mitigated if an effective system of equalizing transfers from the federal government were in place, as discussed in the previous section.

If the state sales taxes take the form of sub-national credit-method value added taxes (VATs), the taxation of interstate trade creates major difficulties. Such transactions can either be taxed on a destination basis (taxing final consumption) such that imports are taxed and exports are zero-rated, or on an origin basis (taxing production) such that both imports and exports are exempted from taxation. Since the use of the destination basis for a VAT requires customs houses at state borders within a federation and thereby works as an impediment to the free flow of goods and services within the nation, a possible alternative is to adopt the 'restricted origin principle', where interstate trade is taxed on the origin principle and international trade on a destination basis. This solution would work well if sub-national units had uniform rates of VAT and if trade flows within and from outside the country were not too uneven across states (see also McLure, 1993). Inefficiencies could result if the taxation basis differed across jurisdictions. For example, state governments might be tempted to use an origin basis for their state taxes rather than a residency one.

Other possible inefficiencies of state sales taxation are related to administrative problems that are likely to be present in developing countries. One has to do with the fact that the broader the base, the more difficult it is to enforce compliance. To get a full general consumption base, including both goods and services, it would be necessary to collect the tax at the level of final sales to the consumer, the retail stage. This increases the compliance costs considerably since the number of taxpayers would be extremely large. Furthermore, enforcement of the tax would be very difficult, and evasion is likely to be high. Some of these difficulties can be avoided by levying the tax at an earlier stage, though at the cost of making the base much narrower.

Another problem with state sales taxes is that it is difficult to avoid some cascading of the tax through purchases of taxed inputs. Systems in which taxes paid on purchases from registered dealers are credited towards or exempted from later levies reduce the incidence of this problem at some administrative cost, but they do not eliminate it entirely. It is also difficult to ensure that sales to buyers outside state boundaries have been purged of taxes on intermediate inputs. These same problems arise at the federal level and are typically addressed by adopting a multi-stage tax such as a value added tax (VAT). Under a VAT, taxes on business inputs are eliminated by the system of crediting for input purchases, exports are given full credit for taxes paid and imports are fully taxed. As noted above, adopting the same remedy at the state level is difficult because of the absence of border controls. Furthermore, since states are inevitably much more open than entire countries, the administrative complexities of operating a system of taxing and crediting on all cross-border transactions would be very high and would be likely to constitute a significant distortion on interstate trade. For these reasons, single-stage state sales taxes may well be preferred.[6]

Quite apart from these difficulties of dealing with cross-border transactions by both producers and consumers, state sales taxes entail a separate layer of administrative machinery on the government side and additional compliance costs for businesses who are required to collect the tax. These costs are especially high in a system in which there are separate sales taxes at the federal and state levels of government.

The practical difficulties associated with the sub-national administration of a multi-stage sales tax are well-illustrated by the Brazilian experience. In Brazil, the federal government levies a manufacturer-level sales tax (IPI), states are assigned a broad-based credit-method VAT (ICMS at 17 per cent rate), and municipalities administer a services tax (ISS). Under the ICMS, interstate sales are taxed on the origin principle (at a 12 per cent rate for north–south and 7 per cent for south–north transactions) and international trade is taxed on a destination basis. Thus in domestic trade, relatively less-developed northern states are given preferential treatment. In international trade, as most of the imports are destined for the southern states and a disproportionate amount of exports go through the northeastern states, most of the revenues are collected by the richer states and export rebates are given by poorer states. Another emerging area of major potential interstate conflict is the use of the ICMS as a tool for state industrial development. Some northeastern states are offering a 15-year ICMS tax deferral to industry. In a highly inflationary environment such as Brazil, unless such tax liabilities are indexed, they could wipe out all ICMS tax liabilities.

Recognizing these difficulties, China introduced a centrally-administered VAT in January 1994 with proceeds to be shared with the provinces on a 50–50 basis. India is facing major difficulties reforming its sales tax system. At present, sales taxes are assigned to the state level, excises are administered by the federal government and the proceeds shared with the states, while the *octroi* is a local tax on intermunicipal trade. Sales taxes are administered on narrow bases; the number of rates vary by state from six in Orissa to 17 in Bihar and Gujarat. Some states consider the sales tax an important element of redistributive policy. To reform the existing sales tax structure, a broad-based national VAT has been proposed but this is strongly opposed by the states. The states are also dissatisfied with the centrally administered excise tax because it limits their powers of taxation. The federal government prefers to raise additional revenues from administered prices rather than from excises because the proceeds from excises have to be shared with state governments. The *octroi* tax on intermunicipal trade is a source of significant revenues for local governments and remains popular in spite of its anti-trade bias.

Excise taxes

Specific excise taxes are also good candidates for decentralization to the states, perhaps better than general sales taxes, although they have much less potential for raising revenues. (Obviously, we are not including customs duties and export taxes in this. They should clearly be federal responsibilities.) Specific excises are unlikely to cause significant impediments to the efficiency of the internal economic union or major misallocations of labour and capital if they are levied on a destination basis. They simply become a form of taxes on residents and are unlikely to be significant enough to cause migration. If they were levied on an origin basis, this might not be the case. Businesses could avoid the tax by moving elsewhere, unless the product taxed depended upon a local resource. An example of the latter might be taxes on oil and gas, to which we return below when discussing resource taxes.

There are two problems of efficiency with excise taxes. First, as with sales taxes, they will give rise to cross-border shopping, possibly on a large scale if the taxed goods are cheap to transport. Tax competition is likely to reduce the importance of this, especially if the fiscal capacities of the states are not too different and if equalizing transfers further reduce discrepancies. Another possible problem is that excise taxes distort the markets for the goods being taxed. This distortion can be significant if states must rely on excise taxes for a large part of their revenues. It could be argued that for some goods (alcohol, tobacco and possibly gasoline) at least some differential tax is justified on the basis of externalities.

Excise taxes may also have an adverse effect on equity to the extent that they are levied on goods consumed by lower-income persons. However, this need not be a telling problem as long as the federal government has other tax instruments (such as the income-based tax-transfer system) for addressing broader redistributive issues. There might, however, be other federal policy objectives which are affected by excise tax policy. For example, the federal government may have a concern with health policy (the effectiveness of which may be influenced by cigarette and alcohol taxes) or with pollution and road use (where gasoline taxes become relevant).

Excises on alcohol and tobacco could be jointly occupied by the federal and provincial levels, as both health care and the prevention of accidents and crimes is usually a shared responsibility in most federations. Games of chance and gambling usually fall within the purview of state and local governments and therefore taxes on betting, gambling, racetracks and lottery revenues would be suitable for assignment to sub-national governments only.

Taxation to control environmental externalities such as congestion and pollution could be suitably imposed by the level of government that is responsible for curtailing such externalities. This would suggest that carbon taxes to combat global and national pollution issues should be a federal responsibility. Btu taxes, taxes on motor fuels and congestion tolls could be levied by all levels in their own sphere of authority. Effluent charges to deal with interstate pollution should be a federal responsibility. Intermunicipal pollution would be a state responsibility but the responsibility to deal with intra-municipal pollution should rest with local governments. Parking fees (to influence inter-modal choices and thereby regulate local traffic congestion) should be a local responsibility.

The administrative problems associated with decentralizing excise taxes are less severe than with other taxes. The difficulties of eliminating taxes on business inputs and on exports that plague general sales taxes do not apply with the same force here. Collection costs may not be excessively high for either the sellers or the government, and enforcement should be no greater problem than with other taxes, especially if the rates are neither too high nor too varied across the federation.

A large variation in excise tax assignment prevails in developing countries. In some countries such as Indonesia and Mexico they are centralized, whilst in others such as Bangladesh and Argentina they are decentralized. In a large majority of developing countries, excise taxes are co-occupied by national and sub-national governments. This is the case in Malaysia, Nigeria and Thailand.

Payroll taxes

Payroll taxes are typically used in industrialized countries for financing social insurance schemes, especially those limited to employees. The sorts of programmes for which payroll taxes are earmarked may be those which are decentralized to state governments, in which case they would be obvious sources of state revenues. However, they can be a useful adjunct to general revenue as well. In either case, they are ideal candidates for state revenue sources. Payroll taxes are relatively easy to administer since they can be collected with minimal cost through payroll deduction. Their base is ultimately almost equivalent to that of general sales taxes. Provided their rates do not differ significantly across states, they are unlikely to cause significant distortions in the labour market.

As well as causing very little distortion of internal labour markets, payroll taxes have minimal redistributive effects. They are not a necessary component of federal redistributive policy instruments and any adverse effect they may have on income distribution can be easily offset by other taxes at the federal level.

Payroll taxes are widely used in Latin American countries, and there is the potential for greater use of this tax instrument by sub-national governments in developing countries.

Resource taxes

The case of taxes on resources is an interesting one since it brings the two economic criteria, efficiency and equity, into direct conflict. On the one hand, since resource endowments are immobile across jurisdictions, state taxes on resources should not distort the internal economic union if designed properly. Indeed, taxes on resource rents would be an ideal tax since they would have no efficiency effects whatsoever.[7] The administrative costs associated with state resource taxes would not be excessive either. However, resources are usually distributed very unevenly across states in a given country, and in those circumstances decentralizing resource taxes to the states would result in significant differences in tax capacities, thus creating fiscal inefficiencies and inequities.

In an ideal world, the decentralization of resource revenues to the states would be accompanied by a set of equalizing federal provincial transfers to alleviate the NFB differences that would otherwise result. However, full equalization of tax capacities is rarely implemented. Thus, one might opt for maintaining federal control of those resources that are more likely to be important and unequally distributed (such as oil and gas), while decentralizing others which are less important (such as mining and perhaps forestry). The decentralization of these resource bases also enables states to engage in resource management and conservation practices within their jurisdictions.

In practice, resource tax bases generally do not coincide with rents and thus resource taxes do have efficiency effects; they often distort capital and employment decisions. States might be tempted to use them as instruments to attract economic activity to their jurisdictions, thereby violating the efficiency of the internal economic union. Thus, what ideally could be a fully efficient source of state revenue could turn out to be a highly distortionary tax. In these circumstances, the case for decentralized control is weakened.

However, some resource taxes, such as royalties and fees and severance taxes on production and/or output, are designed to cover costs of local service provision and could be assigned to local governments. In addition, subnational governments could also impose taxes to discourage local environmental degradation. This rationale explains the practice in Canada, Australia and the USA of having intermediate-level governments (in the USA, local governments as well) impose such taxes on natural resources.

Resource taxes in developing countries are typically a central government responsibility. In a few countries, such as Colombia and the Russian Federation, tax administration is decentralized to sub-national governments. Important exceptions to central domination in this area include Malaysia, where resource taxes are a shared responsibility between federal and state governments, and India, where such taxation is solely a state responsibility.

Property taxes

Taxes on real property are usually mainstays of local finance, and with good reason. Real property is immobile across jurisdictions so the efficiency costs of using it as a tax base are low. Moreover, it can be argued that many benefits of local public services accrue to property owners, so the tax serves as a sort of benefit tax. Of course, there are costs incurred in administering property taxes, and considerable discretion is involved in arriving at property values for taxation. Thus, there is an argument for having states coordinate administration of property taxes, though not necessarily setting local rates.

Just as different states may have different fiscal capacities and can provide different levels of NFBs to their citizens, so municipalities have different fiscal capacities, particularly their real property tax bases. The case for equalizing transfers among municipalities within states is as strong as that for similar transfers across states. Of course, it would be the state which made the transfer rather than the federal government.

In industrial countries, it is common for local governments to require property developers to provide basic infrastructure in a new subdivision – the practice of 'gold-plating' or exactions. Such a practice has potential applications in developing countries.

The assignment of property taxes varies across developing countries. In Indonesia, property taxes are a central government responsibility, whereas in Brazil, China and the Philippines the responsibility is shared among federal, state and local governments. Property taxation is a state-local responsibility in Argentina, Malaysia and Pakistan. In most other developing countries (such as Bangladesh, Colombia, Mexico, Nigeria, Papua New Guinea and Thailand) it is a solely local responsibility. Thus, there is significant potential for decentralizing property taxes in developing countries. Colombia has successfully experimented with a tax on urban property value increases (valorization tax) to finance the infrastructure investment projects which were responsible for the improvements in property values. The city of Jakarta, Indonesia is experimenting with a betterment levy to finance urban infrastructure improvement projects.

Developing countries also frequently levy agricultural land taxes. Taxes based on land area, the market value of agricultural land, the productivity potential and market access of the land have been used as a source of central government revenues in many developing countries. These taxes are more suitably assigned to local governments.

Pricing for public services

A potentially important source of funds for publicly-provided services that are private in nature is pricing those services by user fees and licences. These are especially relevant for local and some state-public services since these are often private. The case for pricing public services is clearest where a service is not provided publicly for redistributive reasons (such as water, garbage, local utilities and recreational facilities). An advantage of pricing for public services is that it can promote efficient use of the services. This can be useful both for rationing available supplies and for determining how many resources to devote to providing the service. That is not to say that pricing is distributionally neutral in these cases. Indeed, many of these services are necessities and form an important part of consumption of lower-income persons. However, in an economy with a well-developed public sector, distributive objectives are probably better left to higher levels of government rather than being a component of each public service provided.

On the other hand, some important quasi-private public services are provided by the public sector largely for redistributive reasons, including health and education. Relying heavily on user fees to finance these services would seem to contradict this objective. That does not preclude limited pricing, for example, to cut down on overuse of medical services. In any case, these sources of revenue are likely to be more important to lower levels of government whose services tend to be private in nature. User pricing should not have an adverse effect on resource allocation nor is it costly to administer since it is simply an application of the fee-for-service principle. As mentioned, any adverse effects on equity can be addressed more effectively by more general policies applied by higher levels of government.

In summary, this discussion of the assignment of taxes makes it clear that the case for decentralizing taxing powers is not as compelling as that for decentralizing public service delivery. Lower-level taxes can introduce inefficiencies in the allocation of resources across the federation and can cause inequities among persons of different jurisdictions. Also, collection and compliance costs can increase significantly. These problems seem to be more severe for some taxes than for others, so the selection of which taxes to decentralize must be done with care. In the end, a balance must be reached between the need to achieve fiscal and political accountability at the lower levels of government and the disadvantages, from a national point of view, of having a fragmented tax system. In virtually all countries, the balance involves a fiscal gap between adjacent levels of government.

The trade-off between increased accountability and increased economic costs from decentralizing taxing responsibilities can be mitigated by the fiscal arrangements that exist between levels of government. As noted above, the system of fiscal transfers can serve to reduce the fiscal inefficiencies and inequities that arise from different fiscal capacities across states. In addition to this, some of the fragmentation that would otherwise occur from decentralizing taxes can be mitigated by joint occupation and harmonization of taxes among different jurisdictions. This will be discussed in the next section.

Co-occupation of tax bases

Taxes need not be exclusively assigned to one level of government or another, but may be occupied simultaneously by both. In some countries, both federal and state governments levy income taxes (United States, Canada), general sales taxes (Canada), payroll taxes (Canada) and excise taxes (Canada, United States). Indeed, even municipal governments may share income or sales tax bases (as in the United States) .

The co-occupation of tax bases can be done with varying degrees of coordination. At one extreme there may be no formal coordination in the sense that each level of government sets its policies independently, although even in this case tax policies will not be completely unrelated. For any given tax base there is a limit to how much it can be exploited for revenue purposes. The amount of 'tax room' available for one level of government will depend upon that occupied by the other. The division of the 'tax room' can affect the degree of harmonization in an otherwise uncoordinated system. For example, the greater the proportion of the 'tax room' occupied by the federal government, the more likely it is that the states will adopt tax structures which are similar to those of the federal government. This may be important for tax bases, like the income tax, that are important instruments for achieving national objectives. Indeed, determining the amounts of 'tax room' of various taxes the federal government should occupy is an important policy decision in a decentralized federation.

Alternative forms of coordination of co-occupied tax bases can exist. At the least there may be an exchange of taxpayer information and other auditing information, and there may be agreement on the formulas for the allocation of tax bases among jurisdictions and on the bounds of tax rates for sales and excise taxes. Common bases may be agreed upon or even common rate structures, and a common collection machinery may be adopted. At the limit, there may be highly centralized tax systems with agreed-upon tax-sharing formulas. The next section considers in more detail the consequences of different degrees of coordination and harmonization.

To summarize this discussion of tax assignment,Table 9.1 presents the main arguments for assignment of the various taxes to the three main levels of government – federal, state and local. A broad view of the extent of decentralization of tax bases in a sample of 15 developing countries is presented in Table 9.2.

Tax harmonization and coordination

The harmonization of tax systems in a federation (like the system of intergovernmental transfers) is a means by which the advantages of decentralized fiscal decision-making can be accomplished without excessively jeopardizing the efficient and equitable functioning of the national economy. In this section, we discuss the general purpose of tax harmonization and outline some of the ways in which harmonization can be achieved.

The objectives of tax harmonization

Tax competition among jurisdictions can be beneficial as it encourages cost-effectiveness and fiscal accountability in state governments. It can also lead to a certain amount of tax harmonization. At the same time, decentralized tax policies can cause certain inefficiencies and inequities in a federation and may lead to excessive administrative costs. Tax harmonization is intended to preserve the best features of tax decentralization while avoiding its disadvantages.

Inefficiencies from decentralized decision-making can occur in a variety of ways. For one, states may implement policies that discriminate in favour of their own residents and businesses. They may also engage in beggar-thy-neighbour policies intended to attract economic activity from other states. Inefficiency may also occur simply from the fact that distortions will arise from differential tax structures chosen independently by state governments with no strategic objective in mind. Inefficiencies also can occur if state tax systems adopt different conventions for dealing with businesses (and residents) who operate in more than one jurisdiction. This can lead to double taxation of some forms of income and non-taxation of others.

Table 9.1 Conceptual basis of tax assignment

Tax type	Determination of base	rate	Collection and adminstration	Comments
Customs	F	F	F	International trade taxes
Corporate income	F	F	F	Mobile factor
Resource taxes				
Rent (profit) tax Royalties/fees: severance taxes	F	F	F	Unequally distributed
production taxes	S,L	S,L	S,L	Benefit taxes
Conservation chgs	S,L	S,L	S,L	Environment preservation
Personal income	F	F,S,L	F	Redistributive, mobility, stabilization
Wealth taxes (capital, wealth transfers, inheritances)	F	F,S	F	Redistributive
Payroll	F,S	F,S	F,S	Social programme
Value-added tax	F	F	F	Admin. costs, stabilization
Single-stage sales				
Option A costs	S	S,L	S,L	Higher compliance
Option B	F	S	F	Harmonized
'Sin' taxes				
alcohol, tobacco	F,S	F,S	F,S	Health care shared
gambling, betting	S,L	S,L	S,L	State and local responsibility
lotteries	S,L	S,L	S,L	State and local responsibility
race tracks	S,L	S,L	S,L	State and local responsibility
Taxation of 'Bads'				
Carbon	F	F	F	Global/national pollution
Btu taxes	F,S,L	F,S,L	F,S,L	By extent of pollution
Motor fuels	F,S,L	F,S,L	F,S,L	Tolls on road use
Effluent charges	F,S,L	F,S,L	F,S,L	By extent of pollution
Congestion tolls	F,S,L	F,S,L	F,S,L	Tolls on road use
Parking fees	L	L	L	Local congestion
Motor vehicles				
Registration	S	S	S	State revenue source
Driver's licences	S	S	S	State revenue source
Business taxes	S	S	S	Benefit tax
Excises	S	S	S	Immobile base
Property	S	L	L	Benefit tax, immobile
Land	S	L	L	Benefit tax, immobile
Frontage/betterment	S,L	L	L	Cost recovery
Poll tax	S,L	S,L	S,L	Non-distorting
User charges	F,S,L	F,S,L	F,S,L	Payment for services

F = federal; S = state; L = local.

Table 9.2   Tax assignment in selected developing countries

Type of tax	Number of countries with sub-national determination of:		
	Base	Rate	Tax collection & administration
Customs	1	1	2
Income & gifts	1	1	6
Estates	4	4	4
Corporate	1	1	4
Resource	3	3	6
Sales	4	5	7
VAT	1	1	4
Excises	8	8	12
Property	11	12	14
Fees	10	10	12
Residual powers	2	2	2

Note: Sample countries (15): Argentina, Bangladesh, Brazil, China, Colombia, India, Indonesia, Malaysia, Mexico, Nigeria, Pakistan, Papua New Guinea, Philippines, Russian Federation, Thailand.

State tax systems may also introduce inequities into the tax system. Different states may have differing degrees of progressivity in their tax structures and these may differ considerably from national equity norms of the federal government. To the extent that one views the federal government as being responsible for redistributive equity, this makes their task more difficult. States may also be induced by competitive pressures to implement tax measures that appear to be regressive from a national perspective. For instance, the mobility of either high-income or low-income persons would encourage them to set tax structures that are less progressive than they would otherwise be.

Administrative costs are also likely to be excessive in an uncoordinated tax system. This is especially true if the states and the federal government both occupy a given tax field. Taxpayer compliance is costly because of the need to deal with more than one tax system. Auditing and collection costs are likely to be higher as well, as taxpayers may be able to avoid taxes by cross-border transactions of a book nature and authorities cannot obtain information from operations in other jurisdictions. In addition, the auditing priorities of state governments may themselves become skewed in favour of generating revenue from non-residents or from residents doing business outside the jurisdiction.

Tax harmonization is intended to eliminate some of these excesses. At the same time, a harmonized tax system can serve as a useful complement to the system of intergovernmental transfers. For one thing, taxes that are harmonized vertically can be used as devices for getting revenues to state governments through tax-sharing. For another, if taxes are harmonized across states, equalizing transfers based on tax capacities of states are easier to implement.

The importance of tax harmonization varies by type of tax. Taxes on businesses, such as corporation income taxes, are good candidates for harmonization to the extent that they are used by state governments. They apply to a mobile tax base and would pose significant administrative costs if uncoordinated. Personal income taxes would also benefit from some harmonization. Compliance costs to taxpayers and collection costs to governments could be reduced, and distortionary treatment of capital income could be mitigated. In addition, national equity objectives could be addressed through harmonization measures. The case for harmonizing sales and excise taxes is less compelling. The main inefficiencies here result from cross-border shopping problems and those are likely to be handled by tax competition among jurisdictions. There could be some administrative savings by having a coordinated system of sales taxes between the federal government and the states to reduce the compliance cost to sellers and to economize on auditing by tax authorities. Some form of harmonization would be virtually mandatory should states attempt to operate a VAT system. In this case, harmonization alone is unlikely to overcome the problems of dealing with cross-border transactions in a federation without border controls. For other tax bases (such as payroll taxes, property taxes and user fees) the advantages of harmonization would seem to be minimal.

Methods of tax harmonization

Varying degrees of tax harmonization are possible depending on the degree of decentralization in the tax system. The following are listed in decreasing order of centralization, focusing largely on systems of harmonization encompassing both the federal government and the states.

At one extreme, a full tax-sharing arrangement may exist whereby the federal government determines the tax base and rate structure (perhaps in consultation with the states) and agrees to share a certain proportion of it with the states. This is basically analogous to an unconditional grant scheme with the size of the grant dependent upon total tax collections. The sharing formula could be based on the principle of derivation or on some other formula (including a simple one like equal per capita shares). Though this scheme is certainly fully harmonized, the states are purely passive recipients of revenues collected by the federal government so there are no advantages to decentralizing tax responsibility. Obviously, a fully uniform tax structure is achieved and national equity and efficiency goals can be pursued at minimal administrative cost. Virtually any type of tax could be shared in this way.

The advantages of a single system can be retained while at the same time allowing the states some responsibility for revenue raised in their jurisdiction. For example, the federal government could determine both the base and rate structure for a particular type of tax and choose the rate level to generate the amount of revenue they need from the tax. The states could then piggyback on the federal base and rate structure by setting a state tax rate to apply to federal tax liabilities that would determine how much revenue is owing to the state. The federal government would collect the tax on behalf of the state and pass on each state's share of the revenue. An allocation formula would be needed to determine allocation of the tax base among states. In the case of personal income taxes, it could be based on the residence of taxpayers. For corporate taxes, the allocation formula might be based on some measure of the profits generated in each state. This is difficult to do with precision given that many corporate activities affect profits across the nation (administrative overheads, research and development, advertising, and so an). Furthermore, allocation by profits would provide an incentive for corporations to engage in book transactions in order to take their profits in low-tax states. Allocation formulas actually used are usually based on the share of payrolls in each state, the share of revenues, the share of capital stock or some combination of those. Such a system combines a high degree of harmonization of the base, rate structure and collection machinery with the devolution of some revenue raising responsibility to the states. It is ideally suited to personal and corporate income taxes where harmonization is desired for national equity and efficiency.

However, it might have some disadvantages. For example, if the states occupy significant 'tax room' for the harmonized tax, they may feel constrained by an inability to use the base or rate structure for policy purposes. In the case of sales taxes, such a system might constrain the type of tax operated by the federal government. For example, if the federal government wished to operate a VAT, it would be difficult to allow the provinces to piggyback on it while setting their own VAT level (let alone exemptions). The process of crediting that is entailed by a VAT would be very cumbersome for intermediate transactions across state borders. An alternative would be to have the states levy single-stage sales taxes with the same final base as the federal VAT and a common collection procedure. The problems with monitoring cross-border transactions would disappear but some of the advantages of a VAT would be lost (such as purging final sales of taxes levied on inputs at earlier stages).

The degree of harmonization could be reduced by allowing states to do more than simply set a rate to apply to federal tax liabilities. States could be allowed to set their own rate structures and apply them to the federal base. Part of this would involve setting their own systems of exemptions, deductions and credits, or alternatively they could be allowed to participate with the federal government in the choice of the base. States could also participate in collection procedures (for example, auditing). Indeed, they may have a great interest in doing so if their taxes include certain items of interest to them but not to the federal government (tax credits, allocations of tax revenue to their jurisdiction, and so forth).

State and federal taxes could coexist in the same area with separate collection machinery but with some agreement over the base, the rate structure and formula for allocating revenues among states. This could give considerable harmonization while retaining a great deal of decentralized responsibility for tax policy. Even this extent of harmonization might be important in fields like corporate and personal income taxes where national efficiency and equity objectives are at stake. Of course, the administrative advantages of having a single tax-collecting authority would be lost.

It is not necessary for the federal government to co-occupy a tax base for harmonization to occur. States may occupy bases by themselves and still have some agreement concerning bases, rate structure, allocation formulas and the like. At the least, they could have agreements to exchange information on taxpayers to improve compliance. Agreements among states to harmonize taxes is analogous to tax treaties among nations.

Finally, harmonization need not require formal agreements among states; tax competition could be relied upon to harmonize certain aspects of taxes, such as income tax bases or indirect tax rates. As mentioned earlier, the disadvantage of this is that it does not rule out the possibility of beggar-thy-neighbour tax policies being implemented by the states.

Implications for tax reform

Much of the above discussion has been abstract and has been based on principles of fiscal federalism that have been conceived largely for industrialized countries. Although the principles are basically universal, their application to developing countries will be constrained by institutional features of those countries. There are some key ways in which the fiscal systems of developing countries differ from those in industrialized countries and may temper reforms.

First, public sectors in developing countries tend to focus on different policy objectives. In industrialized economies, government spending is usually more oriented towards redistributive objectives, using such instruments as transfers, social insurance and provision of basic public services that redistribute in kind. This means that the tax system is relatively less important as an instrument for redistribution. In developing countries, governments are involved more with fostering economic development through participation in industrial projects and the provision of infrastructure and basic public services. The systems of transfers and social insurance are less elaborate or even non-existent. Tax systems differ considerably as well: developing countries tend to rely much more on indirect taxes, including excises and trade taxes, than do industrialized countries, and this hampers their ability to use the tax system for redistribution. The administrative machinery for collecting taxes also tends to be less efficient. Finally, developing countries tend to have fiscal systems that are much more centralized than in developed countries. Even where expenditure responsibilities are decentralized, generally taxation is not. Much of the funding for state and local services often comes from the federal government in a way that impedes lower-level autonomy and fiscal responsibility.

One might expect that, as these economies develop, their fiscal systems would converge with those of industrialized countries. Indeed, there are those who would argue that convergence itself would enhance development by making public sectors more effective. In particular, decentralization of the provision of fiscal services to lower levels of government would make governments more efficient and more responsive to the actual needs of the citizens and the economy. To be effective, this decentralization would have to be accompanied by enough decentralization of revenue-raising responsibilities to make lower levels of government fiscally autonomous and accountable. It would also have to be accompanied by a system of fiscal arrangements which includes both a set of fiscal transfers designed to maintain the efficiency and equity of the internal economic union, and appropriate measures to coordinate tax systems among various jurisdictions.[8]

The process of tax reform is high on the agenda of many developing countries. The existence of multiple levels of government with their own revenue-raising responsibilities will affect the directions of tax reform that are desirable as well as feasible. In this concluding section, we summarize some possibilities for tax reform without reference to any particular country. There will, of course, be institutional or constitutional constraints which limit the extent to which ideal economic systems can actually be implemented.

Tax assignment

To the extent that the assignment of taxes to different levels of government can be chosen, it should be done according to the principles outlined earlier. Efficiency, equity and administrative simplicity are all factors. Efficiency would suggest centralizing taxes applied on more mobile bases. Equity would suggest centralizing taxes that serve a redistributive purpose. The less important cross-border transactions are to the tax base, the simpler it is to decentralize tax administration.

Direct taxes are good candidates for federal assignment, especially corporation taxes, capital taxes, personal income taxes and taxes on wealth and wealth transfers. Taxes on trade should also be federal. The states could use payroll and indirect taxes, both excises (including energy taxes) and general sales taxes. Property taxes are ideally suited for local revenues, although the state government may have a role in assessment and in equalizing municipal revenues. User fees are also a good source of state and local revenue.

Resource taxes are an interesting case. Efficiency considerations would make them suitable for state use since they are immobile. Also, from a resource management point of view, state control might be beneficial. However, in many countries, major resource tax bases (such as oil and gas) are very unevenly distributed so fiscal inefficiencies and inequities can arise from their assignment to state governments. In these circumstances, federal assignment would be desired, whereas those like forestry and minerals could remain with the states. If some or all resource taxes are assigned to the states, it is important that the federal government implement a system of over-arching equalizing transfers as discussed below which includes state resource taxes.

Tax design

The design of particular taxes will depend upon the level at which they are controlled. This is most apparent with sales taxes. At the federal level there are good reasons for using a VAT for general sales taxation; a VAT ensures that traded goods are treated properly and that final sales are purged of all taxes on business inputs. And the tax can be levied at the destination with little difficulty. Compliance problems should be reduced and collection costs minimized for the tax authority (although compliance costs for the private sector will be higher). However, for general sales taxes levied by the states a VAT is much more difficult to administer. There are several reasons for this. First, the system of crediting taxes on inputs becomes complicated on cross-border transactions. Taxes levied on a transaction in one state, in which an intermediate input is sold to a producer in another state, are credited to the tax authority in the latter; the credit should be transferred to the 'exporting' state. Different tax systems among states are complicated to administer, especially without border controls. A second problem also arises from the absence of border controls; cross-border shopping by final demanders is difficult to prevent so it is difficult to tax on a full destination basis. From a practical point of view, taxes on cross-border purchases will accrue to the state of origin rather than that of destination. On the administrative side, the cost of operating several state-level VATs would be quite high. Also, auditing priorities within a given state could be skewed in favour of those things which are likely to generate revenue for a state's own treasury.

The design of destination-based excise taxes by state governments will also be constrained by cross-border transactions. These will limit the extent to which neighbouring states can choose differential tax rates. Cross-border purchases are typically taxed at origin rather than destination. Specific excise taxes could, of course, be levied on an origin basis. While this would avoid the cross-border shopping problem, it could induce inefficiency in the inter-nal common market; also, any tax differentials would give an incentive for producers to locate in the lower-tax jurisdictions. States would thus be more inclined to engage in beggar-thy-neighbour tax competition.

The choice of income tax structures could also be influenced by decentral-ization to the states. Again, tax competition would affect the degree of progressivity of the personal income tax system and the structure of incent-ives for the corporate tax system. Tax administration would also be more complicated, especially for income earned outside the jurisdiction. In the absence of tax treaties and administrative cooperation, it would be very difficult to ensure compliance. Moreover, with independent decision-making, it would be difficult to ensure that income earned outside a given jurisdiction was taxed once and only once within the federation.

The design of some other forms of taxation are much less constrained by decentralization. Payroll taxation avoids most of the above problems since cross-border transactions are a relatively small part of payrolls; most workers reside where they work. Similarly, resource taxes, property taxes and user charges are relatively unaffected by decentralization. The only effect of decentralization is to induce some fiscal accountability through tax competition and that may be beneficial rather than detrimental.

The tax mix

All countries obtain their tax revenues from a variety of sources, even though the bases of some taxes are quite similar. In the absence of federalism considerations, the balance among tax sources depends on a variety of factors. Relying on a mix of taxes ensures that rates for each component tax are lower than they would be otherwise. That makes tax administration less costly by reducing the incentive to evade and avoid taxes. It also broadens the net of taxpayers since those who can avoid one type of tax may end up paying another. The cost of having a mix of taxes, however, is duplication of administrative costs. Also, other goals of government, such as equity, may be compromised by not being able to pursue redistributive policies through a given type of tax.

The decentralization of some tax bases may further constrain the public sector in its choice of tax mix and its ability to achieve its overall goals. For example, if significant tax responsibility is decentralized to the states, the ability of the federal government to choose the optimal mix for the entire federation may be compromised, especially if decentralization is concentrated on one tax type.

Tax harmonization and coordination

Tax harmonization and coordination are important objectives of tax policy; they contribute to the efficiency of the internal common market, reduce collection and compliance costs and help to achieve national standards of equity. Tax harmonization may be horizontal (among states) as well as vertical (between the federal government and the states). In the case of tax bases jointly occupied by the federal government and the states, harmonization can be achieved without sacrificing state fiscal responsibility by having a single centralized collection procedure combined with the ability of the states to decide on their own tax rates. Vertical harmonization can be of varying degrees. The states may simply be required to abide by the federal base but be allowed to impose their own rate structures, or they may be required to abide by the federal rate structure and only be allowed to choose their own rate levels and possible schedules of credits. Fiscal responsibility would require at least that they be able to set their own rate levels. A formula must exist for allocating tax bases among states for those who are taxpayers in more than one state.

It is more difficult to harmonize indirect taxes than direct taxes. On the other hand, harmonization of indirect taxes is not nearly as pressing a need since the efficiency costs of decentralized indirect tax systems is not likely to be high and equity objectives are not likely to be threatened. Since state sales taxes should be single-staged, it would not be possible to operate a joint federal–state VAT system. The best that can be done is to adopt a common base for the state sales tax and the federal VAT and administer them jointly. If the states alone operate general sales taxes, their bases could be harmonized by agreement.

Tax-sharing schemes in which the revenues from a federally administered tax source are shared with the states of origin may be used to address fiscal gaps at the state level. These have the advantage that the tax system remains highly harmonized. However, they have the significant disadvantage that no fiscal responsibility is assumed by the states. It is generally preferable for the states to be allowed to set their own rates within an otherwise harmonized system. If revenue-sharing is used, it is preferable that it not be done on a tax-by-tax basis.

Notes

1   Classic sources include Musgrave (1959), Oates (1972) and Breton and Scott (1978). For more recent general surveys, see Wildasin (1986) and Boadway (1992). The principles applied to developing countries may be found in Boadway, Roberts and Shah (1994).
2   This is an economic principle. There may well be important political constraints that prevent the decentralization of economic power, such as the danger of destabilizing the country. In this chapter, our main concern will be with economic criteria.
3   Though these are stated in terms of federal-state grants, similar arguments apply for the case of state-municipal grants.
4   The exact circumstances in which this will be the case are discussed in Boadway and Flatters (1982); see also Wildasin (1986).
5   See Shah (1991) for a detailed discussion of the appropriate formulas.
6   For a contrary view, see Burgess, Howes and Stern (1993), who have advocated a system of state VATs for India.
7   For a general discussion of the way in which resource taxes could be designed to capture rents, see Boadway and Flatters (1993).
8   A summary of the case for decentralizing fiscal systems in developing countries may be found in Boadway, Roberts and Shah (1994).

References

Boadway, R. (1992) *The Constitutional Division of Powers: An Economic Perspective*, Ottawa: Minister of Supply and Services Canada.

Boadway, R. W. and F. R. Flatters (1982) *Equalization in a Federal State: An Economic Analysis*, Ottawa: Minister of Supply and Services Canada.

Boadway, R. W. and F. R. Flatters (1993) *The Taxation of Natural Resources*, Washington, DC: The World Bank.

Boadway, R., S. Roberts and A. Shah (1994) *The Reform of Fiscal Systems in Developing Countries: A Federalism Perspective*, Washington, DC: The World Bank.

Breton, A. and A. Scott (1978) *The Economic Constitution of Federal States*, Toronto: University of Toronto Press.

Buchanan, J. M. (1950). 'Federalism and Fiscal Equity', *American Economic Review*, vol. 40, pp. 583–99.

Burgess, R., S. Howes and N. Stern (1993) 'The Reform of Indirect Taxes in India', mimeo.

McLure, C. E. Jr. (1993) *Vertical Fiscal Imbalance and the Assignment of Taxing Powers in Australia*, Stanford, Cal.: Hoover Institution.

Musgrave, R. A. (1959) *The Theory of Public Finance*, New York: McGraw Hill.

Oates, W. E. (1972) *Fiscal Federalism*, New York: Harcourt Brace Jovanovich.

Shah, A. (1991) *Perspectives on the Design of Intergovernmental Fiscal Reform*, Washington, DC: The World Bank.

Shah, A. and J. Whalley (1991) 'Tax Incidence Analysis of Developing Countries: An Alternative View', *World Bank Economic Review*, no. 5, September, pp. 535–52.

Wildasin, D. E. (1986) *Urban Public Finance*, Chur, Switzerland: Harwood Academic.

10
Tax Incentives for Investment in Developing Countries
Richard M. Bird[1]

Many papers have surveyed the subject of tax incentives for growth in developing countries over the years.[2] The usual pattern of such surveys is to describe the variety of incentives found in a number of countries and evaluate their likely effectiveness and efficiency. This chapter takes a different tack. Its aim is not to survey tax incentives but rather to reflect on what we know about them as a result of previous studies and to suggest some lessons that might be drawn from this knowledge.

To make the topic more manageable, only selective tax incentives designed to improve the quantity (and perhaps the quality) of investment in developing countries, thus increasing their rate of economic growth, are considered. Neither the incentives (and disincentives) for investment created by different tax structures nor the many special tax incentives intended to foster other policy objectives such as research and development, regional development, employment, exports or savings are discussed at length.[3]

The ruling fiscal orthodoxy is clearly that tax incentives in general are a 'bad thing'. Either they are redundant and ineffective – foregoing revenue and complicating the fiscal system without adding to capital formation – or they are distorting and inefficient – directing investment into less than optimal channels. Studies of countries as different as Indonesia (Gillis, 1985) and Argentina (Sanchez-Ugarte and Zabala Marti, 1986) appear to support these arguments. Even in the successful East Asian countries which have made considerable use of tax incentives in the past, some recent analysts have condemned the tax incentive approach and urged the adoption of a more neutral system.[4]

At one level, such arguments seem convincing. Clearly, tax incentives for investment have sometimes had undesirable effects and have seldom been demonstrated to be effective and efficient. At another level, however, something seems odd about this conclusion. Consider, for example, the five Asian countries usually considered the principal development successes of the postwar period: Japan, South Korea, Taiwan, Singapore and Hong Kong. With the exception of Hong Kong (Krauss, 1983), all these countries have made extensive and prolonged use of specific tax (and other) incentives both before and during their periods of most rapid growth.[5] Moreover, most countries in the world continue to utilize similar special tax incentives for investment, and, in spite of recent moves away from incentives in a few countries, mainly in Latin America (Bird, 1992), most seem likely to continue to do so in the future. If everyone is doing it, can it really be wrong?

The apparently sharp disparity between expert opinion and policy practice leads to several questions. Are the East Asian countries mistaken in thinking that tax incentives and other policies fostering investment had something to do with their growth?[6] Are other countries mistaken in hoping for the same result? Does the 'Hong Kong model' of low and uniform taxes that is currently being urged on such prospective NICs (newly-industrializing countries) as Thailand and Colombia, as well as on such less-developed countries as Malawi and Papua New Guinea, offer a more reliable path to success than the JKS (Japan–Korea–Singapore) model of fiscal (and other) interventionism? Would the East Asian 'tigers' have done as well – perhaps better – without the incentives? Does the apparent failure of superficially similar incentive packages in countries such as Indonesia and Argentina reflect differences in political or social 'culture',[7] the macroeconomic context,[8] or simply differences in the design and implementation of incentives? To put the point at its simplest, in the 1970s would nothing have worked in Argentina and anything have worked in South Korea?

It is not easy to answer such questions. Nonetheless, a review of the growing literature on investment incentives suggests two conclusions. First, although the evidence supporting the case for incentives is not conclusive, neither is the case against them. Our understanding both of what determines investment and of the effects of incentives on investment still leaves much to be desired. The next section of the chapter develops this point.

Second, regardless of how the arguments among the experts are finally resolved, investment incentives are likely to continue to exist in a variety of forms in many developing countries. No matter what one's view of the general efficacy of such incentives may be, it is therefore important to set out as clearly as possible how to make them more efficient and effective. From this perspective the most important (and most neglected) aspect of incentive policy in most countries is an adequate monitoring and review system.

When such a system is combined with appropriate attention to design and implementation, and when fundamentally sound policies (for example, on stabilization) are in place in other areas, there may be a useful, if limited, role for investment incentives in a growth-oriented development policy. In the absence of these conditions, however, even the most generous and well-designed incentives seem likely to prove as ineffective and inefficient in the future as most of them have been in the past. The final section of the chapter develops this argument.

Trends and cycles in investment incentives

The history of investment incentives in developing countries (as in developed countries) in the postwar period may be viewed from two quite different perspectives. One perspective sees this history as a more or less steady trend away from the extensive reliance on incentives that characterized the initial development efforts in many countries in the 1950s and early 1960s, to the nirvana of 'incentiveless' tax systems now commonly recommended by international experts (for example the World Bank, 1991) and, to some extent, put into place in a few countries in recent years.[9] In this view, the palpable failure of central planning in Eastern Europe and elsewhere, the accumulated (though not unquestionable) empirical evidence of the inefficiency and ineffectiveness of incentives (Ebrill, 1987), and the growth of economic knowledge all point in the same direction: away from the sort of interventionist policy represented by incentives and towards the ideal of a uniform 'level playing field' in which market forces, rather than government officials, make investment decisions. The move away from incentives is seen as part of the general move towards market- rather than state-dominated allocative decisions. The truth about incentives has now been revealed to knowledgable experts, and once this truth has been fully absorbed at the policy-making level, the end of incentives will be in sight.

The second perspective on recent changes in attitudes and actions on incentives is quite different. In this view, many different ideas and approaches to incentives may be found in the literature. Which ideas influence policy often depend as much on chance and circumstance as on their inherent merit. Over time both ideas and practices may change. For example, the demise of the central Soviet planning dream supports the current trend away from interventionism and towards the market. However, since the ideas that dominate at any point in time reflect less increments in knowledge than changes in fashion, they may well be reversed a few years down the road.

Which view is correct? Does the recent de-emphasis on investment incentives represent a trend or a cycle? The evidence discussed below suggests that, for better or worse, investment incentives are not dead but, at most, dormant. Wise policy advisers should therefore stand ready to ensure that as and when the reform cycle turns and incentives creep back into practice, the more egregious errors of the past are avoided.

Shah (1995) lists tax holidays in at least 14 developing countries, accelerated depreciation schemes in at least 28, and other investment incentives (credits, reinvestment allowances and so on) in at least 21.[10] Earlier surveys (Lent, 1967; Shah and Toye, 1978; Gandhi, 1987) similarly found widespread use of a variety of tax incentives in all parts of the world. Chia and Whalley (1995) suggest that not only is the variety of tax incentives currently found in developing countries, greater than that in developed countries, but that such incentives are now more common in developing countries than they were a decade ago. Trends appear to have been different in different regions of the world, however, with relatively more use of incentives in Asia, less in Latin America, and little change in Africa.

In contrast, a recent review of tax policy advice found that the attitude to tax incentives in the 1950s and 1960s was markedly different from that which now prevails (Goode, 1993). In the earlier period, reports and advisers frequently favoured tax incentives to channel investment in one direction or another. Later, as scepticism grew about both the efficacy of incentives and the wisdom of interventionist policies in general, attitudes changed, and tax incentives for investment fell into disfavour.[11]

At first, incentives were condemned as ineffective in encouraging investment and costly in terms of revenue foregone (Heller and Kaufmann, 1963). Subsequently, as the neoclassical investment paradigm came to dominate the literature following the pioneering work of Hall and Jorgenson (1967),[12] less emphasis was placed on the ineffectiveness of investment incentives. After all, if investment is assumed to respond to changes in the cost of capital, and incentives change the cost of capital, then incentives must affect investment.

Even if incentives were effective in channelling investment into favoured sectors, however, they might still be inefficient because they distort investment decisions away from those that would have been made in their absence.[13] The ability to channel investments in directions favoured by the authorities is not considered a virtue by those who put their trust in markets rather than governments. In particular, the 'new political economy' with its emphasis on the possibility of destructive rent-seeking behaviour in response to state-granted favours argues against tax incentives as it does against trade protection (Krueger, 1993). Thus, most economists remain sceptical about the usefulness of investment incentives, although the grounds for this scepticism have changed over time.

Recently, however, some developments in economic theory have cast a slightly more favourable light on incentives. The 'new trade theory', for instance, with its emphasis on imperfect markets and external economies, appears to some to have reopened the case for selective government intervention in trade and factor markets. The relevance of these ideas in the real world remains doubtful, owing both to the unclear importance of external economies and the concern that governments may not be capable of implementing even beneficial interventions without opening the doors to dubious special interests.[14] The exacting practical demands of strategic trade theory make it an uncertain basis on which to base an argument for incentives. However, the enthusiasm for such arguments of special interest groups that stand to gain from tax favours seems unlikely to be restrained.

Much the same may be said of the new literature on 'endogenous growth'. Some scholars have already demonstrated in this framework how incentives favouring research and development or machinery and investment may, under certain circumstances, accelerate growth.[15] The fact that a few empirical studies (notably De Long and Summers, 1991, 1992) lend some support to such arguments appears to make the case for interventionist policy stronger, even in the face of the many political and organizational constraints on implementing such policies in developing countries (Levy, 1993).

The partial shift in the ruling paradigm, with some incentives moving back into favour, may be illustrated by contrasting two studies done under World Bank auspices. A 1991 World Bank study reflects the prevailing conventional wisdom with respect to tax incentives: they erode the tax base, reduce investment efficiency (because they often respond to pressure from special interests), are ineffective and often inequitable, and facilitate rent-seeking activities and tax evasion.[16] In contrast, Shah concludes his introduction to an impressive set of empirical studies of tax incentives recently carried out under World Bank auspices as follows:

> Some tax preferences such as expensing, and (refundable) investment tax credits for R&D and machinery and equipment that embody advanced technology have strong theoretical and empirical support.
>
> (Shah, 1995 p. 27)

Expert attitudes to tax incentives may be changing again, whether influenced by changes in theory (endogenous growth), in empirical results (production function studies – see Shah, 1992b), in real world experience (the East Asian 'miracle'), in intellectual fashion, or in all these factors. Whatever the experts say, however, incentives continue to flourish and expand in the real world, as epitomized most recently by the extensive – most would say excessive – proliferation of tax holidays and other incentives in the countries of eastern and central Europe and Asia that are now in transition from command to market economies.[17] Thus, how best to design, implement and evaluate tax incentives remains an important question even for policy economists who are far from convinced that such incentives are worthwhile.

Design and implementation of tax incentives

Should investment incentives be temporary or permanent? Arguments may be made for both positions. Granting an incentive for a limited period may, for example, bring investment decisions forward in time. While timing changes should not affect long-term growth one way or the other, the resulting transitory boost in activity may sometimes be useful. On the other hand, the 'time inconsistency' of the subsequent removal of incentives may reduce their long-term impact in a world of rational optimizers. Indeed, if the announced withdrawal date is fully believed, there may not even be a temporary boost in investment activity. Some potential investors may place considerable weight on temporal consistency and the 'credibility' (permanence) of the low tax rates bestowed by non-time-limited incentives.

From an administrative perspective, time-limited incentives are more costly because it is necessary to decide both the duration of the incentive and to ensure that it is, in fact, limited to that period. On the other hand, the need to monitor what is going on has potential advantages that may be maximized if incentive laws are written in what is called 'sunset' form. A 'sunset' incentive is one that is granted for a limited period of time, for example five years. At the end of this period, it expires unless the investment agency provides a report to parliament demonstrating that the incentive has been working satisfactorily and the law is formally renewed. One difficulty with this formulation is that it is not at all obvious what would constitute 'satisfactory' performance. Nonetheless, such a provision would overcome one of the major weaknesses of virtually all existing incentives not only by requiring information to be collected but also by requiring it to be analysed and discussed publicly, thus ensuring a degree of transparency and reducing the opportunity for abuse.[18] Moreover, while time inconsistency may still be a problem, such arrangements seem likely to serve as something of a guarantee that certainty will prevail, at least during the lifetime of the incentive provision. In the circumstances of many developing countries, measures that increase certainty, even if they imply higher future tax rates, may result in a greater increase in investment than measures that reduce tax rates but increase the uncertainty of the investment environment.

Should incentives be specifically 'targeted'? Narrow targeting – to a particular type of asset or a particular narrowly-defined industrial sector, for example – is probably inadvisable. Detailed interventionism of this sort has largely, and correctly, gone out of fashion everywhere. Governments seem unlikely to be as good at picking 'winners' as unsubsidized investments made by those who must bear the consequences of their mistakes. Nonetheless, evidence suggests that in some circumstances incentives related to investment in machinery and equipment (such as expensing and investment tax credits) may be worthwhile. Moreover, broad asset-related targeting of this sort gives rise to fewer administrative and 'rent-seeking' problems, although it is not free from them (Gravelle, 1993) and is also likely to cost more.

On the other hand, although there may be an even stronger case for some subsidization of 'research and development' owing to the associated spillover effects (Shah, 1995), experience everywhere suggests that attempts to do so through the tax system are not likely to be very effective. They also create substantial administrative complexities and possibilities for evasion and rent-seeking.[19] Such incentives seem especially unlikely to be worthwhile in most developing countries, which would seem better advised to act on the stock of existing knowledge than to spend scarce public funds in the attempt to add to it.[20]

Should incentives be given only to foreign investment? Limiting incentives to foreign investment seems undesirable, although it may appear attractive given the apparent social gain to be reaped from additional foreign investment. Investment incentives are indeed more likely to result in increased capital formation in small open economies than in closed economies (Auerbach, 1995). This increase is not solely the result of additional foreign inflows since, in the absence of the incentive, there would presumably be an increased outflow of domestic savings seeking the higher returns available abroad. If the argument for investment incentives is simply that more investment is assumed to produce more growth, there is no case for discriminating between foreign and domestic investors. Investment is investment, and in a world where capital flight and capital repatriation are common occurrences, the distinction between domestic and foreign investment is not operational.

Nonetheless, current international tax rules make such a distinction, and optimal tax theory suggests that different foreign investors should be treated differently depending on their country of origin (Gersovitz, 1987). Although this complex area cannot be discussed here, it is probably neither advisable nor politically feasible to attempt to discriminate in favour of some foreign investors and against others.[21]

Incidentally, although many writers on tax incentives (for example, Usher, 1977) assert that incentives will be ineffective in attracting investment from abroad in the absence of so-called 'tax sparing' in the investor's home country, this occurs only when investments are financed by new equity from investors in countries which have foreign tax credit systems and no tax sparing, and when such investors both repatriate their profits and have no offsetting 'excess' credits they can use from earnings in high-tax countries. Although this situation arises more frequently with American investors since the 1986 US tax reforms, it is still a considerable exaggeration to present it as the norm. The more common case of direct foreign investment is probably one in which local tax incentives will generally affect reported profits (if not necessarily actual physical investment decisions).[22]

Should incentives be granted automatically? That is, should all those who qualify in terms of the law benefit, as is usually the case with incentives (for example, accelerated depreciation) found in the tax code, or should they be granted only to those who pass some appraisal by an official agency, as is usually the case with incentives (for example, tax holidays) found in separate investment laws and administered by special investment agencies? The argument in favour of the latter approach is essentially a variant of the argument that narrow is more cost-effective. It is also subject to the same criticism: why is the state best able to judge which narrow proposal is better? As mentioned earlier, there seems little to be said in favour of detailed industrial planning by the state, whether directly or indirectly, as through investment agencies approving investment proposals for state aid.

To sum up the preceding arguments, if incentives are to be given for investment they should probably be targeted broadly (for example, machinery and equipment), granted for a fixed number of years subject to periodic evaluation and extension, and given to both domestic and foreign investors if they fulfil the necessary conditions (for example, buy machines). Supporters of detailed interventionist industrial strategies will presumably receive little comfort from this assessment. On the other hand, those who are against all incentives may ask whether there is much to choose between a broad investment incentive and a low-rate, broad-based profits tax.

To put the point another way, given the revenue foregone by a broad investment incentive (which in a given time period has to be recouped by a higher rate on remaining taxable profits), might it not be better to forget the incentive and just cut the tax rate on the resulting broader base? Since most profits accrue to old (existing) capital, and since even the most ardent 'supply-sider' can hardly argue that the supply of old capital can be increased by lowering taxes, the case for focusing any tax concessions intended to expand growth on new investment seems strong.[23]

Suppose this argument is accepted: what is the best way to extend such favours? One of the favourite incentives of developing countries, tax holidays, does not look particularly good from this point of view. Indeed, as Mintz (1995) has argued, in some instances tax holidays may actually discourage investment.[24] Experience suggests holidays are also relatively more costly to administer and more prone to abuse.[25] If so, the choice would seem to be between some form of expensing and an investment tax credit. Given the administrative capacity of most developing countries, full or partial expensing (that is, immediate write-off) of the acquisition cost of machinery and equipment seems preferable (Harberger, 1990). Investment tax credits, particularly refundable credits with basis adjustments, may look better in theory as providing more 'bang per buck' (Meyer, 1993). In practice, however, this degree of refinement seems likely to impose too heavy a load on the weak organizational structure of tax administration to be advisable in most developing countries. Indeed, substantial scepticism has recently been expressed about the practicality of this approach even in developed countries (Gravelle, 1993).

Much the same conclusion emerges when the political economy of incentives is considered. As Levy (1993) has argued, incentive reforms are organizationally and politically difficult in developing countries – and the more they require government officials to make fine discriminatory decisions the more difficult they are to administer. A relatively simple, broadly-targeted incentive administered as part of an existing structure (for example, modifying the depreciation allowances already granted under the profits tax) thus seems more likely to be accepted, and implemented satisfactorily, than a 'new' device such as investment tax credits.

More broadly, if investment incentives in any form are to be granted, this form of incentive also seems to provide something of a compromise between the two quite disparate ways in which the role of government has been viewed in the incentive literature. In some earlier writings (Lent, 1967, for example), government was seen as the wise father dispensing favours. Sometimes mistakes may have been made in the precise design of the fiscal favour and in who got it, but the intentions were presumed to be good and implementation was assumed to be feasible. Some later analysts were more inclined to see either a conspiracy of government and private sector actors laughing on their way to the bank with the money looted from unsuspecting taxpayers, or a naive government vainly wasting money to no avail (Shah and Toye, 1978). Still others went further and saw the potential costs of such 'distortionary' policies as being much greater than the simple transfer of revenue to the unworthy or the increased excess burden arising from inappropriate investment decisions, as the mere existence of incentives may give rise to destructive 'rent-seeking' activities (Krueger, 1993).

Without delving deeper into these complex matters, all these problems may be reduced by keeping any incentives that are granted as general and simple in form as possible and subjecting the entire system of incentives to careful periodic public investigation, perhaps spurred on by an expiry date for the incentive legislation. This proposal is developed further in the last section of this chapter.

Evaluating tax incentives

Curiously, in spite of the widespread use of tax incentives over many years in developing and developed countries, their efficacy has seldom been evaluated. No one has a very clear idea in any country of either the revenue (or other) cost of incentives or of the size of any net economic benefits that may be attributed to them. Three reasons may be suggested for this state of affairs.

First, the data required for such evaluation are almost never collected by the investment promotion agencies that are responsible for initiating and administering incentives. Nor, as a rule, do the tax authorities track the benefits received by the favoured firms.

Second, such data do not exist because there are no incentives for anyone to collect information about incentives. Investment promotion agencies exist to promote investment, not to ask whether their activity is worthwhile. Tax collection agencies exist to collect taxes, not to measure how many taxes they are not collecting. And politicians exist, at least to some extent, by granting favours to special interests, not by demonstrating to those not so favoured that they should not have done so. Major changes in institutional incentive structures are needed to change this situation, as suggested in the next section.

Third, even where information exists it is hard to interpret. None of the models employed for this purpose is flawless, and accepting the results of the existing quantitative work on tax effects on investment as an adequate foundation for reforming incentive policy requires an unwarranted degree of faith in the correctness and completeness of both the underlying model and the data.

Broadly, four approaches have been used to evaluate tax incentives: surveys, econometric studies, simulations, and what may be called 'accounting' studies. Although economists traditionally distrust surveys because they either do not know how to interpret the results or consider them to be inherently biased, this approach continues to be a popular means of evaluating incentives. A well-known recent example of the survey approach is Guisinger (1985), which found, in sharp contrast to earlier surveys such as Reuber (1973), that incentives were decisive in influencing two-thirds of the investment decisions studied, with factor incentives (notably those to capital investment) being especially important in affecting location within countries and between countries in regional markets.

Accounting studies are those which estimate the various costs and benefits of incentives on the basis of information collected by investment and tax authorities. While, for reasons indicated above, there are surprisingly few such studies, they are in any case hard to interpret owing to the 'redundancy' problem emphasized by Usher (1977), namely, the inability to distinguish between investment induced by the incentive and that which would have taken place in any case.

An early study of Jamaica by Chen-Young (1967), for example, which suggested a highly favourable benefit–cost ratio for investment incentives in that country is questionable for this reason. A later, more careful, study of Jamaica by Thirsk (1989), concluded in contrast that the incentives offered in the 1980s were likely net losers, although they might produce a small net gain if exchange rate policy were more appropriate. This conclusion too, however, rests on an arbitrary assumption about the redundancy ratio.

Such 'accounting' information may be used as the basis for simulation studies, which calculate outcomes on the basis of fairly well-founded assumptions about critical variables (see Thirsk, 1989). This approach has been extensively employed to evaluate incentives in recent years in the form of MERT (marginal effective rate of taxation) studies following on the pioneering work of King and Fullerton (1984). Such studies calculate the size of the 'tax wedge' imposed at the margin on an investment with certain characteristics. The resulting numerical estimates have been used both to evaluate alternative incentive arrangements within particular countries (for example McLure and Zodrow, 1992) and to compare incentives across countries (as in Mintz and Tsiopoulos, 1992).

On the whole, MERT studies have not helped the cause of incentives. Since this approach (generally implicitly) posits uniform rates at the margin as desirable, and the intention of incentives as a rule is precisely to make rates non-uniform, it is not surprising that most tax incentives appear to be distorting.[26] On these grounds, for example, the replacement of tax incentives by a more neutral, uniform structure of business taxation was advocated for Colombia by McLure and Zodrow (1992).

The results of such analyses may be interesting, but they are by no means conclusive with respect to the effectiveness and efficiency of investment incentives, even if the characteristics assumed are 'typical' and the underlying assumptions (for example, on the enforceability of legal provisions) reasonable.[27] The reason is simple. Even if a MERT study shows that country A's effective taxes on new investment are lower than country B's by a certain amount, such studies say nothing about how responsive investment is to such differentials – even assuming they exist in practice as they do in the simulation.

Of course, evaluating investment response to tax-induced changes in the cost of capital is precisely the aim of econometric studies of investment functions. Unfortunately, there are major problems in interpreting such studies in developing countries. One is simply that it is far from clear how applicable the underlying neoclassical model is anywhere, let alone in developing countries with imperfect markets. Usher (1977) emphasized this point years ago, and the concerns he expressed remain largely valid. Secondly, there is a variety of econometric and theoretical questions that may be raised about such models even in developed countries, to the point where a recent survey concluded that 'we do not know very much about tax policy and business investment, at least at the aggregate level' (Rushton, 1992).[28] Finally, the policy implications of single-equation estimates of investment functions (for example, with and without incentives) are hard to interpret without the aid of a well-specified (and believable) general equilibrium and macroeconomic framework such as seldom exists in developing countries.[29]

Rules for reformers

To this point, this chapter has presented a condensed and selective review of a vast literature on a vast subject. This final section focuses not on what should be done (or not done) with respect to investment incentives, but rather on how whatever is to be done – if anything – is done. Two levels of such 'process analysis' may be distinguished.

The first level concerns the broad contextual factors that must be satisfied either to reform an existing incentive system or to put into place a better one. Unfortunately, those countries which appear to have the most to gain from well-directed investment incentives (the poorest countries with the most stagnant and often distorted economies) appear to be precisely those that are least likely to be able to adopt and implement such programmes successfully.

Even if the conditions for incentives were propitious in such countries, a second level of 'process' analysis – in the form of a set of rules that should govern those who design and implement tax incentives – leads to much the same conclusion. Once again, the prospects for successful use of tax incentives in the poorest countries are not bright.

Most evaluations of tax incentives have been carried out by fiscal economists. Such studies have focused largely on the design of tax incentives and on the still unresolved question of their effectiveness and efficiency. Recently, however, the considerable extent to which the implementation of reforms is limited by administrative factors has been emphasized. Successful fiscal reform, it has been argued, requires close attention to the administrative dimension (Bird, 1989). Moreover, those who wish to improve tax incentives in any country must also be aware of the major political implications and effects of the measures proposed; in the end, it is those implications that will generally decide the acceptability of the policy proposals. Even a well-designed reform which takes administration fully into account will not be successful unless and until it is politically acceptable.[30]

All three dimensions of tax incentive reform need to be considered simultaneously. The basic questions facing policy advisers may thus be formulated as follows:

- What is the best tax incentive design?
- Can this 'optimal' design be made acceptable to policy-makers? If not, how can it be adjusted to be made acceptable, and is it still the best possible design once these adjustments are made?
- Can even this 'adjusted' design be satisfactorily implemented in practice? If not, what further adjustments are necessary, and what are the implications of such adjustments in terms of both economic desirability and political acceptability?

All three questions are critical: 'good' reforms that will not be accepted or that, if accepted, cannot be implemented, are not really good reforms.

The bad news is that designing a successful tax incentive policy is a complex exercise involving not only considerable economic expertise (see, for example, Ahmad and Stern, 1991), but also considerable skill in handling both the administrative and political dimensions. As Harberger (1993) has recently noted, the 'art' of the economic policy practicioner is both different and more complex than the 'science' of economics alone.

The good news, however, is that reform is possible. Recent experience in a number of developing countries suggests that even major policy reforms can be put into place provided they satisfy three conditions:

1. They solve the problems giving rise to the demand for reform in the first place: for example, incentives are effective in channelling additional investment into desired sectors – for efficiency, of course, they should be the 'right' sectors – or more foreign investment is attracted.

2. They are accepted by those, both politicians and officials, who have the power to ensure their success or failure.
3. They can be implemented reasonably well with the resources at hand: that is, their implementation is not dependent on major, and undoubtedly slow, changes in public administration.

Given the difficulty of assessing the effectiveness of tax incentives, the ease with which they can be perverted to benefit existing special interests rather than serve the general interest, and the resource-intensive nature of good incentive administration, these arguments strongly suggest that incentives should be considered as potentially useful tools of public policy only when a country has not only a non-distorting macroeconomic environment, but also a stable political and administrative system that is committed to fostering economic growth. In the absence of such conditions, developing countries that attempt to emulate the Korean success of the 1970s and 1980s seem all too likely to produce the Argentine disaster of the same era.

What these considerations suggest is that only in a few 'middle-level' developing countries may there be a potentially useful, if limited, role for tax incentives for investment. Such countries, at least in theory, may be able to 'jumpstart' their leap to NIC status through the appropriate use of fiscal incentives and other selective policies – provided that their macroeconomic policies are appropriate and stable, that they have sufficient human and physical infrastructure to support productive investment, that their political environment is sufficiently stable to attract investors, and that their administration is sufficiently competent to administer incentives credibly.

Countries that are either above this level of development – for example, Korea – or below, as is most of Africa, would seem better advised to follow the broad-base, low-rate uniform treatment approach to taxation set out in World Bank (1991). The few 'Koreas' should do so both because of the emerging concern with equity as opposed to growth as a concern of public policy (Choi, 1992) and because of the lower payoff to interventionist policy as they move further up the technological and market curves. The many 'Tanzanias' should do the same, despite their greater need for more higher-productivity investment, because their most pressing problem is to create human, physical and institutional infrastructure rather than to guide how this infrastructure is utilized by private investors – and success in this task will generally require the scarce fiscal and policy resources of the state to be employed in more useful ways than trying to channel non-existent private investment into channels deemed 'better' by some politician or official. A strong state may be able to channel strong market forces to the benefit of all; a weak state that tries to do the same when markets are also weak seems more likely to weaken itself further to no good end.

The 'stage theory' of selective tax incentives suggested above is broadly that such incentives are generally not advisable in very low-income and relatively stagnant countries, that they may possibly be useful in stable and motivated growing countries, and that they are probably not needed in 'successful' developing countries. This approach is of course speculative. Regardless of whether one accepts it or not, however, certain rules may be suggested to guide tax incentive policy in any country that chooses to adopt such measures.[31]

The first rule is simply: Keep it Simple. Complex provisions attempting to 'fine tune' incentives to achieve detailed policy goals are likely to prove costly to administer and unlikely to produce the desired results at a reasonable cost. Few countries have sufficient information to design narrowly-focused incentives. If there are to be tax incentives, they should be few in number and as simple as possible in structure. From this perspective, as noted earlier, expensing investment in machinery or equipment (in whole or part) may, despite its greater revenue cost, prove a more useful approach in the circumstances of most developing countries than a complex scheme of tax holidays for firms that comply with a set of ancillary 'performance requirements' (Guisinger, 1985) or some form of incremental investment tax credit (Meyer *et al.*, 1993).

In any case, whatever the incentive chosen, the second rule is equally simple: Keep Records. Who gets what incentives? For how long? At what estimated cost in revenue foregone? And with what results in terms of investment, employment or whatever else is of interest? There will be problems in interpreting some of this information, as noted earlier. Nonetheless, in the absence of information (the usual state of affairs in most developing countries) there is little reason to think that incentives will play a useful role promoting economic growth. Instead, they are likely to turn out to be, at best, a costly means of advertising for foreign investment[32] and, at worst, a way of rewarding those considered worthy of receiving such favours.

Third, and combining some aspects of the first two rules, incentives should be required to undergo periodic evaluations in as rigorous a way as possible and, if they fail this test, should be terminated. If a country is unable, or unwilling, to put in place such a 'sunset' test of the efficacy of incentives, it should probably not be in the incentive business at all.[33] As with the second rule suggested above, however, at present this rule appears to be honoured in the breach in both developing and developed countries.

The threefold path of wisdom for developing countries that decide to take the incentive path is thus:

1. Avoid detailed, costly and complex attempts to divert private investment into preselected channels;
2. Institute adequate procedures to follow up the results of the incentives implemented; and
3. Eliminate incentives if, after a reasonable period, they do not seem to be achieving their desired ends.

Successful compliance with these apparently simple rules is not easy, as experience around the world suggests. The complex legislation, poor implementation, and complete lack of accountability that presently characterizes most investment incentives in most countries reflect political and institutional factors that seem unlikely to be changed easily or quickly. Nonetheless, in the absence of such changes, any new incentives that may be put into place on the basis of the vision of the Brave New World suggested by some of the recent empirical and theoretical literature will probably soon come to resemble instead the sad and familiar world of all too many existing incentives.

Notes

1 I am grateful to Nelson Dias, Jack Mintz, Sudipto Mundle and Guillermo Perry for helpful comments on an earlier draft of this chapter.

2 For examples, see Heller and Kaufmann (1963), Lent (1967), Shah and Toye (1978), and several of the papers in Gandhi (1987) and Shah (1995a).

3 There are, of course, many studies on each of these subjects. On regional development incentives, for example, see Bird (1966), Modi (1982) and Sanchez-Ugarte (1987); on employment incentives, see Lent (1971) and Bird (1982); on savings incentives, see Byrne (1976) and Ebrill (1987); on export incentives, see Balassa (1975) and De Wulf (1978); and on research and development incentives, see McFetridge and Warda (1983). All but the last of these references deal with developing countries.

4 See Ishi (1993) on Japan and Choi (1992) on Korea.

5 See Ishi (1993) on Japan, Bahl, Kim and Park (1986) and Trela and Whalley (1995) on Korea, Chang and Riew (1990) on Taiwan, and Asher (1988) on Singapore.

6 To quote a recent appraisal: 'Generally, the promotion of investment through the use of incentives has been effective' (Sumantoro, 1993, p. 266). Of course, many other factors were also important in explaining the Asian success stories such as macroeconomic stability, high and growing investment in 'human capital', and the 'market-driven' (export) nature of growth: see Summers and Pritchett (1993). Nonetheless, high investment levels clearly played a critical part, as emphasized by Young (1993).

7 Ishi (1993, p.156), for example, suggests that 'socio-cultural' factors seem more likely to explain high savings rates in Japan than tax incentives.

8 See, for example, Thirsk (1989) on the importance of this factor in evaluating Jamaican incentives. Investment incentives are obviously less likely to be effective in countries with high variability in inflation and growth rates such as Argentina in the 1980s, just as export incentives are unlikely to be very effective in countries with substantial exchange rate instability.

9 The best-known example is probably Indonesia (Gillis, 1985) but similar, if less drastic, moves may be seen in a number of Latin American countries in recent years, including Bolivia, Mexico and Colombia (Bird, 1992). Incidentally, as Asher (1992) notes, even the Indonesian case was not really the 'clean sweep' of incentives sometimes portrayed.

10 Although there is some overlap among the countries thus counted, other studies (e.g. Mintz, 1995) list various incentives in a number of countries not included in the figures cited from the introduction to Shah (1992a), so the figures mentioned do not exaggerate the variety and spread of tax incentives around the developing world.

11 Compare, for example, the discussion of incentives in Colombia in Bird (1970) with that in McLure and Zodrow (1992).

12 For an extensive review of this literature, see Jorgenson and Yun (1991). For more critical appraisals, see Bosworth (1984) and Chirinko (1987).

13 On the other hand this approach has appeal if – and only if – one believes that real-world markets correspond reasonably well to the theoretical conditions of perfect information, rationality, competition and mobility. This comment seems even more applicable in the circumstances of developing countries.

14 See, for example, the interesting papers by Krugman (1993) and Krueger (1993). As Krugman (p. 364) puts it: 'Free trade [read uniform factor taxation] is a pretty good if not perfect policy, while an effort to deviate from it in a sophisticated way will probably end up doing more harm than good.'

15 See, for example, Barro and Sala-i-Martin (1992) and Perroni (1993). Although there is no necessary implication in these models that increased growth results in increased welfare, policy-makers looking for a rationale for doing something they want to do have never worried about such refinements in the past, and they seem unlikely to do so in the future.

16 Despite these harsh words, the 'reference set' of taxes proposed in World Bank (1991) recognized that there may still be tax preferences in some cases, although it argued any incentives should be both limited in duration and – in line with the MERT analysis discussed below – distributed more evenly across sectors and assets.

17 For some examples, see Mintz and Tsiopoulos (1993) on eastern Europe.

18 On the other hand, the recipients of incentive benefits may legitimately object to having their private tax affairs publicized: the public need for transparency has to be sensibly tempered by the private need for confidentiality. Of course, this problem is hardly unique to tax incentives.

19 For example, Canada undoubtedly has the highest level of tax subsidization of such investment among developed countries and one of the highest in the world, yet there is almost no evidence that such incentives have yielded benefits equal to their cost (McFetridge and Warda, 1983).

20 The popular argument that only those who play the R&D game are able to reap the full benefit of advances in knowledge rests on tenuous grounds even in advanced countries – see, for example, the review of the literature in Bird *et al.* (1986). This argument is even less likely to be persuasive in the circumstances of most developing countries.

21 See Bird (1987) for further discussion; also Brean, Bird and Krauss (1991).

22 For two useful, and very different, treatments of these complex international tax questions, see Frenkel, Razin and Sadka (1991) and Piciotto (1992); see also Bird (1987) and Brean, Bird and Krauss (1991).

23 Note that the argument is *not* that tax incentives to investment will necessarily increase growth – a proposition that is, as indicated earlier, far from proven (see also Bosworth, 1984, and Gravelle, 1993) – it is simply that more new investment per dollar of revenue foregone is likely to result from tax concessions to new capital alone (e.g. accelerated depreciation or investment credits) than from concessions to both new and old capital (e.g. rate cuts).

24 See Wen (1992) for a more favourable view of tax holidays which suggests they may be effective in inducing investment to the extent that the 'signal' they give concerning government's commitment to pro-market (low-tax) policies plus the direct financial benefit conferred is sufficient to offset the fact that tax rates can (and likely will) be raised later, given the adjustment costs once capital is committed.

25 This judgement is based on various case studies reported in the survey papers and country studies cited elsewhere in this chapter as well as on unpublished evaluations carried out at various times by the author and others in a number of countries (e.g. the Philippines, Indonesia, Egypt and Jamaica).

26 See, for recent examples, Agell (1986), Pellechio *et al.* (1990) and McLure. (1989). For an analysis that is more favourable to incentives, see Mintz and Tsiopoulos (1992).

27 See also the comment in note 13 above. Much the same may be said (for different reasons) about the very different simulation approach of CGE (computable general equilibrium) analysis utilized by, for example, Clarete (1995) and Trela and Whalley (1995). As Shoven and Whalley (1992, p. 3) emphasize, while CGE models very usefully make '. . . explicit the implications of alternative courses of action within a framework broadly consistent with that currently accepted by many microeconomic theorists', they do not provide empirical tests of hypotheses about the effects of incentives on investment.

28 Much the same conclusion was reached in the earlier survey of the literature in Bird (1980).

29 In this regard, it is still a useful and sobering exercise to consider the disparate analyses of this issue in the early study edited by Fromm (1967): cf. also Bosworth (1984) and Rushton (1992) for later, and equally bleak, appraisals of the state of knowledge in this field. The last two decades has improved the techniques but not resolved the basic problems of such studies.

30 What determines the acceptability in developing countries of policy innovations in a number of fields has recently been considered by Nelson (1990) and Grindle and Thomas (1991): similar analysis is clearly needed with respect to incentive reform.

31 For an earlier version of these rules, see Bird and Oldman (1990), pp. 131–2.

32 This signalling or 'tax competition' aspect of incentives has not been discussed here: see Mintz and Tsiopoulos (1992), Shah (1995) and Wen (1992) for discussion.

33 By this test, most incentives in developed countries should also not exist. See, for example, the evaluations of Canadian incentives in Bird (1980) and Rushton (1992). Interestingly, the Canadian government did at one point, after considerable parliamentary pressure, set up a Tax Measures Evaluation Unit in the Department of Finance to evaluate tax incentives. None of the initial studies undertaken by this unit, however, were particularly favourable to the incentives being reviewed, so it was not surprising that this unit was among the first to be abolished as part of a recent 'expenditure reduction' effort. Officials and politicians do not like having their judgement questioned, even (or especially) by other officials.

References

Agell, J. N. (1986) 'Subsidy to Capital through Tax Incentives', in P. Shome (ed.), *Fiscal Issues in South-east Asia*, Singapore: Oxford University Press, 1986.

Ahmad, E. and N. Stern (1991) *The Theory and Practice of Tax Reform in Developing Countries*, Cambridge: Cambridge University Press.

Asher, M. (1988) 'Fiscal System and Practices in Singapore', in M. G. Asher (ed.), *Fiscal Systems and Practices in ASEAN: Trends, Impact, and Evaluation*, Singapore: ASEAN Economic Research Unit, Institute of Southeast Asian Studies.

Asher, M. (1992) 'Reforming the Tax System in Indonesia', unpublished; World Bank.

Auerbach, A. (1992) 'The Cost of Capital and Investment in Developing Countries', in Shah (1992a).

Bahl, R., C. K. Kim and C. K. Park (1986) *Public Finances During the Korean Modernization Process*, Cambridge, Mass.: Harvard University Press.

Balassa, B. (1975) 'Reforming the System of Incentives in Developing Countries', *World Development*, vol. 3, pp. 365–82.

Barro, R. J. and X. Sala-i-Martin (1992) 'Public Finance in Models of Economic Growth', *Review of Economic Studies*, vol. 59, pp. 645–61

Bird, R. M. (1966) 'Tax-Subsidy Policies for Regional Development', *National Tax Journal*, vol. 19, pp. 113–24.

Bird, R. M. (1970) *Taxation and Development: Lessons from Colombian Experience*, Cambridge, Mass.: Harvard University Press.

Bird, R. M. (1980) *Tax Incentives for Investment: The State of the Art*, Toronto: Canadian Tax Foundation.

Bird, R. M. (1982) 'Taxation and Employment in Developing Countries', *Finanzarchiv*, vol. 40, pp. 211–39.

Bird, R. M. (1987) *The Taxation of International Investment Flows: Issues and Approaches*, Wellington, NZ: Institute for Policy Studies.

Bird, R. M. (1989) 'The Administrative Dimension of Tax Reform', in M. Gillis (ed.), *Tax Reform in Developing Countries*, Durham: Duke University Press.

Bird, R. M. (1992) 'Tax Reform In Latin America: A Review of Some Recent Experience', *Latin American Research Review*,

Bird, R. M. and O. Oldman (eds) (1990) *Taxation in Developing Countries*, Baltimore: Johns Hopkins University Press.

Bird, R. M. *et al.* (1986) *Industrial Policy for Ontario*, Toronto: Ontario Economic Council.

Bosworth, B. P. (1984) *Tax Incentives and Economic Growth*, Washington, DC: The Brookings Institution.

Brean, D. J. S., R. M. Bird and M. Krauss (1991) *Taxation of International Portfolio Investment*, Ottawa: Centre for Trade Policy and Law and Institute for Research in Public Policy.

Byrne, W. J. (1976) 'Fiscal Incentives for Household Saving', *International Monetary Fund Staff Papers*, no. 23, pp. 455–89.

Chang, C.-H. and J. Riew (1990) 'Tax Policy and Business Investment – The Case of Taiwan's Manufacturing Industry', paper presented at Conference on Tax Policy and Economic Development among Pacific Asian Countries, Taipei.

Chen-Young, P. (1967) 'A Study of Tax Incentives in Jamaica', *National Tax Journal*, 20: 292–308.

Chia, N. C. and J. Whalley (1995) 'Patterns in Investment Tax Incentives among Developing Countries', in Shah (1995).

Chirinko, R. (1987) 'Will the Neoclassical Theory of Investment Please Rise? The General Structure of Investment Models and their Implications for Tax Policy', in J. M. Mintz and N. Bruce (eds), *The Impact of Taxation on Business Activity*, Kingston: John Deutsch Institute for the Study of Economic Policy.

Choi, K. (1992) 'Tax Policy and Tax Reforms in Korea', unpublished; World Bank.

Clarete, R. (1995) 'General Equilibrium Effects of Investment Incentives in the Philippines', in Shah (1995).

De Long, J. B. and L. H. Summers (1991) 'Equipment Investment and Economic Growth', *Quarterly Journal of Economics*, vol. 106, pp. 445–502.

De Long, J. B. and L. H. Summers (1992) 'Equipment Investment and Growth: How Strong is the Nexus?' *Brookings Papers on Economic Activity*, Washington, DC: The Brookings Institution.

De Wulf, L. H. (1978) 'Fiscal Incentives for Industrial Exports in Developing Countries', *National Tax Journal*, vol. 31, pp. 45–52.

Ebrill, L. (1987) 'Are Labor Supply, Savings, and Investment Price-Sensitive in Developing Countries? A Survey of the Empirical Literature', in Gandhi (1987).

Frenkel, J., A. Razin and E. Sadka (1991) *International Taxation in an Integrated World*, Cambridge, Mass.: MIT Press.

Fromm, G. (ed.) (1967) *Tax Incentives and Capital Spending*, Washington, DC: The Brookings Institution.

Gandhi, V. P. (ed). (1987) *Supply-side Tax Policy: Its Relevance to Developing Countries*, Washington, DC: International Monetary Fund.

Gersovitz, M. (1987) 'The Effects of Domestic Taxes on Foreign Private Investment', in D. Newbery and N. Stern (eds), *The Theory of Taxation in Developing Countries*, London: Oxford University Press.

Gillis, M. (1985) 'Microeconomics and Macroeconomics of Tax Reform: Indonesia', *Journal of Development Economics*, vol. 19, pp. 221–54.

Goode, R. (1993) 'Tax Advice to Developing Countries: An Historical Survey', *World Development*, vol. 21, pp. 37–53.

Gravelle, J. G. (1993) 'What Can Private Investment Incentives Accomplish? The Case of the Investment Tax Credit', *National Tax Journal*, vol. 46, pp. 275–90.

Grindle, M. S. and J. W. Thomas (1991) *Public Choices and Policy Change: The Political Economy of Reform in Developing Countries*, Baltimore: Johns Hopkins University Press.

Guisinger, S. (ed.) (1985) *Investment Incentives and Performance Requirements*, New York: Praeger.

Hall, R. E. and D. Jorgenson (1967) 'Tax Policy and Investment Behavior', *American Economic Review*, vol. 57, pp. 391–414

Harberger, A. C. (1990) 'Principles of Taxation Applied to Developing Countries: What Have We Learned?' in M. J. Boskin and C. E. McLure, Jr. (eds), *World Tax Reform*, San Francisco: ICS Press.

Harberger, A. C. (1993) 'The Search for Relevance in Economics', *American Economic Review, Papers and Proceedings*, vol. 83, pp. 1–16

Heller, J. and K. M. Kaufmann (1963) *Tax Incentives for Industry in Less Developed Countries*, Cambridge, Mass.: Harvard Law School International Program in Taxation.

Ishi, H. (1993) *The Japanese Tax System*, revd edn, London: Oxford University Press.

Jorgenson, D. and K.-Y. Yun (1991) *Tax Reform and the Cost of Capital*, Oxford: Clarendon Press.

King, M. A. and D. Fullerton (eds) (1984) *The Taxation of Income from Capital*, Chicago: The University of Chicago Press.

Krauss, M. (1983) *Development without Aid*, New York: McGraw-Hill.

Krueger, A. O. (1993) 'Virtuous and Vicious Circles in Economic Development', *American Economic Review, Papers and Proceedings*, vol. 83, pp. 351–5.

Krugman, P. (1993) 'The Narrow and Broad Arguments for Free Trade', *American Economic Review, Papers and Proceedings*, vol. 83, pp. 362–6.

Lent, G. E. (1967) 'Tax Incentives for Investment in Developing Countries', *International Monetary Fund Staff Papers*, no. 14, pp. 399–417.

Lent, G. E. (1971) 'Tax Incentives for the Promotion of Industrial Employment in Developing Countries', *International Monetary Fund Staff Papers*, no. 18, pp. 399–417.

Levy, B. (1993) 'An Institutional Analysis of the Design and Sequence of Trade and Investment Policy Reform', *World Bank Economic Review*, no. 7, pp. 247–62.

McFetridge, D. G. and J. P. Warda (1983) *Canadian R&D Incentives: Their Adequacy and Impact*, Toronto: Canadian Tax Foundation.

McLure, C. E., Jr. (ed) (1989) *The Taxation of Income from Business and Capital in Colombia*, Durham: Duke University Press.

McLure, C. E., Jr. and G. Zodrow (1992) 'Tax Reform in Colombia: Process and Results', unpublished; World Bank.

Meyer, L. H., J. L. Prakken and C. P. Varvares (1993) 'Policy Watch: Designing an Effective Investment Tax Credit', *Journal of Economic Perspectives*, vol. 7, pp. 189–96.

Mintz, J. M. (1995) 'Tax Holidays and Investment', in Shah (1995).

Mintz, J. M. and T. Tsiopoulos (1992) 'Contrasting Corporate Tax Policies: Canada and Taiwan', *Canadian Tax Journal*, vol. 40, pp. 902–17.

Mintz, J. M. and T. Tsiopoulos (1993) 'Corporate Income Taxation and Foreign Direct Investment in Eastern Europe', Occasional Working Paper no. 4, Foreign Investment Advisory Service, World Bank, Washington, DC.

Modi, J. R. (1982) 'Narrowing Regional Disparities by Fiscal Incentives', *Finance and Development*, vol. 19, no. 1, pp. 34–7.

Nelson, J. M., (ed.) (1990) *Economic Crisis and Policy Choice*, Princeton: Princeton University Press.

Pellechio, A., G. P. Sicat and D. Dunn (1990) 'Effective Tax Rates under Varying Tax Incentives', in Bird and Oldman (1990).

Perroni, C. (1993) 'Endogenous Growth and the Choice of Tax Base', unpublished; University of Western Ontario, London.

Piciotto, S. (1992) *International Business Taxation*, London: Weidenfeld & Nicolson.

Reuber, G. (1973) *Private Foreign Investment in Development*, Oxford: Oxford University Press.

Rushton, M. (1992) 'Tax Policy and Business Investment: What we Learned in the Past Dozen Years', *Canadian Tax Journal*.

Sanchez-Ugarte, F. (1987) 'Rationality of Income Tax Incentives in Developing Countries: A Supply-Side Look', in Gandhi (1987).

Sanchez-Ugarte, F. and A. Zabala Marti (1986) 'Argentina: Tax Incentives to Promote Investment', Washington, DC: International Monetary Fund.

Shah, A. (1995) 'Overview', *Fiscal Incentives for Investment and Innovation*, World Bank and Oxford University Press.

Shah, A. (ed.) (1992b) 'Tax Policies and Investment in Physical and R&D Capital', unpublished; World Bank.

Shah, S. M. S. and J. Toye (1978) 'Fiscal Incentives for Firms in Some Developing Countries: Survey and Critique', in J. Toye (ed.), *Taxation and Economic Development*, London: Frank Cass.

Shoven, J. B. and J. Whalley (1992) *Applying General Equilibrium*, Cambridge: Cambridge University Press.

Sumantoro (1993) 'Investment Incentives and Controls', in E. Quah and W. Neilson, (eds), *Law and Economic Development: Cases and Materials from Southeast Asia*, Singapore: Longman.

Summers, L. H. and L. H. Pritchett (1993) 'The Structural-Adjustment Debate', *American Economic Review, Papers and Proceedings*, vol. 83, pp. 383–9.

Thirsk, W. R. (1989) 'Jamaican Tax Incentives', in R. Bahl (ed.), *The Jamaican Tax Reform*, Cambridge, Mass.: Lincoln Institute of Land Policy.

Trela, I. and J. Whalley (1995) 'Taxes, Outward Orientation and Growth Performance in the Republic of Korea', in Shah (1995).

Usher, D. (1977) 'The Economics of Tax Incentives to Encourage Investment in Less Developed Countries', *Journal of Development Economics*, vol. 4, pp. 119–48.

Wen, J.-F. (1992) 'Tax Holidays in a Business Climate', Discussion Paper no. 864, Institute for Economic Research, Queen's University, Kingston.

World Bank (1991) *Lessons of Tax Reform*, Washington, DC: World Bank.

Young, A. (1993) 'Lessons from the East Asian NICs: A Contrarian View', Working Paper no. 4482, National Bureau of Economic Research, Cambridge, Mass.

Index